CULTURAL TRANSLATION IN EARLY MODERN EUROPE

This groundbreaking volume gathers an international team of historians to present the practice of translation as part of cultural history. Although translation is central to the transmission of ideas, the history of translation has generally been neglected by historians, who have left it to specialists in literature and language. This book seeks to achieve an understanding of the contribution of translation to the spread of information in early modern Europe. It focuses on non-fiction: the translation of books on religion, history, politics and especially on science, or 'natural philosophy' as it was generally known at this time. The chapters cover a wide range of languages, including Latin, Greek, Russian, Turkish and Chinese. The book will appeal to scholars and students of the early modern and later periods, and to historians of science and of religion, as well as to anyone interested in translation studies.

PETER BURKE is retired Professor of Cultural History at the University of Cambridge and Life Fellow of Emmanuel College. His most recent publications include *What is Cultural History?* (2004) and *Languages and Communities in Early Modern Europe* (2004).

R. PO-CHIA HSIA is Edwin Erle Sparks Professor of History at Pennsylvania State University. He is the author and editor of numerous books, including *The World of Catholic Renewal, 1540–1770* (2nd edition, 2005) and the sixth volume of *The Cambridge History of Christianity: Reform and Expansion, 1500–1660* (2007).

CULTURAL TRANSLATION IN EARLY MODERN EUROPE

EDITED BY

PETER BURKE

AND

R. PO-CHIA HSIA

CAMBRIDGE UNIVERSITY PRESS
Cambridge, New York, Melbourne, Madrid, Cape Town, Singapore, São Paulo

Cambridge University Press
The Edinburgh Building, Cambridge CB2 8RU, UK

Published in the United States of America by Cambridge University Press, New York

www.cambridge.org
Information on this title: www.cambridge.org/9780521862080

First published 2007

Printed in the United Kingdom at the University Press, Cambridge

A catalogue record for this publication is available from the British Library

ISBN 978-0-521-86208-0 hardback

Contents

Notes on contributors   *page* vii

Introduction
Peter Burke and R. Po-chia Hsia   1

PART I   TRANSLATION AND LANGUAGE   5

1   Cultures of translation in early modern Europe
    Peter Burke   7

2   The Catholic mission and translations in China, 1583–1700
    R. Po-chia Hsia   39

3   Language as a means of transfer of cultural values
    Eva Kowalská   52

4   Translations into Latin in early modern Europe
    Peter Burke   65

PART II   TRANSLATION AND CULTURE   81

5   Early modern Catholic piety in translation
    Carlos M. N. Eire   83

6   The translation of political theory in early modern Europe
    Geoffrey P. Baldwin   101

7   Translating histories
    Peter Burke   125

8   *The Spectator*, or the metamorphoses of the periodical:
    a study in cultural translation
    Maria Lúcia Pallares-Burke   142

PART III   TRANSLATION AND SCIENCE   161

9   The role of translations in European scientific exchanges
     in the sixteenth and seventeenth centuries
     Isabelle Pantin   163

10   Scientific exchanges between Hellenism and Europe:
     translations into Greek, 1400–1700
     Efthymios Nicolaïdis   180

11   Ottoman encounters with European science: sixteenth-
     and seventeenth-century translations into Turkish
     Feza Günergun   192

12   Translations of scientific literature in Russia from the
     fifteenth to the seventeenth century
     S. S. Demidov   212

Bibliography   218
Index   238

Notes on contributors

GEOFFREY BALDWIN studied at Cambridge and was the Lloyd Fellow of Christ's College, and lectured at Cambridge and Yale before his appointment as Lecturer in the Department of History, King's College London. He has published on early modern intellectual history and political thought.

PETER BURKE studied at Oxford and taught at the University of Sussex before moving to Cambridge, where he was Professor of Cultural History until his recent retirement. He is a Life Fellow of Emmanuel College, Fellow of the British Academy and Academia Europea. He has studied the transmission of knowledge in Europe from the Renaissance to the Enlightenment and published *A Social History of Knowledge* (2000). He has been working on the social history of language for nearly thirty years and his publications on the subject include *Languages and Communities in Early Modern Europe* (2004).

SERGEI SERGEEVICH DEMIDOV studied at M. V. Lomonosov University, Moscow. He is Director of the Department of the History of Mathematics, the S. I. Vavilov Institute for the History of Science and Technology of the Russian Academy of Sciences and holds the chair of the History of Mathematics and Mechanics of the Faculty of Mathematics and Mechanics at M. V. Lomonosov University. He was vice-president of the International Academy of the History of Sciences (1997–2005). He is the author of more than 200 studies in the history of science.

CARLOS M. N. EIRE is the T. Lawrason Riggs Professor of History and Religious Studies at Yale University. Before joining the Yale faculty in 1996, he taught at St John's University and the University of Virginia. He is the author of *War Against the Idols* (1986), *From Madrid to Purgatory* (1995) and *Reformations: Early Modern Europe 1400–1700* (forthcoming, 2007). His memoir of the Cuban Revolution, *Waiting for Snow in Havana* (2003), won the National Book Award for non-fiction.

FEZA GÜNERGUN (born Baytop) is Professor of History of Science at Istanbul University. She graduated from the Faculty of Chemical Engineering (Istanbul University) in 1980 and started research on the inorganic drugs used in Ottoman medicine during the fourteenth to seventeenth centuries for her doctoral study. Her current researches focus on the history of science in Turkey during the modernization period (eighteenth to twentieth centuries) of the Ottoman Empire with a special emphasis on the introduction of modern sciences to Turkey. She has also published articles on the history of chemistry and medicine in Turkey. She is the founder and editor of the Turkish academic journal *Osmanli bilimi arastirmalari* (Studies in Ottoman Science).

R. PO-CHIA HSIA is Edwin Erle Sparks Professor of History at the Pennsylvania State University. He has published extensively on the history of the Reformation, Christian–Jewish relations, and on the cultural encounter between early modern Europe and China. His latest publications include *Jesuit Missionaries in China and Vietnam* (2006) and the edited volume, *Cambridge History of Christianity*, vol. VI: *Reform and Expansion, 1500–1660*. He is an elected member of the Academia Sinica, Taipei.

EVA KOWALSKÁ, Senior Research Fellow at the Institute of History, Slovak Academy of Sciences in Bratislava, studied history and philosophy at the Comenius University there. She specializes in religious and cultural history in early modern Hungary, focusing recently on the confessional exile in Central Europe in the seventeenth century. She has written two monographs, one on the public school reforms of Maria Theresa and Joseph II (1987) and the second on the Lutheran community in Slovakia in the eighteenth century (2001). She has also published more than ninety articles and chapters in books (most recently in the *Concise History of Slovakia*, 2001).

EFTHYMIOS NICOLAÏDIS was born in Athens, studied in France and took his doctorate at the Ecole des Hautes Etudes en Sciences Sociales. After working at the National Observatory of Athens (1979–84), he joined the programme of the history of science of the National Hellenic Research Foundation in 1984, becoming its director in 2003. He is Secretary General of the International Union of the History and Philosophy of Science / Division of History of Science and Technology. His main publications are concerned with the history of science during the Byzantine and the Modern Greek period (Ottoman period and Greek state) and on the spreading of European (classical) science towards the periphery.

MARIA LÚCIA PALLARES-BURKE studied and taught in the Faculty of Education, University of São Paulo, before coming to England where she is Associate of the Centre for Latin American Studies, University of Cambridge. Her doctoral thesis, published in 1995, was a study of the English journal *The Spectator*. Since then she has published *Nísia Floresta, O carapuceiro e outros ensaios de tradução cultural* (1996); a collection of nine interviews with historians, *The New History: Confessions and Conversations* (English version, 2002); and an intellectual biography of the young Freyre, *Gilberto Freyre: um Vitoriano dos trópicos* (2005).

ISABELLE PANTIN is Professor of Renaissance Literature at the University of Paris X-Nanterre, and she participates in the research programme of the Observatoire de Paris (CNRS, SYRTE), in the section dedicated to the history of astronomy and related fields. Besides critical editions of works by Galileo and Kepler, she has published *La poésie du ciel en France* (1995) and *Les Fréart de Chantelou: une famille d'amateurs au XVIIe siècle* (1999). Her current project is a study of cosmological thought in Renaissance northern Europe, from Regiomontanus to Tycho Brahe.

Introduction

Peter Burke and R. Po-chia Hsia

Just as the Tower of Babel collapsed because its builders were dispersed by the diversity of tongues, the House of the European Community would surely fall if deprived of its army of interpreters: for who would know the differences between cod, *kabeljauw*, *morue* and *bacalhau* (the most dedicated gourmands excepted) and be able to smooth over rival national claims to fishing rights and sauce preparations but the dedicated translators and interpreters of the EU?

If communication between languages and cultures is an assumed and accepted fact in our contemporary world, it was by no means self-evident in the past. Yet all major cultural exchanges in history involved translation: be it the rendering of Buddhist texts from Sanskrit and Pali into Chinese during the early medieval period; or the transmission of Greek philosophy into Arabic in the early medieval, and the subsequent translation of the same texts from Arabic into Latin during the high medieval centuries; or the more recent translations of Western texts into Japanese and Chinese that marked the modernization of those two East Asian civilizations in the late nineteenth and early twentieth centuries.

All the same, it was Europe that represented the scene of the most sustained and intense cultural transfers throughout its long history, a process marked by an enormous effort in translation: of religious, scientific, political and literary works from a large variety of vernaculars into Latin and vice versa, and of vernaculars crossing national and linguistic boundaries.

The essays in this book, which emerged out of a series of workshops on cultural exchange funded by the European Science Foundation, are concerned with what might be called the cultural history of translation, especially in early modern Europe, from the Renaissance to the Enlightenment. The idea that translation has a history is an old one, but until quite recently this history was an academically marginal activity, pursued on the fringes of literary and religious history.

I

Studies of comparative literature, for instance, have long been concerned with the reception of famous authors in other countries, such as Ariosto in France, Cervantes in England or Richardson in Germany.[1] Literary studies of the Renaissance focused on translations from the classics into the vernacular, like the versions of Plutarch by Jacques Amyot or Thomas North, together with a few famous translations from one vernacular to another, like John Florio's English version of Montaigne.[2] Studies of the Reformation noted the importance of translations of the Bible by Luther and his followers in England, Denmark, Sweden and elsewhere.[3] Alternatively, following the model of comparative literature, they discussed the influence of Luther in France or Erasmus in Spain.[4]

To give translation a more central position in academe was the aim of the movement for Translation Studies in the later 1970s. Two ideas discussed at this time are particularly important for the cultural history of translation. Earlier books on the art of translation were generally normative, but the focus of Translation Studies – like that of sociolinguistics – was and is descriptive, stressing what translators actually do rather than what they should do. In the second place, where earlier studies had focused on the source, such as Ariosto or Calvin, the new studies – like the theory of 'reception' and the history of reading – focused on the audience, viewing translations as 'facts of the culture which hosts them' and as agents of change in that culture.[5] Cultural exchange was viewed from a new perspective, that of the horizon of readers and their culture, whether we call it the 'host culture' or the 'target culture'.[6]

In a famous early map of the new field, James Holmes distinguished between theoretical and descriptive studies of translation, but allocated little or no space to history. The early years might be described as the 'theoretical moment' in Translation Studies, a time of an emphasis on systems associated with Itamar Even-Zohar and Gideon Toury.[7]

Since that time, however, what might be called a 'historical turn' has begun, a growing awareness of the historicity of what a recent study calls 'constructed – and often contingent – linguistic equivalences'.[8] Some leading figures in the new field, notably Antoine Berman, Theo Hermans, Lawrence Venuti, Anthony Pym and members of the Göttingen school such as Wilhelm Graeber and Geneviève Roche, take history seriously.[9] The

---

[1] Cioranescu (1938); Fitzmaurice-Kelly (1906); Beebee (1990).
[2] Matthiessen (1931); Highet (1949), 104–26.   [3] Stolt (1983).   [4] Moore (1930); Bataillon (1937).
[5] Holmes (1972); Toury (1995), 7–19, 24, 27.   [6] Liu (1995), 26–8.
[7] Basnett (1980); Munday (2001).   [8] Liu (1999), 5.
[9] Berman (1984); Hermans (1985); Graeber and Roche (1988); Venuti (1995); Pym (2000).

FIT (Fédération Internationale des Traducteurs) has set up a Committee for the History of Translation, and a Directory of Historians of Translation has been published.[10]

Even today, though, workers in this field have less to say about the contrasts between cultures than between individual translators, less about long-term trends than about short-term processes, and less about the history of practice than about the history of theory.[11] It is hoped that the essays in this volume (by ten contributors who between them speak nine native languages) will do something to fill these gaps.

In any case, the turn towards history within Translation Studies has not yet been matched by a turn towards the study of translation on the part of historians, even cultural historians. A second aim of this volume is therefore to encourage a dialogue between workers in Translation Studies and in cultural history. Central to such a dialogue is the notion of translation between cultures as well as between languages, in other words the adaptation of ideas and texts as they pass from one culture to another. This notion informs the chapters by Burke, Hsia, Baldwin and Pallares-Burke in particular.

A third aim of the volume is to complement existing work on the history of translation by compensating for absences. Where earlier work privileged literary translation, this volume privileges non-fiction, the transmission of information and knowledge from one language to another. One chapter focuses on political texts (Baldwin), another on historical texts (Burke), a third on periodicals (Pallares-Burke). Where earlier work on religious texts privileged the translation of the Bible and of the writings of the reformers, in this volume Eire focuses on the diffusion of works of piety (examined from an international viewpoint), while Kowalská views the Czech Protestant Bible from a Slovak perspective. Four chapters (Demidov, Günergun, Nicolaïdis and Pantin) are concerned with the translation of works of science or 'natural philosophy', as it was generally known in the early modern period. They contribute to the understanding of the role of interlingual translation in that larger movement of the 'making of natural knowledge', the translation of local knowledge into universal science.[12]

So far as different languages are concerned, earlier work has concentrated on translations from Latin and Greek into the vernacular.[13] This volume, by contrast, emphasizes translations between vernaculars and also

[10] Delisle and Woodsworth (1995).
[11] On the history of theory, Kloepfer (1967); Kelly (1979); Ballard (1992); Robinson (1997).
[12] Golinski (1998).   [13] Bolgar (1954); Schweiger (1830–4).

the neglected yet important topic of translation from the vernaculars into Latin (Burke). The contributors (especially Demidov, Günergun and Nicolaïdis) examine European peripheries as well as centres and extend their researches to the world beyond Europe (Hsia).

Earlier studies of translation have concentrated on printed translations, though the history of interpreting has been studied by some scholars, including one of the participants in our workshops, Dejanirah Couto.[14] However, three contributions to this volume (once again, Demidov, Günergun and Nicolaïdis) emphasize the importance of manuscripts in the so-called 'age of print', especially in the eastern half of Europe.

There remains much work still to be done on the cultural history of translation. The purpose of this volume is to make better known what has been done already, to offer a few more contributions to encourage readers to enter this fascinating field.

---

[14] Couto (2001).

PART I

Translation and language

Cultures of translation in early modern Europe

Peter Burke[1]

> Translation is always a shift not between two languages but between
> two cultures   (Umberto Eco)

This essay has two aims: to present a general survey of translating in early
modern Europe and to discuss translation between languages in the context
of translation between cultures. Differences between cultures as well as
languages reduce what has been called the 'translatability' of texts. A major
problem for anyone translating comic literature, for instance, is that the
sense or senses of humour of different cultures, 'cultures of laughter', as
they have been called, are very different. Jokes fail to cross frontiers. In
similar fashion they often go stale over the centuries or become unintelligible, like the references to the horns of husbands in Shakespeare, which
may have had Elizabethan audiences rolling in the aisles of the Globe, but
are greeted with silence today.[2]

I

If the past is a foreign country, it follows that even the most monoglot of
historians is a translator.[3] Historians mediate between the past and the
present and face the same dilemmas as other translators, serving two masters
and attempting to reconcile fidelity to the original with intelligibility to
their readers.[4]

For example, should one speak of the 'policy' of a medieval king? The
word does not occur in medieval texts. It was not necessary, since a
medieval king did not have to convince voters to elect him by presenting
them with a programme for future action. A policy in the sense of some

[1] I should like to thank my colleagues in the ESF project on cultural exchange, the Royal Library in The Hague, The Netherlands Institute for Advanced Study, Mark Goldie of Churchill College and Aleka Lianeri of Darwin College for helping me in different ways in the writing of this essay.
[2] Unger, Schultze and Turk (1995).   [3] Cohen (1997), 297.   [4] Evans (1994).

principles or strategies underlying everyday political action, from doing justice to extending his realm, he may have had, but a policy in the modern sense of programme is an anachronistic concept.

Again, can a historian speak of 'propaganda' for Louis XIV? In its political sense, the term was coined in the late eighteenth century in order to compare techniques of political persuasion with techniques of religious conversion as practised by the Catholic Church and its institutions 'for the propagation of the faith' (*de propaganda fide*). On the other hand, writers and artists in the service of Louis not only glorified the king in general but justified particular actions such as the expulsion of Protestants from France in 1685.[5] I would therefore argue that to speak of 'propaganda' for Louis is culturally appropriate even if it is technically anachronistic. It is a free translation but not an unfaithful one.

The term 'cultural translation' was originally coined by anthropologists in the circle of Edward Evans-Pritchard, to describe what happens in cultural encounters when each side tries to make sense of the actions of the other.[6] A vivid example, famous among anthropologists, is Laura Bohannan's account of how she told the story of *Hamlet* to a group of Tiv in West Africa and heard the story 'corrected' by the elders until it finally matched the patterns of Tiv culture.[7]

Working as they often do in situations where the cultural distance between themselves and their informants is unusually great, anthropologists are well aware of the problem of untranslatable terms (some of which, like 'totem' and 'taboo', they have introduced into European languages) as well as the more general problem of communication between natives of one culture and natives of another. They are becoming increasingly conscious of both the linguistic and the wider cultural problems involved in turning conversations with informants into their own academic prose.[8]

The concept of cultural translation has recently been taken up by a group of literary scholars concerned with the translatability of texts.[9] It may also be used to refer to visual images (discussed by Hsia below) and to everyday life. It has often been suggested, from August Schlegel through Franz Rosenzweig to Benvenuto Terracini, Octavio Paz and George Steiner, that understanding itself is a kind of translation, turning other people's concepts and practices into their equivalents in our own 'vocabulary'. As

---

[5] Burke (1992).
[6] Beidelman (1971); a critique in Asad (1986); cf. Pálsson (1993), Kissel (1999), Howland (2001); and Rubel and Rosman (2003).
[7] Bohannan (1971).   [8] Sturge (1997); Tihanyi (2004).   [9] Budick and Iser (1996).

Paz puts it, 'learning to speak is learning to translate' (*aprender a hablar es aprender a traducir*).[10]

Within contemporary Western culture, for instance, most people do not understand the technical language used by lawyers, doctors and many different kinds of scientist. This was already becoming a problem in the seventeenth century, when the Dutchman Adriaan Koerbagh published a dictionary of legal terms in the vernacular in order to help ordinary people avoid being manipulated by the lawyers.[11] The task of translating law or medicine in the sense of taking legal or medical ideas across linguistic as well as social frontiers is even more difficult.[12] So is the translation of gods, to be discussed below in the context of Christian missions in Asia and the Americas.[13]

Translation implies 'negotiation', a concept which has expanded its domain in the last generation, moving beyond the worlds of trade and diplomacy to refer to the exchange of ideas and the consequent modification of meanings.[14] The moral is that a given translation should be regarded less as a definitive solution to a problem than as a messy compromise, involving losses or renunciations and leaving the way open for renegotiation.

In the case of the early modern period, the idea of negotiated translation seems particularly appropriate to the mission field. Christian missionaries had to decide how far they could go in adapting (or as was said at the time, 'accommodating') the Christian message to the culture in which they were working. In China, for example, Matteo Ricci discovered that if he dressed as a priest no one would take him seriously, so he dressed like a Confucian scholar instead, thus 'translating' his social position into Chinese. He allowed the Chinese whom he converted to pay reverence to their ancestors in the traditional manner, arguing that this was a social custom rather than a religious one. He translated the word 'God' by the neologism *Tianzhu*, literally 'Lord of Heaven', and allowed Chinese Christians to refer simply to *Tian*, 'Heaven', as Confucius had done (further discussion below, pp. 39–51).

In Rome, the Jesuits were accused of having been converted to the religion of the Chinese rather than converting them to Christianity. What appeared in Beijing to be a good cultural translation looked more like a mistranslation in Rome.[15] Other missionaries refused to go so far as Ricci, keeping their traditional black robes and also the Latin word *Deus*,

[10] Glatzer (1953), 255; Terracini (1957), 39; Paz (1971), 7; G. Steiner (1975), 1–48.
[11] Israel (2001), 187.
[12] On law, Liu (1999) and Legrand (2005); on medicine, Chen (1999). On justice as itself a kind of translation, White (1990).
[13] Assmann (1996).   [14] Pym (1993); Eco (2003).   [15] Gernet (1982).

glossing rather than translating it (below, p. 48). These conflicts offer the most vivid early modern examples of the problems of both interlingual and intercultural translation.

Another way of discussing cultural translation is to speak of a double process of decontextualization and recontextualization, first reaching out to appropriate something alien and then domesticating it. Interlingual translation may be regarded not only as an instance of this process but also as a kind of litmus paper that makes it unusually visible – or audible. It may be illuminating to attempt to look at the process from a double viewpoint. From the receiver's point of view it is a form of gain, enriching the host culture as a result of skilful adaptation. From the donor's point of view, on the other hand, translation is a form of loss, leading to misunderstanding and doing violence to the original.

II

In any history of cultural exchange, translation between languages is obviously of great importance. The relation between linguistic translation and cultural translation has recently been the concern of a number of perceptive studies focused on the movement of ideas such as liberty, individualism and democracy from the West to China, Japan, West Africa and elsewhere.[16] The focus of these studies on translation between continents is no accident. The greater the distance between the languages and cultures involved, the more clearly do the problems of translation appear. All the same, this approach may usefully be extended to cultural exchange within Europe.

The translation of texts was central to the great cultural movements of early modern Europe, the Renaissance, the Reformation, the Scientific Revolution and the Enlightenment. In the Renaissance, for instance, translations from the classics (including translations from Greek into Latin) take pride of place, but translations of major works of vernacular literature, from the *Orlando furioso* to *Don Quixote*, were also influential. In the Reformation and Counter-Reformation, as we shall see in Eire's chapter (below, pp. 83–100), translations of Erasmus, Luther, Calvin, Luís de Granada, Roberto Bellarmino and others played an important role. The spread of the Scientific Revolution (discussed below, pp. 161–217) can to some degree be measured by the translations of Galileo and Newton, and that of the Enlightenment by those of Montesquieu and Locke.

---

[16] Liu (1995); Sakai (1997); Schaffer (1998); Howland (2001).

Translations from the classics, like translations of major works of vernacular literature, have often been studied. Hence this chapter, like the rest of the volume, will concentrate on what has tended to be neglected, translations of non-fiction written either in the vernaculars of early modern Europe or in neo-Latin (studied in more detail below, pp. 65–80). A definitive study, if such a thing is possible, will have to wait until a census has been made of all the translations produced in early modern Europe, a task beyond the powers of a small team, let alone an individual.

What can be done here is to place these texts in their cultural context, including the systems or 'regimes' of translation prevalent in this period, in other words the rules, norms or conventions governing its practice, both the ends (or 'strategies') and the means (the 'tactics' or 'poetics').[17] The following overview of these regimes, or as I prefer to call them, the 'cultures of translation', in early modern Europe offers provisional answers to the following six large questions: Who translates? With what intentions? What? For whom? In what manner? With what consequences?[18]

III

Who translates? The thousands of translators in Europe in this period may be classified in various ways. For example, most translations were the work of individuals, but teamwork can also be found at this time, as it had been in the Middle Ages (in Toledo, for instance, and also in the Swedish monastery of Vadstena). Thus the German publisher Zacharias Palthen organized a team to translate the works of Paracelsus into Latin (below, p. 173), while the poet Alexander Pope employed a team of collaborators to help him translate Homer.[19]

Collaborative translation was especially common in the case of the Bible, not only because the text was so long but also by reason of the responsibility involved in interpreting the word of God. The English Authorized Version and the Czech Kralicy Bible as well as a Dutch, a Danish, a Swedish and a Finnish Bible produced in the early modern period were all the work of committees of scholars (in the English case, six 'companies', two based in Oxford, two in Cambridge and two in London). The establishment of these groups followed the model of the famous Septuagint, the seventy-two scholars who were supposed to have assembled in Alexandria in order to translate the Old Testament into Greek.

[17] Pym (1998), 125–42.   [18] Lambert (1993).   [19] Pantin (below).

Another useful distinction between translators divides the amateurs from the professionals. The vast majority of translators engaged in this activity only once or twice in their lives. The amateurs include a number of rulers or future rulers, among them Queen Elizabeth, James I, Philip IV and Philip V of Spain and Ludwig Prince of Anhalt. Devotional writers often translated other devotional writers (Luís de Granada and the Jesuit Emmanuel Nieremberg, for instance, both translated Thomas Kempis). Physicians translated herbals and works on anatomy (Annibale Briganti, for instance, translated the herbals of García de Horta and Monardes into Italian). Historians translated other historians, as Leonardo Bruni translated or adapted Polybius and Procopius, while Johann Sleidan translated Commynes. Artists and connoisseurs translated treatises on art and architecture (Richard Haydocke, a physician who was also an engraver, translated the Italian art theorist Lomazzo into English).

Women were relatively prominent in this field, probably because translation was considered more compatible than original writing with female modesty. The tradition lasted a long time: in early twentieth-century Germany, 40 per cent of the literary translations from English were the work of women.[20] In the early modern period, female translators included the Italian Giuseppa-Eleonora Barbapiccola, the Pole Maria Sipayllówna, the Germans Eleonora von Sporck and Louise Gottsched, the Danes Dorothea Biehl and Birgitte Thott, the Swedes Catharina Gyllengrip and Catharina and Maria Gyllenstierna and the Frenchwomen Geneviève Chappelain, Anne Dacier, Susanne Du Vergerre, Octavie Belot and Emilie Marquise du Châtelet. In England – to mention only the best-known names – there were Margaret Beaufort, Aphra Behn, Elizabeth Cary, Ann Cook, Ann Lok, Jane Lumley, Margaret Roper, Mary Sidney and Margaret Tyler.

By contrast with the many amateurs, a relatively small number of translators were professional, at least in the general sense of devoting a considerable amount of their life to this task, often for money. Translators of texts were among the first authors to be paid for their work and most early modern writers who aspired to live by their pen, from Erasmus to Dr Johnson, engaged in translation among other literary activities. By the end of the period a few of them were able to make a reasonable amount of money in this way. The group included one woman, Elizabeth Carter, who was said to know ten languages and translated from four of them – Greek, Latin, French and Italian. Carter earned 1,000 guineas from her translation

[20] Pym (1998), 144.

of Epictetus, while Alexander Pope received £4,500 for the English *Odyssey*, passing on a fraction of that sum to his collaborators.

The professionals include a substantial number of oral translators. Interpreters were often appointed by governments and sometimes trained in special schools, in Vienna, for instance, in Venice, or in Paris, where the students were known as 'les jeunes de langues'.[21] Their position might be hereditary, as in the case of the Russian-speaking interpreters in Sweden or the Dutch-speaking *tsujis* of Deshima, the island to which foreigners were confined by the Japanese government from the early seventeenth century to the 1850s.[22]

The record for the number of texts translated in this period is held by the Frenchman Gabriel Chappuys, who translated some eighty texts from Italian or Spanish. The Dutchman Jan Hendriksz Glazemaker translated over sixty works from Latin, French, German and Italian. The German Christian Weisse translated forty-eight works from English. The Swede Eric Schroder translated over forty works, mainly from Latin, while the Dutchman Vincentius Meusevoet translated over thirty-five, mainly from English.

All the same, it is more exact to call these people 'semi-professional', since it was common at this time to combine the career of translator with teaching languages, interpreting, acting as a secretary, compiling dictionaries or with writing for money (even today, only a minority of translators work full-time).[23] Thus Meusevoet was a Calvinist pastor, Chappuys a royal secretary and interpreter. Weisse was active as an editor and a writer as well as a translator. Schroder occupied the position of royal translator, but he was also a proof-corrector at the royal press in Stockholm and at one time ran his own press as well.

For some rare examples of full-time salaried translators, we need to turn to eighteenth-century Russia, where they were employed by the Academy of St Petersburg and held regular meetings to discuss their problems. As a speech he made in 1735 shows, Vasilij Trediakovsky in particular had a strong sense of the translator's mission, in this case to transmit Western European culture to Russia.[24]

The scarcity of resources available to assist translators in the early modern period deserves to be emphasized.[25] The lack of bilingual dictionaries of European vernaculars is particularly striking. Take, for example, the situation of the English translator. For a French–English dictionary

[21] Dupont-Ferrier (1923); Lewis (1999).   [22] Tarkiainen (1972); Goodman (1967).
[23] Pym (1998), 162.   [24] Marker (1985), 52–3.   [25] Kelly (1979), 126–30.

it was necessary to wait until 1580, for Spanish–English until 1591, for French–German until 1596, for Italian–English until 1598. In the case of Sweden, it was necessary to wait till 1694 for a French–Swedish dictionary, till 1734 for English–Swedish, and till 1749 for German–Swedish. Before those dates translators who encountered problems with a particular language had either to work via Latin or to turn for help to a native speaker.

Two semi-professional groups stand out from the rest. The first, predictably, is that of émigrés, amphibians who were unusually well qualified for their task and often made a career of mediating between their two countries. These European amphibians, like the professional interpreters of the time, have not been studied as intensively as their equivalents in the Americas, the Portuguese Empire and elsewhere. In the Ottoman Empire, for instance, interpreters were often 'renegades', in other words converts from Christianity to Islam, while the Portuguese interpreters in India were often 'new Christians', generally of Jewish origin.[26]

As for translators of texts, sixteenth-century examples include two Londoners with Italian parents, John Florio – a hybrid name expressing what was probably a hybrid identity – and Lodowick Bryskett, otherwise known as Lodovico Bruschetto. Italian Protestant refugees were especially prominent among translators into Latin (below, p. 70).

In the seventeenth century it was the turn of French Protestant refugees to enter the field of translation, whether from English into French or the other way round. Pierre Coste, the translator of Locke and Newton, was a Huguenot in exile in Amsterdam and Essex.[27] Jean Baptiste de Rosemond became an Anglican clergyman and translated his new colleagues such as Gilbert Burnet and Edward Stillingfleet. On the other hand, Pierre Desmaizeaux, the translator of Bayle, Fénelon and Saint-Evremond, and John Desaguliers – another hybrid name – translator of works on fortification and natural philosophy, preferred to turn French texts into English. Desmaizeaux also acted as a cultural translator in a broader sense by acting as the English correspondent for the learned periodical *Nouvelles de la république de lettres* and sending information about new publications.[28]

In the case of the Netherlands, returned immigrants form a special category, notably those who fled to England in the days of the Duke of Alba's persecution of Protestants and later returned to their native country to become Calvinist ministers. The prolific translator Vincentius Meusevoet, for instance, lived for some years in Norwich. Michael Panneel lived in Ipswich. Johannes Beverland lived in Yarmouth. Jan Lamoot went to school

[26] Karttunen (1994); Ács (2000); Couto (2001).   [27] Rumbold (1991).   [28] Almagor (1984).

in London. Willem Teelinck studied in St Andrews, lived in Banbury and married a woman from Derby. These personal experiences of Britain surely helped the translators in their task of cultural negotiation.

A second group that deserves mention here, alongside the refugees, is that of the cosmopolitan order of the Jesuits. Jesuits were of course specialists in cultural translation who had been instructed by their founder Ignatius Loyola (in the words of St Paul) to be 'all things to all people' (*omnia omnibus*). In that sense Ricci's strategy of dressing as a Chinese scholar was typical of his order.

Translation between languages formed part of the Jesuit strategy of conversion. More than 250 Jesuit translators were active between the foundation of the order in 1540 and the end of the eighteenth century, translating especially though not exclusively from the vernacular into Latin and concentrating on texts by other Jesuits. The highest number of texts translated by a single individual is thirty (in the case of the Fleming Frans de Smidt), followed by twenty-three (the Pole Simon Wysocki), nineteen (the German Conrad Vetter), eighteen (the northern Netherlander, Jan Buys) and seventeen (both the Frenchman Jean Brignon and the Czech Jiři Ferus). Jesuit translation was particularly important in East-Central or Eastern Europe. Thus Jacob Szafarzyński translated his colleague Rivadeneira into Polish, Balthasar Hostovinus translated letters from the Jesuit missions into Czech and so on.[29] Jesuit translators were also active in China, as Hsia shows (below, p. 44).

Besides the translators themselves it is necessary to take into account the patrons in the sense of 'the powers (persons, institutions) that can further or hinder the reading, writing and rewriting of literature'.[30] Some of them were leading figures in the Church. The humanist pope Nicholas V commissioned a number of translations of Greek classics into Latin. Cardinal Jiménez de Cisneros was patron of a polyglot edition of the Bible, as well as of a number of works of piety (below, p. 92), while the Cardinal of Lorraine encouraged the translation of devotional works from Spanish into French.[31]

Other important patrons were rulers. Already in the thirteenth century, King Alfonso X of Castille, known as 'the wise' or 'the learned' (*el sabio*) had commissioned a number of translations, mainly of Arabic texts on astrology, while some thirty texts were turned into French at the command of King Charles V.[32] Circulating in manuscript, these texts reached a limited audience. In the age of print, Gustav Adolf in Sweden and Peter

[29] Burke (2006).   [30] Lefevere (1992), 11–25, at 15.   [31] Martin (1969), 12.   [32] Pym (2000), 56–79.

and Catherine the Great in Russia initiated similar campaigns of translation which reached far more people (below, p. 18).

The example of Catherine reminds us that women were prominent as patrons, encouraging men to translate particular authors into particular languages. The Spanish and English versions of Castiglione's *Cortegiano* were the result of suggestions by two noblewomen, Gerónima Palova de Almogáver and Elizabeth Marchioness of Northampton. John Florio dedicated the three parts of his translation of Montaigne's *Essays* (1603) to six noblewomen. The third French translation of Paolo Sarpi's *History of the Council of Trent* was made at the command of the Queen of England (below, p. 139).

There were also the entrepreneurs of translation, the printers – some of whom were particularly interested in this kind of book. For example, Gabriel Giolito of Venice founded a series of translations of classical historical works (below, p. 126), as well as employing the Spaniard Alfonso de Ulloa to translate from Spanish. Theodor de Bry and his son Johann Theodor commissioned German and Latin translations of travel books. Printers who practised translation themselves included William Caxton in London, Etienne Dolet in Lyon and Barezzo Barezzi in Venice. It was largely thanks to printers that a few large cities became centres of translation, in particular Venice, Paris, London and Amsterdam.

IV

With what intentions or strategies were translations undertaken?[33] The most obvious and perhaps the most important projects were religious ones. The parallel as well as the connection between the work of translators and missionaries is worth noting. Missionaries such as Ricci translated religious texts as a means of conversion, but they sometimes found themselves translating their religion as well, in the sense of adapting it to the local culture, and even converting their language, in the sense of introducing into it words and phrases from Tupí, Japanese and so on.

There was a good deal of missionary activity in Europe as well as in other continents and here too translation played an important role. In the world of the Catholic Counter-Reformation, there was what might be called a 'translation policy', associated with attempts to make converts from

---

[33] The importance of intention has been emphasized by the so-called 'skopos' theorists: Reiss and Vermeer (1984), 95–104.

Protestantism or Orthodoxy. The policy is particularly clear in the case of the catechism written by Roberto Bellarmino, which was translated into twenty European languages (or twenty-two if Piedmontese and Sicilian, which are now treated as dialects, are included).[34]

In Rome, a number of translations, including an Arabic version of the church history of Cardinal Baronius, were financed and published by the Congregation 'for the Propagation of the Faith' (*de propaganda fide*) and published by their special press from 1626 onwards.[35] In the case of the Jesuits in particular, it is tempting to speak of a conspiracy of translation, or at any rate of a translation policy, of books produced not only *Ad majorem dei gloriam* ('to the greater glory of God', the Jesuit motto) but also to the greater glory of the order.

The many versions of the Bible made by Protestants, from Luther onwards, offer another obvious case of a conscious strategy. So do the production of Lutheran texts, especially catechisms, in many languages. The first texts ever printed in Latvian (1525), Estonian (1535), Lithuanian (1547) and Sami (1649), as well as an early Russian text, printed in Stockholm in 1625, were all translations or paraphrases of works by Luther.[36]

Again, when we find that theological and devotional works by the Puritan William Perkins were translated into Dutch and Hungarian at a time when few books by Englishmen were translated into any foreign language, the explanation that immediately springs to mind is that Calvinists too must have had a policy or strategy of translation. The speed with which Paolo Sarpi's anti-papal *History of the Council of Trent* appeared in its English, French, German, Dutch and Latin translations (in 1620 and 1621, following the original Italian edition of 1619), once again suggests co-ordinated action in the Protestant world.

Secular strategies or policies of a similar kind can also be found in this period. For example, Luis de Avila's official history of the emperor Charles V's war against the Protestant princes in 1546–7 was published not long after the events not only in the original Spanish but also – in the same year – in Italian, French, Flemish, Latin and English. This co-ordination suggests that the initiative for translation came from the emperor's circle.

In England in the age of Henry VIII, William Marshall translated Lorenzo Valla, Marsilio of Padua, Martin Luther and Martin Bucer in order to support the Reformation and was himself supported by the

---

[34] Sommervogel (1890–1900). [35] On 'translation policy', Toury (1995), 58; Henkel (1972).
[36] Burke (2004), 78.

king's minister Thomas Cromwell, though it seems that the initiative for translation came from Marshall himself and not from the government.[37] In similar fashion, in the reign of Elizabeth, Richard Hakluyt seems to have encouraged translations of travel books, for instance by his assistant John Pory (who translated the description of Africa by Leo Africanus) and also by William Phillip.

In the case of seventeenth-century Sweden, on the other hand, although the initiative came from a private individual, Schroder, who set out his plan in a book dedicated to Karl IX in 1606, it would not be far from the mark to speak of an official 'translation campaign' in the age of Gustav Adolf, undertaken with the aim of helping the Swedes to catch up with cultural developments elsewhere in Europe. In the eighteenth century, too, it was the state (more exactly, the Chancery College) that commissioned the Swedish translation of Locke's *Second Treatise on Government*.[38]

In the case of eighteenth-century Russia it is even more appropriate to speak of a translation campaign. Translators worked for the College of Foreign Affairs, as they had already done earlier (below, p. 132). In 1698, Ilya Kopievich was commissioned to translate no fewer than twenty-one titles.[39] Translations in Peter the Great's time were mainly military, scientific and technical, reflecting the tsar's interests and policies. They included works of anatomy (Vesalius), cosmology (Huyghens), geography (Varenius) and architecture (Vignola, supposedly translated by Peter himself). History was represented by Curtius's life of Alexander the Great, who was doubtless a role model for Peter, and by Pufendorf's survey of European states, a textbook in courses at the Naval Academy.[40]

This campaign increased in scale after Peter's death, but technical books were replaced by works of literature, reflecting a 'self-conscious attempt' by Catherine to create a lay vernacular culture in Russia via foreign models, whether classical (Horace, Virgil) or French (Boileau, Fénelon). Eighteenth-century Russia offers a vivid early modern example of the importance of translation in cases where a given literature is 'young', weak and peripheral.[41] Translators now worked for the Russian Academy. In 1768, the Society for the Translation of Foreign Books began its activities, and 154 translations were published in the following twelve years. In the

---

[37] Alec Ryrie (2004), 'William Marshall (d. 1540?)' in *Oxford Dictionary of National Biography* (Oxford).

[38] Hansson (1982), 70; Hallberg (2003), 57n.   [39] Hughes (1998), 317.

[40] Marker (1985), 29, 248.   [41] Even-Zohar (1979).

period 1756–75, 765 translations were published. French books accounted for 402 of these, German books for 175, Latin and Italian for 54 apiece and English for 36, though texts were not always translated from their original language.[42]

In short, Sweden and Russia exemplify the importance of cultural contributions from the periphery. Sweden effectively entered the European Republic of Letters in the seventeenth century and Russia in the eighteenth. The elites felt that they needed to catch up with Western Europe, and translation was the means. Hence translation was more highly organized and had a higher status, and the state was more closely involved with the enterprise than it was elsewhere.

Elsewhere the term 'campaign' seems less appropriate in this period, although the ideal of spreading enlightenment by means of translation was widespread. On one side, translations into Latin were made to give the scholarly community access to works written in vernaculars they did not know, as in the case of the translations of antiquarian works from Italian made in the Dutch Republic on the initiative of Johan Georg Graevius (below, p. 68). Conversely, translations were made into different vernaculars from Greek and Latin in order to allow groups excluded from a classical education to have access to the wisdom of the ancients. Didactic and economic motives were intertwined in the projects of Giovanni Battista Ramusio, Richard Eden, Richard Hakluyt, Theodore de Bry and others to give Europeans a better knowledge of other continents.

Another important motive for translations into vernaculars was what has been described as 'cultural nationalism'. Translators often used the language of rivalry. Sir Thomas Hoby, for example, was aware that Castiglione's *Courtier* had been translated into Spanish and French before he began his English version.[43] Gavin Douglas translated Virgil's *Aeneid* into what he called 'the langage of Scottis natioun', contrasting it with Caxton's translation of the poem into English.[44]

The translations of vernacular classics, including the epic poems of Ariosto and Tasso, into dialects such as Bergamask, Bolognese and Neapolitan may have been made for similar reasons to Douglas's, out of local pride. They may also represent a form of learned playfulness, the early modern equivalent of the twentieth-century Latin version of *Winnie the Pooh*, which was produced by a Hungarian living in Brazil.

---

[42] Marker (1985), 50–8, 88, 91.   [43] Ebel (1969).   [44] Corbett (1999), 42.

V

What was translated? From the point of view of a cultural anthropologist or a cultural historian, translation reveals with unusual clarity what one culture finds of interest in another, or more exactly what groups from one culture (or individuals such as Peter the Great) find of interest in another. One might say that the choice of items for translation reflects the priorities of the recipient culture, though 'refraction' might make a more appropriate metaphor.[45] The point is that works seem to be selected for translation on two opposite principles. In the first place, unsurprisingly, to fill gaps in the host culture.[46] For example, in 1700 Russia lacked books on mathematics, science and technology and so Peter the Great set out to remedy this deficiency.

The second principle, however, is the opposite of the first. It might be called the principle of confirmation, according to which people in a given culture translate works that support ideas or assumptions or prejudices already present in the culture. If they do not support ideas of this kind, the translations are modified, directly or indirectly (via 'paratexts' such as prefaces or letters to the reader) in order to give the impression that they do, as in the case of what might be called the 'Protestantization' of the Italian historians Francesco Guicciardini and Paolo Sarpi (below, pp. 134ff.).

In early modern Europe the most translated text was, unsurprisingly, the Bible. Translations of Scripture were published in fifty-one languages between 1456 and 1699, including classic versions such as Luther's German Bible, the Czech Kralicy Bible, the English Authorized Version and the Dutch 'States' Bible'.[47] As might have been expected during the Renaissance, the Greek and Latin classics were frequently translated. Between 1450 and 1600, around a thousand translations of the Greek and Latin classics were published in five vernaculars alone.[48] After the Bible, the *Imitatio Christi* (often attributed to Thomas Kempis) was well ahead of the field, with at least fifty-two translations into twelve languages, including Breton, Catalan, Czech, Hungarian, Polish and Swedish, all published before 1700. Among modern authors, Luther and Erasmus were among those most often translated (below, p. 83).

Works of modern literature were often turned into other languages. They are passed over rapidly in this volume not because they were unimportant in the period but because they have been studied much more intensively than works of non-fiction. Tasso's *Gerusalemme liberata*, for

---

[45] Lefevere (1992).   [46] Toury (1995), 27.   [47] Nida (1939).   [48] Bolgar (1954), appendix 2.

instance, was translated into Latin, Spanish, English, French, German and Polish. *Don Quixote* had already appeared in French, Italian, English and German by 1648. Guarini's *Pastor fido* appeared in nine foreign languages by the end of the seventeenth century: French, Spanish, English, Dutch, Croat, Greek, German, Polish and Swedish. The translations from English into Latin made in this period included versions of the *Shepherd's Calendar, Paradise Lost,* the *Essay on Man* and the *Elegy in a Country Churchyard* (below, p. 75).

The translation of works of history, politics, piety and especially science will be discussed in later chapters of this volume. Travel and geography were also popular in translation. For example, the travels of Ludovico de Varthema, first published in Italian in 1510, had been translated into five languages by 1600. Giovanni Botero's *Relazioni,* or descriptions of the different parts of the world, were translated wholly or partially into German, Latin, English, Spanish and Polish. Contemporary interest in China is revealed by the many translations of Marco Polo, of the description of China by the Augustinian friar Juan González de Mendoza and of the history of the fall of the Ming dynasty written by the Italian Jesuit Martino Martini (below, p. 129).[49]

VI

For whom were translations made? Translations were clearly made for different publics with different levels of education, as may be seen from the coexistence of two trends in this period. The first is that of translations from Greek and Latin into the vernaculars. The second, little studied despite the importance of the phenomenon, is the reverse, translations into Latin, not only from Greek but from the vernaculars as well. Over 1,100 translations from the vernaculars into Latin were made between the invention of printing and 1799, with a peak of more than 350 texts in the fifty years 1600–49 (below, p. 68).

Translations in manuscript should not be forgotten, like the general circulation of manuscripts in early modern Europe, emphasized in some important recent studies.[50] These manuscript translations include Spanish versions of More's *Utopia,* Sidney's *Defence of Poetry,* Montaigne's *Essays,* Cambini's history of the Turks, Spandugino's account of the Turks, the two Guicciardinis, Francesco and Ludovico (both translated by King

---

[49] Of all these authors, Machiavelli has been studied with most care: Gerber (1911–13).
[50] Love (1993); Bouza (2001).

Philip IV), and Maffei's history of the Indies.[51] Again, a German translation of the Italian historian Sabellico (by Thomas Murner, more famous
as a critic of Luther), like an English translation of the history of England
by the Italian humanist Polydore Vergil, remained unpublished in the early
modern period. In Russia and the Ottoman Empire, where there were few
printed books until the eighteenth and nineteenth centuries respectively,
translations generally circulated in manuscript (below, pp. 192ff., 212ff.).

The question, for whom? requires a geographical as well as a social
answer. Translations into Latin were made primarily so that educated
men whose first language was Germanic or Slav could have access to
works written in Italian, French or Spanish (below, p. 71). As for translations from one European vernacular into another, they may be analysed
according to both their original language (a sign of its prestige or cultural
hegemony) and their target language (a sign that that culture was open to
ideas from outside). In other words the 'political economy of translation',
both the imports and the exports, makes a revealing cultural indicator.[52]

Few attempts have been made to compile complete lists of translations
from one vernacular into another, so the conclusions that follow are
necessarily impressionistic and provisional.[53] Translations were made into
many languages in this period, whether European (Basque, Breton, Croat
and so on) or non-European (Armenian, Aymara, Chinese etc.), but only a
few languages were the vehicle for many translations.

Looking at the 'balance of trade' between vernaculars it is no surprise to
find a high level of Italian exports, especially in the Renaissance. Less
predictably, Italian imports were also high, especially in the sixteenth
century and from Spanish, a sign of Spanish cultural hegemony at that time.

In France, imports from Italian and Spanish were high in the late
sixteenth and early seventeenth centuries.[54] In the later seventeenth century,
French culture gradually opened to translations from English, a generation
or so before the notorious 'Anglomania' of the eighteenth century. Hobbes,
Locke, Richard Baxter, Thomas Browne, Thomas Gage, Richard Allestree,
William Temple and Gilbert Burnet were among the authors translated
into French between 1650 and 1700. The growing prestige of French is
revealed by its use as an intermediary, for English books to be translated into
German, for instance, and sometimes into Spanish, Italian or Russian.[55]

---

[51] On More, Bouza (2001), 48; on Sidney, Buesa Gómez (1989); on Montaigne, Marichal (1971); on the
Turks, Lawrance (2001), 18–19.
[52] Jacquemond (1992), 139.
[53] Existing studies include Scott (1916); Balsamo (1992); Hausmann (1992).
[54] Balsamo (1998).   [55] Blassneck (1934).

In the case of Spain, both imports and exports seem to have been lower than in Italy or France, although they were higher than traditional stereotypes of a 'closed country' might suggest. Erasmus was translated into Spanish relatively early, along with Renaissance Italians such as Ariosto, Castiglione, and even Aretino and Machiavelli (though not the *Prince*). It was only after 1550 that the culture began to close.

As for Renaissance England, imports from Italian, Spanish and French were quite high (from the period 1550–1660, about 450 published translations from Italian have been identified).[56] On the other hand, exports were extremely low before the 1660s. The few cases include the travels of Francis Drake, Martin Frobisher and Walter Raleigh, as well as texts by Francis Bacon, Philip Sidney, James I, William Perkins and Joseph Hall. These translations were often made by Englishmen, since most continental Europeans did not know English.[57] From the later seventeenth century onwards, on the other hand, translations from English became increasingly common, from the *Pilgrim's Progress* and *Paradise Lost* to works by Locke, Addison, Fielding and Richardson (on *The Spectator*, see pp. 142ff. below).[58]

In the sixteenth century, imports into German were lower than into English, though they did include the Spanish play *Celestina* (1534), Castiglione's *Cortegiano* (translated twice, in 1565 and 1593), Guicciardini (1574) and Rabelais (1575). German exports were helped by interest in Luther, but hampered by the fact that few foreigners outside the Netherlands and Central Europe knew the language.

Dutch imports were much higher than their exports, as one might have expected from a small nation that was also a trading nation with a culture that was relatively open to foreign influences. The Dutch translated a good deal from French, German, Italian, Spanish and even English. A study of this topic notes no fewer than 641 translations from English into Dutch (mainly of works of piety) made between 1600 and 1700, and it is possible to add a few items to the list.[59]

In Eastern or East-Central Europe, imports were higher than exports – as one would expect in a situation of power imbalance – but both were relatively low. Translations tended to be made from modern Latin texts (by Erasmus, for example, Calvin and Lipsius) rather than vernacular ones. Translation into Czech was important in the sixteenth century, including works by Petrarch, Erasmus and Luther and reflecting the high prestige of that language among its Slav neighbours. On the other hand, it declined

---

[56] Scott (1916).   [57] Burke (2004), 115–17.
[58] Price and Price (1934); Graeber and Roche (1988); Fabian (1992).   [59] Schoneveld (1983).

rapidly in the seventeenth century, following the Germanization of Bohemia after the Battle of the White Mountain in 1620.

The place of Czech was taken by Polish, which was on the rise as a literary language in the later sixteenth century. Castiglione's *Cortegiano* was turned into Polish, together with Ariosto, Tasso and the political writers Botero and Fadrique Furió Ceriol (below, p. 113). In the seventeenth century, translations from Latin into Russian were made via Polish, indicating the importance of Poland for Russians at that time as a cultural intermediary with the West.

In Scandinavia, exports were virtually non-existent and imports were low until the seventeenth-century campaign described above. Of the 335 translations into Swedish printed in the course of that century, 203 (or 61 per cent) were from German, 14 from French and 11 from English (translation from Latin accounting for most of the rest).[60]

'Uneven flows' of this kind demand explanation and have been explained in terms of the place of different countries in the centre or on the periphery or semi-periphery of a world system.[61] What was translated from one language into another at a given time offers a valuable clue to the dominant cultural model, whether it was Italian, Spanish, French or came from another culture. In the case of Sweden, for instance, translations suggest that the model was Germany.

The history of what was not translated, like other absences, also offers valuable clues to differences between different parts of early modern Europe. For example, translations of the Bible into Spanish were published in this period but only outside Spain (in Antwerp in 1543, in Ferrara in 1553 and in Basel in 1569). Montaigne's *Essays* were not publicly available in Spanish in this period (although two manuscript translations have survived), and they did not appear in print in German until 1797. For translations of Shakespeare, readers and listeners had to wait until the middle of the eighteenth century, the one exception to this rule being a seventeenth-century Dutch version of *The Taming of the Shrew*.

VII

In what manner were translations made? What theories, explicit or implicit, did translators follow in this period? We have reached what might be called the 'tactics' of translation, as opposed to the 'strategy' discussed above.[62]

---

[60] Hansson (1982).   [61] Heilbron (1999); cf. Milo (1984).
[62] On 'translation tactics', Lefevere (1992), 97–108.

These tactics should be understood not in the sense of rules to be followed mechanically but rather as what the French social theorist Pierre Bourdieu called a 'habitus', in other words a principle underlying and controlling spontaneity and improvisation.[63] Translation theory is not new, even though it is currently enjoying a massive revival. In the 1420s, for instance, the Italian humanist Leonardo Bruni produced what has been called 'the first substantial theoretical statement on translation since St Jerome's letter to Pammachius', a short treatise entitled *De interpretatione recta*, 'On correct translation'.[64] After 1500, such statements multiplied, among them Martin Luther's *Sendbrief vom Dolmetschen* (1530); Etienne Dolet's *La manière de bien traduire* (1540); and Gaspard de Tende's *Règles de la traduction* (1660), as well as general prefaces to particular translations such as Nicolas d'Ablancourt's *Tacitus* (1640) or John Dryden's *Ovid* (1680).[65]

Debates revolved around the distinction between translating word for word – often denounced as 'slavery', 'servility' or 'superstition' – and translating the sense of a given text. A phrase from Horace about the 'faithful translator', *fidus interpres*, the equivalent for translation theory of his phrase *ut pictura poesis* in Renaissance art criticism, was discussed over and over again.[66]

The idea of untranslatability, a result of the specific genius of each language, was also discussed at this time, long before the well-known statements of Benedetto Croce and José Ortega y Gasset.[67] In Poland, for instance, Jan Seklucjan argued that 'There are many properties in a given language which it is difficult to express in another language with an equally important word.'[68] In France, the scholar-printer Etienne Dolet and the poets Joachim Du Bellay and Jacques Peletier du Mans made similar points: 'chacune langue a ses propriétés' (Dolet); 'chaque langue a je ne sçay quoy propre seulement à elle' (Du Bellay); 'les mots et manières de parler sont particuliers aux nations' (Peletier).[69] In England, Florio's preface to his Montaigne lamented that 'The Tuscan altiloquence ... the sharpe state of the Spanish, the strong significancy of the Dutch [probably meaning German] cannot from here be drawn to life.'

The variety of terms employed in different languages in the early modern period to describe the practice that we know as translation is worth noting

---

[63] Bourdieu (1972).   [64] Viti (2004); Copenhaver (1988), 82.
[65] Larwill (1934); on Luther, Stolt (1983); on Dolet, Worth (1988); on Tende and D'Ablancourt, Zuber (1968); on Dryden, T. Steiner (1975), and Kitagaki (1981).
[66] Norton (1984).   [67] Stankiewicz (1981); Trabant (2000).   [68] Quoted in Mayenowa (1984), 345.
[69] Dolet (1540), 15; Du Bellay (1549), Book 1, chapter 5; Peletier (1555), 110.

here because it provides clues to how the practice was viewed at the time. The terms 'translate', *traduire, tradurre, traducir, transferre* (an irregular Latin verb with a past participle *translatus*), *übersetzen* and so on were coming into use (the Italian *tradurre* is recorded in 1420, for instance, and the French *traduire* from 1480).[70]

However, these terms coexisted with words which were vaguer and so seem to license a free or domesticating approach. In German, for instance, there was *verdeutschen*, 'to make German', *gedolmetschen*, 'to interpret', *versetzen* and *ümgesetzen*, as well as circumlocutions such as 'ins Teutsche gebracht'. In Latin, there was *versio*, 'a turn', *convertere*, 'to convert' and *interpretare* (reminding us of the links between interpreters and interpretations). In English, there was 'done into English', 'reduced into English' (Geoffrey Fenton's phrase for his translation of Guicciardini) or simply 'englished'. In Italian there was *volgarizzare*, to turn into the vernacular (*il volgare*); in Spanish, *vulgarizar* or *romanzar*, 'turn into a Romance language'.

Turning from theory to practice, it seems possible – at least as a first approximation – to distinguish a medieval regime or culture of translation from a post-medieval one. Although specialists have rightly noted 'the heterogeneity and complexity of the medieval tradition', it may still be suggested that the medieval regime was dominated by 'word-for-word' translation (*verbum pro verbo*, in Cicero's famous phrase), though it did allow the incorporation of glosses to the text without signalling that these were additions by the translator.[71] As Theo Hermans puts it, literalism was the 'hard core' of the medieval regime.[72]

One result of this literalism, whether or not this was intended, was what translation theorists such as Lawrence Venuti call 'foreignizing'. The term, itself a translation of the German verb *verfremden*, refers to the introduction of words from the donor culture into the receiver culture, producing in the reader a sense of distanciation or estrangement.

By contrast to medieval practice, translators from Leonardo Bruni onwards emphasized the need to translate sense for sense (*sensum de sensu*).[73] Despite frequent references to the 'laws' of translation, the early modern culture of translation was one of relative freedom. Translators generally followed what Venuti calls the 'fluent strategy', the one that 'domesticates the foreign text', offering the reader 'the narcissistic experience of recognizing his or her culture in a cultural other'.[74] If they still used

---

[70] Folena (1991); some criticisms on the basis of Spanish material in Pym (2000), 109–31.
[71] Copeland (1991), 222; Pym (2000), 46–51, 72.   [72] Hermans (1992), 99.
[73] Viti (2004); Folena (1991), 60–6.   [74] Venuti (1992), 5.

that once fashionable term, anthropologists might describe what these translators were doing as a form of 'acculturation'.

Translations were often made indirectly, at second hand. The unashamed references to this process on title-pages indicate a different culture of translation from the one which became dominant in the nineteenth century.[75] In England, for instance, Greek, Italian and Spanish texts were often translated via French. Bacon's *Essays* were rendered into French from Italian and his *Considerations Touching a War with Spain* (like Locke's *Concerning Human Understanding*) into Italian from French. Dutch was the medium through which some translations of devotional works by William Perkins and others travelled on their way from English into German. In the seventeenth and eighteenth centuries, many translations of English texts into German (among them Hall's *Characters*, Bayly's *Praxis of Piety* and Locke's second *Treatise on Government*) were made via French.[76]

There were even translations at third or more hands. A version of the Koran in German published in 1688 announced that it had been translated from the Dutch translation of the French translation from the Arabic. However, this was closer to the original than the Dutch Koran of 1641, made from the German translation of an Italian translation of the Latin translation.[77] A still more extreme example is that of the fables of Bidpai. In this case Sir Thomas North produced what has been described as 'the English version of an Italian adaptation of a Spanish translation of a Latin version of a Hebrew translation of an Arabic adaptation of the Pahlevi version of the Indian original'.[78]

All the same, practices of translation in the early modern period varied considerably more than general theories suggest. As often happens, different norms coexisted and competed, so that we may speak of cultures or sub-cultures of translation.[79] Individual translators were not forced to be free. The variety of sixteenth-century practice may be illustrated from different versions of a passage from the famous Italian conduct book *Il galateo*, where the subject is language itself. The text argued that Lombards, for example, should speak their own dialect because they speak it better than Tuscan. The English and French translations retained the Italian example, while the German translator replaced it with a roughly equivalent reference to High German and Saxon.

---

[75] Stackelberg (1984).   [76] Blassneck (1934); Stackelberg (1984); Graeber and Roche (1988).
[77] The last example is quoted by Pym (2000), 13.   [78] Matthiessen (1931), 63n.
[79] Toury (1995), 53–69; Schäffner (1999).

A number of writers distinguished between approaches to different kinds of text – religious and secular, verse and prose – just as Jerome himself had done when he recommended the literal translation of the Bible but a freer translation of other texts. The higher the status of the text, the greater was the pressure on the translator to follow the original wording closely.

The admiration for Cicero during the Renaissance encouraged some humanists to translate texts – including the Bible – into a prose that was closer to Cicero than the original had been. However, Sébastien Castellion's translation of Scripture into Ciceronian periods was generally condemned. Following a foreignizing strategy, some translations of the Old Testament into English and Dutch (the Authorized Version and the States' Bible, for instance), took pains to imitate Hebrew formulae and syntax, making great use of the conjunction 'and' as well as repetitions such as 'to thee this day, even to thee'.[80]

Differences in styles of translation expressed diverse views of the Church. Translations of the New Testament were criticized by radical Protestants for not being literal enough, for example for translating *episkopos* as 'bishop' rather than 'overseer' or *ekklesia* by 'church' rather than by 'congregation'. In the case of the Old Testament, Szymon Budny coined the word *ofiarnik*, 'sacrificer', to replace the traditional rendering, *kaplan*, 'chaplain', 'because', as he put it, 'some simple uneducated people may understand that such saintly men as Samuel and Zacharias . . . were equal to our contemporary Roman priests, yet the two kinds are different as day differs from night'.[81]

Placing Calvin on the same level as Scripture, the English translator Thomas Norton claimed that he would 'follow the words so near as the phrase of the English tongue would suffer me'.[82] As Hermans has noted, the strategy of literalism often expresses a sense of inferiority to a given text, author or language.[83]

All the same, some Bible translators, from Luther to Castellion, chose the fluent strategy. Luther, for instance, rejected the literal translation of biblical phrases such as 'the abundance of the heart' or 'full of grace'. One reformer, Matthias Flacius, in his 'Key to the Bible' (*Clavis scripturae*, 1567) described a close adherence to words at the expense of the meaning as a kind of 'superstition'. The foreword to the Authorized Version criticized the 'scrupulosity of the Puritans' who 'put washing for Baptism'.

---

[80] Hammond (1982), 210.   [81] Quoted in Borowski (1999), 29.   [82] Quoted in Kelly (1979), 208.
[83] Hermans (1992), 108.

Faced with the problem of translating Christianity beyond Europe, different missionaries chose different options. In Japan, some of them treated the word *Deus* as untranslatable, leaving it in Latin.[84] In the Philippines, they used the Spanish words 'Dios', 'Espíritu Santo' and 'Jesu-Cristo', whether to avoid the risk of misunderstanding or because they believed in the superiority of Spanish. In Mexico too the Franciscans used the term 'Dios'.[85] In Brazil, the Jesuit José de Anchieta, who wrote hymns in Tupí, introduced into that language Portuguese words for concepts that the Indians apparently lacked, notably 'grace' (*graça*), 'virgin' (*virgem*) and 'sin' (*pecado*).[86]

Only a few bold missionaries, generally Jesuits, rendered keywords of Christianity by apparent equivalents from the culture of their audience, such as 'heavenly way' (*tento*) in Japanese and 'heaven' (*tian*) in Chinese.[87] It may well be significant that these exceptions come from fields in which the missionaries lacked the support of a colonizing power such as Spain or Portugal and were dependent on the good will of their hosts.

The majority of examples support the generalization that colonizing states forced the colonized to view their own culture through the lens of the dominant power.[88] All the same, the force of the arguments in favour of these tactics should not be forgotten. Like other translators, the missionaries were forced to make the always difficult choice between foreignizing and domestication – their situation being the reverse of the usual one for translators, since the donor culture in this case was their own and the recipient culture that of the 'other'.

Next on the scale of respect after religious texts came the Greek and Latin classics. For example, the relatively free translations of Aristotle produced in the Renaissance by Leonardo Bruni and Johannes Argyropulos were criticized by other humanists such as Alonso de Cartagena (Bishop of Burgos and translator of Cicero). Bruni was a purist who objected to Latin terms such as *democratia* because they were hybrid, or as he put it, 'half Greek', while Cartagena preferred the borrowing of such technical terms to paraphrasing.[89] In similar fashion William Caxton's translation of the *Aeneid* was criticized for its freedom by the early sixteenth-century Scottish translator Gavin Douglas.[90]

In seventeenth-century France, a famous debate centred on the new translations of the classics by Nicolas d'Ablancourt. These free and fluent

[84] Elison (1988).   [85] Rafael (1993), 20; Pym (2000), 148.   [86] Anchieta (1984), 157, 171, 178.
[87] Elison (1988); Higashibaba (2001), 39. On China, see Hsia's essay in this volume.
[88] Rafael (1993); Cheyfitz (1991); Niranjana (1992).   [89] Pym (2000), 122–6.
[90] Burrow (1997), 22–3.

versions provoked the critic Gilles Ménage to refer to the *belles infidèles*, comparing translations to women and claiming that the beautiful ones are not faithful, while the faithful ones are not beautiful.[91] Replying to his critics and secularizing a traditional phrase of religious reformers like Flacius (above, p. 28), D'Ablancourt attacked what he called the 'Judaic superstition' of following the original text word by word. 'I do not always stick to the author's words or even to his thoughts,' he declared. 'I keep the effect he wanted to produce in mind.' What he advocated was what we might call cultural translation, giving the old metaphor of a language as a form of clothing a new twist and arguing that 'Different times do not just require different words but also different thoughts, and ambassadors usually dress in the fashion of the country to which they are sent.'[92]

The freedom claimed by D'Ablancourt was criticized by other writers such as Gaspar de Tende, who stressed *fidélité*.[93] Ménage raised the issue of anachronism, condemning 'translations that outrageously modernized their text'.[94] However, even D'Ablancourt argued for the retention of some technical terms such as 'cohort' or 'centurion' when translating ancient writers, since their armies were very different from 'ours'. The reason for this temporary shift into foreignization, which led D'Ablancourt to provide his translation of Appian with a glossary, was probably that he was writing for noblemen who took considerable interest in the details of military organization.[95]

So far as relatively modern texts were concerned, the early modern regime of translation was characterized by even greater freedom than has been described so far, allowing plenty of scope for reworking. Modern texts were not infrequently considered capable of improvement by their translators. Thus Jean Martin, the translator into French of the Italian romance *Polifilo*, boasted – with some justification, it is true – that 'from a more than Asiatic prolixity he has reduced it to a French brevity' (*d'une prolixité plus que Asiatique il l'a reduict à une brieveté françoise*), while Pierre Boiastuau called Matteo Bandello's stories *mieux poly* ('better polished' or 'more polite') in his French version than in the original Italian.

The borderline between translation and imitation was drawn less sharply than it would be in the nineteenth century, though it was drawn in different places by different individuals. What the sixteenth-century French poet Joachim Du Bellay called 'imitation' was described as translation a

---

[91] Mounin (1955); Zuber (1968); Guillerm (1996).   [92] Zuber (1968).

[93] Mounin (1955); Zuber (1968), 165–279; Guillerm (1996). On Tende, Ballard (1992), 186–97.

[94] Quoted in Zuber (1968), 195.   [95] Zuber (1968), 122–3, 139, 175, 211.

hundred years later by Nicolas d'Ablancourt and his English contemporaries, such as John Dryden.[96] The Spanish version of Garzoni's *Piazza universale*, describing all the world's occupations, was described on its title-page as 'in part translated from the Tuscan and in part an original composition' (*parte traduzida del toscano y parte compuesta*).

The crucial point is that what were described at the time as 'translations' often differed from the originals in major respects, whether they shortened the texts or amplified them. Changes of this kind were often made without warning the reader, although the French critic Jean Chapelain, translator of the Spanish romance *Guzmán de Alfarache*, declared with some pride that he had cut, added, moved, strengthened and weakened passages from the original as well as changing metaphors and phrases, producing a text that was longer than the original (*J'ay transposé, restably, retranché, adjousté, uny, separé, renforcy, affoibli le discours, changé les metaphores et les phrases . . . et plustost augmenté que diminué*). The poet Abraham Cowley was even more frank in the preface to his version of the Greek poet Pindar: 'I have in these two odes of Pindar left out and added what I pleased.'

Contraction, the freedom to subtract, took different forms. Long texts might be abridged in translation, reduced to as little as half of their original length. Other omissions were a form of bowdlerization. It has been noted, for instance, that the Italian humanists who translated Plato's *Republic* into Latin avoided his reference to the community of women. Where Plato wrote *sunoikein*, 'cohabit', the translators preferred vaguer terms such as *habitare*, 'inhabit', or *adherere*, 'join'.[97] Again, the Latin version of Machiavelli's *Principe* by Silvestro Teglio 'omits key sentences, as in chapter 18 on how princes are to keep faith'.[98] Passages might be omitted – without warning to readers – for religious, moral or political reasons. Thus the Dominican friar Francesco Pipino's translation of Marco Polo's travels deletes a passage in praise of Buddha as well as eliminating some of the rhetoric of chivalry.[99]

Bowdlerization was equally common in translations into the vernacular. Johann Fischart, better known for his amplifications, omitted some passages in Rabelais discussing religion. The German translation of *Lazarillo de Tormes* omitted some anticlerical remarks.[100] The Italian translation of Bacon's *Essays* left out one essay altogether, dealing with religion and superstition, while the French version – made from the Italian – suppressed some of Bacon's references to recent French history.[101] The Spanish

---

[96] Hermans (1992); Toury (1995), 132.   [97] Hankins (1990), vol. II, 424–6.
[98] Anglo (2005), 441.   [99] Larner (1999), 76, 104, 107, 113.   [100] Brancaforte (1983), xv.
[101] De Mas (1975), 160; Lawton (1926).

translation of the *Wealth of Nations* removed Adam Smith's approving references to toleration.[102]

The liberty of Renaissance translations also included the freedom to add material, or as the rhetoricians put it, to 'amplify'. It was not uncommon for translators to render one word in the original by two, perhaps out of insecurity, though possibly because conjoint phrases pleased the ears of readers of the period. A number of translators of the *Cortegiano* produced doublets of this kind, rendering the key term *sprezzatura* (more or less 'negligence') as *mespris et nonchalance* or *Verachtung oder Unachtsamkeit*. Again, Florio translated Montaigne's *simptome* as 'a Symthome or passion' and his *siècle debordé* as 'an irregular and licentious age'.[103]

Amplifications might introduce new messages as well as reinforcing existing ones. Pipino's translation of Marco Polo, for instance, inserted condemnations of Islam. Jacques Gohorry's translation of Machiavelli's *Discorsi* announces on the title-page that the discourses have been 'revised and augmented' (*reueuz et augmentez*). The translation of Erasmus's *Enchiridion* by Alonso Fernández has become as notorious for its amplification of the original text as for its omissions.[104] It was not an aberration but simply an extreme example of a general tendency to be found in the Renaissance culture of translation.

The most famous example of amplification is probably Fischart's translation of Rabelais, the *Geschichtsklitterung* (1575). In this case the rivalry between translator and author is particularly clear. For example, the already long lists dear to the original author, like the 200-odd games played by the young giant Gargantua, are expanded still further in the translation. Fischart never used one word when two or three would serve his purpose, out-rabelaising Rabelais and inventing a grotesque polysyllabic language of his own. He was emulated in this respect in the following century by the Scottish translator Sir Thomas Urquhart. The extra material was sometimes derived from other texts that the 'translator' assembled in a kind of collage, a practice that the German translator Aegidius Albertinus already described as *Colligiren*.

In some cases the action of dialogues, plays and stories was shifted from one locale to another, a process that may be described in musical terms as 'transposition' or – following the practice of current translators of software – as 'localization'.[105] Translated plays, for instance, were placed in new settings that were more familiar to the new audiences. Péter Bornemisza's

---

[102] Lai (1999), xix.   [103] Toury (1995), 102–12; on Castiglione, Burke (1995), chapter 4.
[104] Russell (1985), 52.   [105] On transposition, Jakobson (1959), 234; on localization, Pym (2000), 117.

Hungarian version of *Electra* set the play in Hungary, while a Polish translation of Plautus's play *Trinummus*, Cieklinski's *Protrójny* (1597), relocated the action to Lwów. Fischart moved the settings of chapters of Rabelais from France to Strassburg or Basel. Abraham Fraunce went still further in a translation of Tasso into which he inserted a new character, 'Pembrokiana', in honour of his patroness Mary Sidney.

A similar procedure was followed in the case of non-fiction. For example, the Spanish humanist Juan de Lucena adapted a text by Bartolomeo Fazio on the happy life, moving the dialogue from Ferrara to the court of Castille. The translation of Machiavelli's *Arte della guerra* into Spanish displaced the dialogue from Italy to Spain and turned the speakers into two Spaniards, the Great Captain Gonzalo Fernández de Cordoba and the Duke of Najara, perhaps because Spanish readers of the period would not have expected to learn anything about war from Italians. The Polish version of Castiglione's *Cortegiano* made by Łukasz Górnicki relocated the dialogue from Urbino to a villa near Kraków.

Again, the translation into English by Ludovic Bryskett in 1608 of a dialogue on civil life by the Italian Giambattista Cinthio Giraldi transposed the setting of the conversation from Italy to Ireland and introduced English participants such as the Archbishop of Armagh and the poet Edmund Spenser. Actually, the book was not presented as a translation either on its title-page or in its dedication. Only at the end does the reader learn that Bryskett had 'Englished' the work, 'for my exercise in both languages', and that he had omitted passages and added others because 'I would not tie myself to the strict laws of an interpreter.'

Even more shocking for modern readers, translators of works of history or natural philosophy sometimes allowed themselves to express opinions that the original author would have repudiated. When Thomas Dale translated a dialogue on physics by the French Cartesian Noël Regnault, for instance, he introduced the ideas of Newton into the notes. With characteristic boldness, when Cardinal de Retz, who had been a rebel himself, translated Agostino Mascardi's history of the conspiracy by Count Fieschi, he contradicted his source text by turning the protagonist from a villain into a hero.[106]

These translations were extremely creative. Indeed, they might be described more exactly as 'tradaptations', as Michel Garneau puts it.[107]

---

[106] Watts (1980), 134.
[107] On the need to relate conceptions of translation to conceptions of intellectual property, Hermans (1992), 133; Garneau quoted in Baker (1998), 8.

Conversely, as John Florio pointed out in his preface to his translation of Montaigne's *Essays*, so-called original works might be described more exactly as translations. 'If nothing can be now sayd, but hath beene saide before ... What doe the best then, but gleane after others harvest? borrow their colours, inherit their possessions? What doe they but translate?'

At this point it may be useful to step back from the examples for a moment in order to consider their significance. The freedom of translators may be compared with the freedom of scribes. It was not uncommon for copyists of poems, for instance those of John Donne (which circulated in manuscript at the beginning of the seventeenth century), to leave out stanzas or even to insert new ones. Manuscript was what we might call an 'interactive' medium.[108] Like these scribes, early modern translators of medieval or modern works seem to have viewed themselves as co-authors with the right to modify the original text. In the early modern period it was only very gradually that the idea of a text as both the work and the property of a single individual imposed itself.

This free or open regime of translation continued into the eighteenth century.[109] Thus Rawlinson's version of Lenglet du Fresnoy, published in 1728, was described on the title-page as 'translated and improved', like the late eighteenth-century version of Richardson's *Pamela*. The most that could be said about a trend over time is that the seventeenth-century debate reveals a sharper awareness of the dilemmas that face translators. Dryden's distinction between 'metaphrase' (a literal translation), 'paraphrase' (defined as 'translation with latitude') and 'imitation' is a famous example of such awareness.[110] Domestication ruled.

It is true that a few examples of foreignization can be found, as was noted earlier, in the religious domain, as in the case of texts concerned with the Ottoman Empire (below, p. 79).[111] Some translators of the Bible refused to commit anachronisms such as translating the New Testament Greek term *presbyteros* by 'priest'. This refusal, generally motivated by a belief that the Church of their own time was corrupt and that a return to the 'primitive church' was necessary, also reveals a sense of distance between past and present in contrast to the medieval assumption that past and present were close to each other.[112]

All the same, it was only around the year 1816, the year of the publication of important statements on translation by Friedrich Schleiermacher and Wilhelm Humboldt, that the self-conscious attempt to give readers a

---

[108] Love (1993); Marotti (1995).   [109] Stackelberg (1971).   [110] G. Steiner (1975), 253–6.
[111] Burke (forthcoming).   [112] Burke (1969).

sense of the alien quality of the original text became a major trend in translation history.

As Schleiermacher put it, the translator's choice was between taking the reader to the writer or taking the writer to the reader (*Entweder der Übersetzer lässt den Schriftsteller möglichst in Ruhe, und bewegt den Leser ihm entgegen; oder er lässt den Leser möglichst in Ruhe und bewegt den Schriftsteller ihm entgegen*). In his opinion, the translator should prefer the first alternative. The new ideal was to give the translation what Wilhelm von Humboldt called 'a kind of foreign colour' (*eine gewisse Farbe der Fremdheit*), translating Homer or Dante into medieval English or French or imitating ancient Greek syntax in German.[113] The hybridization of language condemned by Bruni now became a virtue, at least for a minority of translators.

In other words, changes in translation practices fit the model proposed by Michel Foucault in which 1800 marks a major break in what he calls the European 'episteme'.[114] The rise of foreignization is part of the rise of romanticism and historicism, including the idea that different languages express different world-views and that the past is a foreign country. The view expressed by Dryden, that Virgil should be presented in translation as if he had been born 'in this present age', was now rejected.[115]

Germans played a prominent part in this trend, reacting against a French cultural hegemony associated with the emphasis on universal values such as clarity and reason.[116] In this regard Herder's comment on translations of Homer is revealing. 'Homer must enter France a captive, clad in the French fashion, lest he offend their eye . . . We poor Germans, on the other hand . . . just want to see him as he is.'[117] In other words, at the end of the eighteenth century the Germans viewed domestication as foreign!

VIII

A final question: what were the consequences of translation? Like other forms of speech and writing, translating is a kind of action. As we have seen, rulers and churches patronized translation in order to change the world, to convert the heathen or to help Sweden or Russia catch up with Western Europe.

The contribution of translation to the spread of knowledge is obvious enough, but something should also be said about misunderstanding, a

---

[113] G. Steiner (1975); Berman (1984); Venuti (1995).   [114] Foucault (1966).
[115] Quoted in G. Steiner (1975), 256.   [116] Mannheim (1927).
[117] Herder quoted in Robinson (1997), 59.

topic that has not yet received from cultural historians the attention that it deserves. A small but typical example is that of the sixteenth-century French artist Bernard Palissy, whose belief that fossils were a result of the Flood derived from a misunderstanding of a passage in a treatise by the Italian natural philosopher Girolamo Cardano that Palissy read in French translation.[118] On a grander scale, the English translator of Philibert de Vienne's satire *Le philosophe de court* took literally what the author had meant to be taken ironically and so recommended precisely what the original author condemned.[119]

In the case of the Bible, the translator's choice of key terms might have far-reaching consequences, whether in the case of *episkopos* (above, p. 28), or in that of the passage in Exodus often rendered 'Thou shalt not suffer a witch to live' – though Johan Weyer and Reginald Scot claimed that 'poisoner' was a better translation than 'witch' for the Hebrew *chasaf*. In a still more radical fashion the Dutch freethinker Adriaan Koerbagh claimed that the Hebrew word in the Old Testament generally translated as 'devil' actually meant 'accuser' or 'libeller'.[120]

The translation movement of the period had major consequences for the languages of early modern Europe. The literary theorist Mikhail Bakhtin drew attention to 'the immense importance of translations' in the Renaissance in what he variously called (in Russian) the interaction, 'interorientation' and 'interanimation' of languages.[121] The translation of the Bible and the classics into the vernaculars of Europe helped raise the status of these languages. It also enriched them thanks to the neologisms coined by translators who found no terms appropriate to render the religious vocabulary of the Old Testament, for instance, or the philosophical vocabulary of Aristotle (including political terms such as *oligarchia* and *democratia*). The period 1570–1630, when the English vocabulary expanded most rapidly, was also a great age of translation.

When Alberti's treatise on architecture was translated into French in 1553 the dedication to the king drew attention to the translator's enrichment of the language. In order to translate Rabelais, Fischart invented many German words. The poet George Chapman's version of Homer introduced many new words into English. Many of these words did not take root, so that modern editors of Chapman consider it necessary to provide a glossary. On the other hand, a number of the neologisms coined by Florio in his translation of Montaigne have become part of the language, among them amusing, conscientious, efface, effort, emotion, endear, facilitate and

---

[118] Rudwick (1972), 41.   [119] Javitch (1971).   [120] Israel (2001), 405.   [121] Bakhtin (1965), 470.

regret. Again, John Shute's version of Andrea Cambini's history of the Turks introduced into English such Ottoman terms as *aga, cadi, seraglio, spahi* and *vizier*.

That the increased accessibility of texts from other cultures widened the horizons of readers seems plausible enough, even if this widening cannot be measured. At this point we may return to the reception of the Renaissance, the Reformation and the Enlightenment and the way in which translation made something happen, multiplying the effect of certain important texts at the price of changing their meaning.

In the case of the Renaissance, the many translations of the classics into vernacular languages have been mentioned already. The translation of Italian treatises on the arts encouraged the adoption of the new classicizing style, and both the plans and the details of a number of sixteenth-century buildings in England, France and elsewhere have been traced back to illustrations in the treatise on architecture by Sebastiano Serlio, which had appeared by 1611 in Dutch, German, French, Spanish, Latin and English as well as in the original Italian. Turning to political and social thought, we find that More's *Utopia*, written in Latin, was available in six printed translations before the end of the sixteenth century (one each in German, Italian, English and Dutch and two in French).

In the case of the Reformation, translation was even more important. Erasmus wrote in Latin in order to be read all over Europe, but to reach ordinary people he needed the help of translators. His *Enchiridion militis christiani* appeared in nine vernaculars in the sixteenth century – in chronological order they were Czech, German, English, Dutch, Spanish, French, Italian, Portuguese and Polish.[122] Works by Luther, notably his catechisms, were translated into ten vernaculars between 1517 and 1546. In order of importance these languages were Dutch, Danish, French, Czech, English, Italian, Polish, Spanish, Swedish and Finnish.[123] As for Calvin, eighteen translations of his work into Dutch had been published by 1600, nineteen into Italian, thirty-two into German and ninety-one into English.[124]

During the Enlightenment, translation was once again essential to the spread of ideas. In the eighteenth century, Montesquieu's *Esprit des lois* circulated in English, Dutch and Italian as well as the original French. Locke's *Second Treatise on Government* circulated in French, German and Swedish, his *Essay on Human Understanding* in French, Latin and German

---

[122] Haeghen (1897–1907).   [123] Seidel Menchi (1977); Higman (1984); Moeller (1987).
[124] Higman (1994).

and his *Thoughts on Education* in Dutch, French, German, Italian, Swedish and Russian. Although it was published in 1776, Adam Smith's *Wealth of Nations* was already circulating in German, French, Danish, Italian, Spanish and Dutch by the end of the eighteenth century.

These translations had their price. Translators have their own agenda which may differ from those of the original writer, a point exemplified below (pp. 134ff.) by the reception abroad of the Italian historians Guicciardini and Sarpi. Even when translators tried to be neutral, the language they used was not. Take the case of Adam Ferguson's *Essay on the History of Civil Society*. In German the key concept was rendered as *bürgerliche Gesellschaft*, assimilating it to the German legal tradition and eliminating the 'original civic, activist meaning' of the term 'civil'.[125]

Whether translators follow the strategy of domestication or that of foreignizing, whether they understand or misunderstand the text they are turning into another language, the activity of translation necessarily involves both decontextualizing and recontextualizing. Something is always 'lost in translation'. However, the close examination of what is lost is one of the most effective ways of identifying differences between cultures. For this reason, the study of translation is or should be central to the practice of cultural history.

[125] Oz-Salzberger (1995), 142–8.

The Catholic mission and translations in China, 1583–1700

R. Po-chia Hsia

Between the establishment of the Catholic mission in China by the two Italian Jesuits Michele Ruggieri and Matteo Ricci in 1583 and the apex of its success around the year 1700, European missionaries composed and published c. 450 works in Chinese.[1] Of this total, some 120 texts deal with European science, technology and geography; another 330 are religious texts. This chapter will investigate the role of translations in this Sino-European cultural exchange: What texts were translated? Who were the translators? What were the different processes of translation? And what impact did translations exert in the cultural reception of Europe in early modern China?

Our first task, to determine the exact number of translations, involves some explanation. It can be established that of the 450 texts, at least 50 are translations in the modern sense, i.e. the adaptation of a text in whole or in parts from one language into another. There is, for example, the 1607 translation of Euclid's *Elementa*, undertaken jointly by Matteo Ricci and Paul Xu Guangqi, or the partial translation of Thomas Aquinas's *Summa theologica* by Ludovico Buglio SJ, completed between 1654 and 1678.

There were other methods of rendering European texts into Chinese that did not follow exact translations. European missionaries presented titles that paraphrased, compiled and summarized the original texts, taking account of which would substantially expand the body of translated works. In other words, in addition to translation in the strict sense, there were two further methods of textual transmission. The second method consisted in

---

[1] A complete bibliography of Christian works in Chinese for the Ming and Qing dynasties is being compiled under the direction of Nicolas Standaert at the University of Leuven. Until the completion of this work, the most reliable and convenient reference work is Xu (1949). Xu arranges the Jesuit Collection at Zikawei (Shanghai) in the year 1940 according to subject matter. All prefaces of each title are published in addition to brief biographies of Jesuit authors. In addition to the selection of the most significant titles at Zikawei Library, Xu Zongze also included partial bibliographies of the Chinese Christian collections at the Bibliothèque Nationale de France in Paris (now the Bibliothèque de France) and at the Vatican Library, Rome.

the compilation of translated or paraphrased passages from European texts into a single Chinese work, an example being Ricci's highly successful *Jiren shipian* (1608) or *Ten Essays from a Remarkable Man*, with translated passages from Aesop and Epictetus.

The third method was represented by synopsis. The Italian Jesuit Giulio Aleni published in 1635 a text *Tianzhu jiangsheng yanxing jilüe* or *The Birth, Life and Sayings of the Lord of Heaven*, which, as its title indicates, represented a synoptic presentation of the Gospels.[2] More ambiguous are Chinese texts authored by European missionaries that are based essentially on one or more European texts, making a precise conceptualization of 'translation' problematic when we consider the corpus of European cultural production in early modern China. One may assume that all scientific works produced in Chinese represented paraphrases or adaptations from existing European texts, if not outright translations.

SUBJECTS

Translated books can be divided into three large subject categories: religion, science and humanism. The first two categories are by far the more important and can be subdivided into more detailed genres. Translations on religion, for example, included prayers, liturgical texts (missal, breviary), works of theology, hagiographies, catechisms, rules of confraternities and devotional texts. Scientific translations covered astronomy, geometry, arithmetic, hydraulics, weaponry, anatomy, optics, falconry and musicology. Finally, there are a handful of texts that introduced fragments of Graeco-Roman works to Chinese readers of the seventeenth century.

Religious texts included translations from the Roman liturgy for the use of the Chinese Church (a special Chinese language liturgy was authorized in 1615 by the papacy but rescinded in the late seventeenth century). Works translated included the *Missale romanum* (1670), *Breviarium romanum* (1674) and the *Manuale ad sacramenta ministranda juxta ritum S. Romae Ecclesiae* (1675), all translated by Ludovico Buglio. Prayer translations and accompanying commentaries included the Lord's Prayer, the Rosary and the Credo. A compilation of Christian prayers, the *Tianzhu shengjiao nianjing zongdu* published by the Jesuits in 1628, contained the usual daily prayers in addition to many texts by the Spanish devotional writer Luís de Granada.[3] The most important theological work to be translated

---

[2] Bibliothèque de France (BF), Chinois 6756.　　[3] Standaert (2002), 616. Text in BF Chinois 7345.

were parts of Aquinas's *Summa theologica*, which we will discuss in detail in a later section.

In addition to works introducing the lives of the Virgin Mary and Joseph (the patron saint of China), Jesuits also published a Saints' Life and separate lives of St Josephat, St Jan Nepomuk, St Francis Borgia, St Francis Xavier, St Stanislas Kostka and St Aloysius Gonzaga. These texts were based on European originals, although the precise texts still need to be established. Devotional texts included the *Imitatio Christi*, translated by the Portuguese Jesuit Emmanuel Diaz in 1640, and aphorisms by St Teresa of Avila and St Bernard.

Like Tridentine Catholicism in Europe, the China mission did not emphasize the transmission of the Bible. A full translation of the New Testament and portions of the Old Testament were published only in the late eighteenth century by the ex-Jesuit Louis de Poirot, who based his translation into colloquial Mandarin (as opposed to the classical written style) on the Vulgate. Before this text, the only partial biblical translation was the 1730 Chinese text of Tobit, entitled *Xunwei shenbian*, completed by the French Jesuit François-Xavier Dentrecolles.[4]

In the absence of a full Bible translation, the story of the Passion was transmitted by other methods. The most successful introduction of the *Passio Christi* was represented by a pictorial translation: Giuglio Aleni's *Tianzhu jiangsheng chuxiang jingjie* (1637), based on fifty-five illustrations from Jerónimo Nadal's *Evangelicae historiae imagines*, first published in Antwerp in 1595.[5] The copper engravings of Nadal were copied by Chinese artisans, who reproduced them in cheaper woodcuts. This is the best example of pictorial translation, involving a technical reproduction (from engraving to woodcut) and a stylistic interpretation (from European to Chinese motifs).

In the translations of scientific texts, the most important works were in the fields of astronomy and mathematics, all completed before 1640, during the early decades of the Jesuit mission. A list of the European texts and their Chinese translations is presented below:[6]

> Christophorus Clavius, *Euclidis elementorum libri XV*, 1574. Chinese translation by Matteo Ricci and Xu Guangqi: *Jihe yuanben*, 1607.
> Christophorus Clavius, *Geometria practica*, 1604. Chinese translation by Matteo Ricci and Xu Guangqi: *Celiang fayi*, 1608.

---

[4] BF Chinois 6782. [5] BF Chinois 6750. [6] Standaert (2002), 739–40.

Christophorus Clavius, *Epitome arithmeticae practicae*, 1583. Chinese translation by Matteo Ricci and Li Zhizao: *Tongwen suanzhi*, 1614.

Christophorus Clavius, *In sphaeram Ioannis de Sacro Bosco commentarius*, 1570. Chinese translation by Matteo Ricci and Li Zhizao: *Yuanrong jiaoyi*, 1614.

John Napier (1550–1617), *Rabdologiae, seu numerationis per virgula libri duo*, 1617. Chinese translation by Giacomo Rho and Adam Schall: *Chousuan*, 1628.

Galileo Galilei, *Le operazioni del compasso geometrico e militare*, 1606. Chinese translation by Giacomo Rho and Adam Schall: *Biligui jie*, 1630.

Bartholomaeus Pitiscus (1561–1613), *Trigonometriae*, 1612. Chinese translation by Johann Terenz Schreck: *Da ce*, 1631.

Christophorus Clavius, *Geometria practica*, 1604. Chinese translation by Giaocomo Rho: *Celiang quanyi*, 1631.

Under the Qing emperor Kangxi (reigned 1662–1722), several Jesuits served as imperial tutors. Although several European mathematical texts were translated for the instruction of the emperor, they were never published. The second period of the Jesuit mission saw few scientific translations. One exception was in the theory of painting: the Jesuit painter Giuseppe Castiglione collaborated with Nian Xiyao to translate the *Perspectiva pictorum* (1706) of the Jesuit artist Andrea Pozzo; the Chinese work, *Shixue*, appeared in 1729 and contributed to the reception of painting in perspective in eighteenth-century China.

Only a very small fragment of the Graeco-Roman textual corpus was translated into Chinese. These texts, based on the humanistic curriculum of the *Ratio studiorum*, familiar to all Jesuit missionaries, could further be divided into the genres of rhetoric and philosophy. Ricci's highly successful *Jiaoyou lun* (1595) or *De amicitia* was based on Andreas Eborensis's *Sententiae et exempla*, an aphoristic collection from the writings of Cicero, Seneca and other classical authors.[7] Another of Ricci's texts, the *Ershiwu yan* (1605), or *The Twenty-Five Sayings*, represented a translation of a Latin version of the *Encheiridion* of Epictetus.[8]

If Chinese readers were offered snippets of Epicurean and Stoic texts, they were treated to a much larger serving of Aristotle. The Portuguese Jesuit Francisco Furtado and the Italians Alfonso Vagnone, Aleni and Francesco Sambiasi translated several Aristotelian texts and commentaries. The commentaries on Aristotle used at the Jesuit College at Coimbra were translated: *De coelo, Universa dialectica Aristotelis, Isagoge Porphrii, Categoriae, Analytica priora*. The three Italian Jesuits translated parts of

---

[7] For full classical references in Ricci's text, see the critical edition by Mignini (2005).
[8] Standaert (2002), 605.

De coelo et mundo, Meteorologica, De anima, Parva naturalia and the *Ethica Nicomachea.*

All translations were effected within a relatively short period between 1623 and 1639. Chinese literati converts collaborated closely on these texts as co-translators or stylistic editors: Xu Guangqi, Li Zhizao (1565–1630), his son Li Cibin, Han Lin (1601–44) and Duan Gun (d. 1641); two others, Wei Douxu and Zhu Sihan, were not known as converts.

Many of these texts were not translated in full, but offered as paraphrased synopses or partial translations. The translation of Aristotle accompanied the transmission of European scientific texts, which provided the motivation for someone like Li Zhizao, who was first attracted to Catholicism through his interest in European science. In his preface to *Mingli tan* (1631), the Chinese title of the first part of Aristotle's *Dialectica*, Li stressed that true knowledge of the material world depended on proper classification and concepts. Hence, terms such as *genus, species, differentia, proprium, accidens* and *categoria* aided the Confucian literati in pursuing natural philosophy (literally, *gewu qiongli zi dayuanbin*, meaning the 'origins of measuring things and exhausting principles').[9]

In turn, knowing the natural world leads to a higher form of knowledge, that of metaphysics and of God. In the preface to *Huanyou quan* (1628), the Chinese translation of *De coelo*, Li Zhizao elaborated that a true knowledge of nature and metaphysics was essential in combating the Buddhist fabrication of a myriad cosmos.[10] On this important task, Li continued in his preface, he and Furtado laboured for five years on account of the conceptual and linguistic difficulties. The presentation of the initial results in 1628 offered a first taste of much more to come; and the Chinese texts also served the function of an introduction to the language for European missionaries.

Li Zhizao died two years later, leaving the translation a fragment. A complete translation of the *Dialectica* was not effected until 1684, when Ferdinand Verbiest presented a manuscript copy to Emperor Kangxi, who denied Verbiest's request for publication, citing the uselessness of the text. Thus ended the reception of Aristotle in seventeenth-century China.

No texts by Plato or Neoplatonic works were translated into Chinese. Unlike the Aristotelian corpus, Plato was not essential reading in the humanistic curriculum of early modern Europe. Moreover, Plato's idea of the transmigration of souls was reminiscent of the Buddhist doctrines of

---

[9] Preface printed in Xu (1949), 194.   [10] Preface printed in Xu (1949), 199.

karma and reincarnation, against which the first Jesuit missionaries and their converts fought an intense polemical battle.

TRANSLATORS

With a handful of exceptions, the Jesuit mission was responsible for the production of translations into Chinese in late Ming and early Qing China. For this reason, I shall use the term 'Jesuits' to designate European missionaries in this discussion. For the period up to 1720, the Society of Jesus furnished more than two-thirds of all the European missionaries sent to China. Between 1583 and 1723, a total of 563 Jesuits left Europe for China: a few perished en route and some eventually worked in India, South-East Asia or Japan, leaving a final minimum figure of 288 European Jesuits active in the China mission in this period.[11]

Not all Jesuits participated in the production of books. The impressive Jesuit Chinese corpus was in fact produced by only fifty-nine European fathers, with eighteen engaged in translation. According to their nationality, the breakdown of Jesuit authors is as follows: Italians eighteen, Portuguese seventeen, French fourteen, Belgian four, German three, and one each from Spain, Poland and Austria. Among the eighteen Jesuit translators, eight were Italians, five Portuguese, three French and two Belgians.[12]

At first glance, the national representation of Jesuit authors/translators seems to match the overall national strength in the China mission: the three major nationalities – Portuguese, French and Italian – are prominently present. But when we actually compare these figures with the precise number of Jesuit missionaries working in China (the overall figures by Dehergne as revised by Girard, see note 11) we come up with a more nuanced picture.

In the period 1583 to 1723, a total of 129 Portuguese Jesuits, by far the strongest national representation, worked in China and Macao. Of this total only 17 fathers published texts, of whom 5 engaged in translations. The French Jesuits, who were relative latecomers in the China Mission, would dominate the foreign missionary presence in the course of the eighteenth century; overall they came in second numerically. During this

---

[11] Figures from Dehergne (1973) as revised by Girard (1999), 171–3. Girard includes only the major nationalities in her revised calculation; a handful of Polish and Swiss Jesuits are not included in her list. The actual number of Jesuits working in China would be slightly higher when they and the Macaist Jesuits are included.

[12] Calculated from Xu (1949).

earlier period, there were fifty-eight French Jesuits of whom fourteen were authors (four translators among them). Italian Jesuits occupied the third position, with fifty-six in the mission but with the highest number of authors – eighteen authors altogether with eight translators among them. Noteworthy was the textual production of Jesuits from the two Belgian provinces: five out of fourteen in this period wrote and/or translated texts into Chinese. As we shall see later, they also played a key role in the translation of Chinese texts into Latin. Another way to look at these figures is through the percentages of Jesuits in China of any particular nationality who also engaged in textual production; the top five ranks are as follows: Belgians (35.7%), Germans (33%), Italians (32%), French (24%), Portuguese (13%).

A further set of statistics is of interest. In the number of Chinese texts the Jesuit missionaries produced, the Germans averaged 12.3 works, the Italians 9.26, the Belgians 7, the Portuguese 3 and the French 3. Two Jesuit directors of the Imperial Observatory and the Tribunal of Mathematics were among the most prolific authors: the German Johann Adam Schall von Bell and his successor, the Belgian Ferdinand Verbiest, authored twenty-five and twenty works respectively, most of which were scientific texts (calendars, astronomical observations, mathematical tables etc.). Among individuals, Italian Jesuits were the most prolific: Giuglio Aleni authored twenty-six texts, Ludovico Buglio and Giacomo Rho twenty-one texts each, Ricci accounted for nineteen works and Alfonso Vagnoni fifteen texts. They out-produced the most prolific Portuguese Jesuit, Emmanuel Diaz, who had thirteen works to his credit.

The French Jesuits made a modest but respectable contribution to the output of Jesuitica sinensis; they also played the leading role in the introduction of Chinese texts and culture to an eighteenth-century European public, which explains the focus of their literary work and the relatively modest Chinese output.

The relationship between the production of Chinese books (from writing, translating or paraphrasing) and the production of *Sinica* (translations from Chinese texts into European languages and writings about China published in Europe) is in fact a highly interesting question. In general, the first period of the Jesuit mission from the 1580s to c. 1680 saw the greatest production of Jesuit Chinese writings. Almost all important texts and translations were completed in this period; they ranged from scientific works and moral philosophy to standard liturgical texts, such as the Roman *Missale* and *Breviarum*, as well as the translations of the works by Aquinas and Aristotle.

The second period, from the 1680s to the dissolution of the Society of Jesus, was characterized by a significant drop in the production of Chinese titles, the narrowing of subject matter (focusing on catechistic and devotional works), more publications in the colloquial language and the translation of a small body of Christian texts into Manchu, the language of the Qing conquest dynasty.

Also significant in this second period was the transmission of Chinese texts and culture to Europe. Beginning with the translation of the Confucian Four Books (*Great Learning, Golden Mean, Analects, Mencius*) under the editorship of the Belgian Philippe Couplet,[13] French, German and Austrian Jesuits continued to add to the corpus of *Sinica* through the eighteenth century. If 1580–1680 was the European century for China, the following hundred years represented the Chinese century for Europe.

PROCESS AND RECEPTION

Some preliminary conclusions can be drawn from the above presentations. Although the Jesuit mission in China was under the Portuguese *padroado*, and taking into consideration the numerical predominance of Portuguese Jesuits and the Portuguese enclave of Macao on the south China coast, Portugal failed to play the crucial role one would have expected in Sino-European cultural exchange. Instead, Italian and Belgian Jesuits represented the driving force in the transmission of European texts to China up to 1723. Thereafter, French Jesuits played an increasingly dominant role.

This is not to say, however, that the Jesuits could claim all the glory. Chinese collaborators, both converts and sympathizers, often played a crucial role, in both Jesuit compositions and translations, as indicated in prefaces to many of the texts. For translations, there were three possible scenarios. First, the Jesuits themselves undertook to translate the European texts into Chinese. Second, the Jesuit translator explained the European texts orally to his Chinese collaborator, who set down the Chinese version in writing; the text was subsequently examined jointly, until a final translated text was agreed upon. Third, a Jesuit translator composed a draft translation, which was then revised for style by a Chinese collaborator.

Of these three scenarios, the second – Jesuit oral translation and Chinese written composition – was by far the most significant. This represented the ordinary method of translation during the first fifty years of the Jesuit mission in China for very good reasons. For one, it was the most efficient

---

[13] *Confucius* (1687).

way of translation, allowing the relatively few Jesuit missionaries to produce a large body of Chinese texts. For another, close collaboration with Chinese literati offered an opportunity for proselytizing or for strengthening the bonds between missionary and convert. A third reason was that this method of collaboration allowed for the greatest accuracy and elegance in translation, maximizing the Jesuit understanding of European texts and the Chinese mastery of stylistic elegance. Ricci's preface to the translation of Euclid is instructive:

Since my arrival in China, I have seen that there are many scholars and works on geometry, but I have not seen any fundamental theoretical works . . . I had then entertained the wish to translate this book for the use of the gentlemen of our times, in order to thank them for their trust in a traveller. Nevertheless, I am of little talent. Moreover, the logic and rhetoric of East and West are so supremely different. In searching for synonyms, there are still many missing words. Even if I can explain things orally with an effort, to put it down in writing is extremely difficult. Ever since then, I have met colleagues who assisted my progress left and right, but whenever there is a difficulty I would stop, advancing and stopping thrice already.[14]

The difficulty was only overcome after a meeting with Xu Guangqi, sometime leading minister at the Ming court, who became one of Ricci's most valuable converts and a leader in early Chinese Catholicism. In discussing Christianity and Western science, Xu urged Ricci to complete the translation, 'commanding him to transmit (the text) orally, and receive (the text) in writing, turning the text over and over in order to reflect on its meaning, resulting in its publication only after three versions'.[15]

An example of a text entirely undertaken by Jesuits is the partial translation of the *Summa theologica* by St Thomas Aquinas. By far the most ambitious project in the Jesuit mission, this translation occupied the Italian Ludovico Buglio more than twenty years between 1654 and 1678. Even so, only a small portion of the *Summa* was translated. Buglio concentrated on the *Pars prima*. The first ten *juan*[16] appeared in 1654: they deal with the nature of God, the Trinity and the Creation. In 1676, another six *juan* on angels and the Creation were finished. The third instalment appeared in 1677/8 and consisted of a further ten *juan* on Man, the soul, the body and human lordship over all things. All were drawn from the *Pars prima*. While the *Pars secunda* remained untranslated, a small portion of the *Pars tertia* – six *juan* on the Birth of Christ and the Resurrection (the latter

---

[14] Xu (1949), 261–2.   [15] Xu (1949), 262.

[16] *Juan* was the basic unit of a Chinese book, ranging from twenty to thirty leaves.

translated by the Portuguese Jesuit Gabriel de Magalhães) – was completed in 1677/8.

Aside from the sheer volume of the text, the *Summa* presented a particular difficulty because of its technical theological language, an obstacle lightly touched upon in Buglio's preface to the 1654 edition. After commenting on the significance of Aquinas to Christian learning and offering the obligatory and polite self-deprecation, Buglio described the difficulty of rendering the *Summa* into Chinese: 'languages differ from land to land, and words are limited; after repeated endeavours, new words are added, and the *Pars prima* is accomplished with great effort. Yet I dare not say that I have exhausted the meaning of the original text.'[17]

This passage reflects a common problem in all translation projects: whether to render equivalent concepts by neologisms. Whether one opts for creating new words in the host language while risking unintelligibility, or rendering the original concept in terms familiar to the host culture and thereby losing perhaps the original signification, it is a daunting task.

The latter option was the one adopted by Ricci. In translating the Latin word *Deus* into Chinese, Ricci avoided a pitfall by creating a new term, *Tianzhu*, the Lord of Heaven, by combining two terms from the ancient Confucian canon familiar to the Chinese literati.[18] A graceful stylist, Ricci adopted Chinese syntax and idioms, trying to persuade by means of a Christian discourse decorated by Chinese rhetorical flourishes. Successful while this might have been with the Chinese literati, this accommodation-ist translation was sharply contested by Niccolò Longobardo and other Jesuits in China and Japan.

Suppressed in favour of the Riccian method for the sake of internal unity, this controversy would resurface later and land the Jesuits in trouble, as rival Dominican missionaries accused the Society of mixing idolatry with true religion by linguistic and cultural accommodation. The famous Chinese Rites Controversy was essentially about translation: whether Chinese terms used by the Jesuits (*Tian* meaning Heaven and *Shangdi* meaning God on High) could adequately represent the notion of Christian divinity, and whether Chinese ancestral rituals were to be read as civic or religious, hence, idolatrous, liturgy.

Buglio's translation of Aquinas ran into the opposite problem: unin-telligibility. Titled in Chinese *Chaoxing xueyao*, or *Summary of Nature-Surpassing Learning*, Buglio chose to render Latin terms into equivalent

---

[17] Xu (1949), 190. A copy of Buglio's long translation is available at BF Chinois 6907–9.
[18] For the most recent work, see Kim (2004).

Chinese sounds. Thus 'Spiritus Sanctus' became *si-pi-le-do-san-du*, 'theologia', *dou-lu-ri-jia*, 'philosophia', *fei-lu-suo-fei-ya* and so forth. In translating religious texts, preserving the aura of authenticity by sacrificing intelligibility was not necessarily flawed.

On the other hand, sound-approximation translations of Sanskrit chants and prayers hardly impeded the widespread expansion of Buddhism in medieval China. Moreover, many key Buddhist concepts such as *Buddha*, *bodhisattva*, *asura* were rendered by sound-approximation and became accepted terms in Chinese Buddhist sutras. Unintelligibility, in fact, might well have added to the aura of sutra recitation.

Buglio's translation suffered from something more serious: poor syntax and style. Translating the scholastic Latin of Aquinas into classical Chinese was something like rendering Aquinas intelligible to Cicero. The abundance of neologisms, subordinate clauses and dialectical demonstrations made the *Chaoxing xueyao* a very difficult if not unintelligible text to Chinese readers of the late seventeenth century. There is no evidence of its reception and it was not reprinted until 1932.[19]

CONCLUSION

Did translations of European texts exert any cultural influence in early modern China? If so, what subjects or books were preferred? The answer to these questions depends on the definition of the reading public. Within a narrow definition of the sphere of reception, one can speak of a high degree of success when focusing on the use of translated texts within the Chinese Catholic Church. Hence prayer books, devotional works, catechisms, European visual images copied in China and theological works served the convert population that grew to a peak of 200,000 in 1700 before entering into a period of slow decline. The existence of reprints and multiple extant copies of these works in major Chinese and European libraries testifies to their function and success.

Outside Chinese Catholic circles, the question of reception is more difficult to investigate. There are two indices of the general reception of European texts (both composed and translated) that provide some answers: private collections and the Imperial Encyclopedia, the *Siku quanshu*, compiled between 1772 and 1784.

In the case of private collections, Nicolas Standaert has searched ten published catalogues of large collections of the seventeenth and early

---

[19] For extant editions and the history of editions see Chan (2002), 284–7.

eighteenth centuries. A total of ninety-six Jesuit works showed up in these
catalogues, of which c. 70 per cent represented scientific texts. Religious
and moral texts were not unknown, but essentially limited to the writings/
translations of Matteo Ricci.[20]

This result is collaborated by surveying the Table of Contents of the
Imperial Encyclopedia. Approximately 13,000 titles were collected in this
official project under the Qianlong emperor.[21] A selection was made to
represent 'proper learning': 3,488 books altogether were collected in full,
6,783 titles were recorded and commented on; other texts deemed politi-
cally or intellectually subversive were either destroyed or left out. Thirty-six
Catholic texts were included in the Comprehensive Table of Contents of
the *Siku Quanshu*; again, scientific texts comprised the majority and texts
by Ricci represented the large majority of philosophical and religious texts.

Taken together, the evidence from private collections and from the *Siku
Quanshu* indicates that the reception of European writings was largely
represented by scientific texts, that works published in the early seventeenth century were best represented and that no fewer than seven texts by
Matteo Ricci received a commentary by the imperial editors or were
reproduced in full.

When we reflect on this conclusion in the larger context of this chapter,
several points become apparent. The translation of European texts into
Chinese involved a sustained and continuous effort on the part of
European Jesuits and their Chinese collaborators. The success of this
translation project was very much in evidence for the internal textual
consumption of the China mission.

Outside convert communities, European texts made a considerable
impact in the early decades of the seventeenth century, especially on
calendar reform, astronomy, mathematics and other sciences. In addition,
several texts by Matteo Ricci on both Graeco-Roman and Christian topics
enjoyed a wide circulation among the literati circles of urban areas owing to
his reputation. However, in the course of the later seventeenth century and
the eighteenth century, the 'market' for European texts became increasingly restricted to Christian circles.

In selecting texts for translation, Jesuit missionaries fell back on those
titles most familiar to them through their education and milieu: Aristotle
in the general philosophical curriculum, and Jesuit writers on more specialized subjects (Clavius on mathematics and Pozzo on perspective). The
most systematic effort was in the translation of religious works for the

---

[20] Standaert (1985). [21] On the Imperial Encyclopedia Project see Guy (1987).

liturgical and devotional life of the China mission. Chinese converts had access to a long list of prayer books and liturgical texts, although the Bible was not translated (in stark contrast to Protestant efforts in the nineteenth century).

Interest in scientific and philosophical works was concentrated in the first half of the seventeenth century, both inside and outside the convert community. The decline in the interest in European texts went in parallel with two other processes: the disenchantment of the Confucian literati elites in the late seventeenth century, a process accentuated by the Chinese Rites prohibition by the papacy in 1704; and the declining social status of Christianity after the imperial prohibition of conversions in 1724.

Compared to the focused translation of Chinese texts into Latin, which inspired a sustained 'China-wave' in Europe between Leibnitz and Voltaire, the much greater effort at translations into Chinese reaped a relatively meagre cultural harvest for the Jesuit mission. The extant titles and collections remained, nonetheless, a monument to cultural exchange sustained by many generations of cultural pioneers.

CHAPTER 3

Language as a means of transfer of cultural values

Eva Kowalská

As was suggested in chapter 1, from the point of view of a cultural historian what is not translated into a given language may be as significant and as revealing as what is translated. In the case of the Slovaks in the early modern period, the significant absences include the most translated text of all, the Bible. Why this was the case will be explained in the course of the chapter.

The use of the vernacular in the liturgy and especially its use as a means of access to divine revelation – the Bible – was a basic characteristic of Protestantism from the time of the Reformation onwards. However, a vivid discussion about the accessibility of the Bible as a source of true faith has already taken place in the Middle Ages, in which English and German authors were the first to take part.[1] There was serious anxiety about the laity or ignorant priests reading the Scripture, while it was feared that vernacular translations could change the meaning of the text, by using inappropriate metaphors, for instance.[2]

The English and the German translations of the Bible were not the only ones to be widely discussed. Bohemia was another important centre of these discussions, from Jan Hus onwards.[3] Despite this, the neighbouring region of Hungary, including modern Slovakia, accepted the *Devotio moderna* movement rather than the teaching of Hus himself.[4] In the Kingdom of Hungary, the social consequences of the activities of Hus were mainly negative. The population experienced destructive Hussite raids rather than the message of faith and the word of God in the language of the people.[5] After the Reformation, the Slovak population was in the same position as the other ethnic groups in the kingdom.

The basic starting point of the Reformation was access to the Scriptures as the source of true faith. However, it was not easy to meet this challenge.

---

[1] Mackenzie (2002); Long (2001), at 120–32, 204–11.   [2] Marsden (1996).   [3] Kyas (1997).
[4] Sopko (1997).   [5] Bartl (1996).

The language of Slovak Lutheranism was affected by the Latin education of the elite as well as by theological problems. The first confessions of faith, dating from the middle of the sixteenth century, were compiled in Latin, and it was another three decades before religious texts of various types appeared in a language accessible to the people.[6]

For ethnic Slovaks, the Reformation did not encourage the vernacular in an immediate and unambiguous manner, as it did in the case of the Germans and Hungarians, and it did not lead to the identification of the ethnic group with its spoken language.[7] These facts are interesting not only from the point of view of the history of religion, but also from that of the functioning of language, the transmission of cultural values and the formation of modern nations, a process that began at this time.

Anyone concerned with the beginnings of the formation and development of subordinate ethnic groups in Central Europe in the early modern period encounters an interesting phenomenon in the case of the Slovaks. In spite of the absence of a lively historical tradition, of an institutional basis for the development of cultural or political activities and even of a single form of written language, the Slovaks had a relatively strong ethnic identity and were later able to develop into a modern nation.

It might be supposed that the impulses for this process started from the Church as an institution and symbol of ethnic unity. However, religious allegiance could not become a unifying factor. The Lutheran Church was dominant after the Reformation, but in the course of the seventeenth century it retreated under pressure from the movement of re-Catholicization, which led to a change in the confessional composition of the population. At the beginning of the seventeenth century, non-Catholics, mostly Lutherans, still formed about 90 per cent of the population of Upper Hungary, but the situation was reversed in the course of the eighteenth century, and non-Catholics became (in Slovakia as in the Kingdom of Hungary in general) a marginalized minority of about 20 per cent. Members of this minority were not allowed to hold public office (royal or municipal) and their civic rights were limited.

At the same time, the widening, strengthening or defence of confessional identity represented a basic value and indeed a mission for members of a given community. Identification with a confession was extremely important,

---

[6] Bodnárová (1998). However, the first original texts, the hymns written by Johannes Silvanus, were published only in 1571 in Prague. The first books printed in Czech used by Slovaks were the translations of Luther's Catechism published in Bardejov in 1581 and probably in 1583 in Hlohovec: Ďurovič (1940), 38–43.

[7] Bitskey (1999).

especially when it was threatened, for example when membership could not be supported by religious institutions, but only through informal signs of identification. Thus, the distinction between the two confessional camps was not expressed at the level of doctrine alone. The two confessions also began to distinguish themselves by using different forms of written language. They began to prefer different historical traditions and develop opposing ideas about the character of their own ethnic group. This led to a sharp differentiation between the two camps – Lutheran and Catholic – in the framework of one ethnic unit, each of them showing a strong collective identity.

The acceptance of Czech – a comprehensible language, but still that of another ethnic group – as the liturgical language of the Slovaks may be regarded as an important factor of differentiation within the ethnic group. This was both a result of the development of the Lutheran confession among the Slovaks and a stimulus to their specific development. Czech was not only the language of the Bible, catechisms and religious services, it also gradually became the symbol of the connection and relationship of its Slovak users with the ethnic group from which they appropriated historical traditions. These traditions did not derive from direct experience over the generations or from popular traditions mentioned in medieval chronicles. They were an artificial construction by the intellectuals.[8]

An example of this process is the claim that Hussitism was the direct forerunner of Lutheranism, which found a response in Slovakia in spite of the fact that no direct continuity between the Hussites and the Reformation existed there. Language also allowed the idea of a direct relationship between the Slovaks and Czechs to enter the collective consciousness. The concept of a united Czechoslovak tribe within the framework of the Slavonic group, which later played an important role in the process of the formation of the modern nation, already appeared in the early modern period as part of the idea of Baroque Slavism.[9]

The acceptance of a foreign language as a means of cultivated communication is not at all unusual. It is enough to mention Latin as the lingua franca of the whole of Europe in the medieval and early modern periods. However, the identification of an ethnic group or an important part of it with the living language of another ethnic group and the declaration that this form of speech is the mother tongue represents a different phenomenon. This process had several causes, derived from specific developments in the whole Kingdom of Hungary after the Reformation.

---

[8] On the construction of history in early modern Europe, Bahlcke and Strohmeyer (2002).
[9] Brtáň (1939).

In the case of the Slovaks, it is especially necessary to emphasize that the Reformation did not mean an automatic impulse for the production or translation of liturgical and other literary texts into their own spoken language. The bearers of the ideas of the Reformation among the Slovaks were the burghers and gentry, that is, the social groups whose education oriented them towards humanist Latin culture. Teaching in urban schools took place entirely in Latin.[10] In addition, most cities still had close and direct connections with German regions and German was one of the languages of the town councils.[11] Thanks to this the ideas of the Reformation spread in their original form and the magistrates corresponded on matters of religion with the centre of the Lutheran Reformation in Wittenberg and its leaders, especially Philipp Melanchthon.[12]

The teachings of the Reformation were therefore initially received in German and Latin. For example, the confessions of individual urban associations used to gain legal recognition of the new church synods and their organizations, together with their rules, were written in these languages. As a result appeals to the unchanged character of texts became an important political factor at the time of forcible re-Catholicization and the cancellation of guarantees for the functioning of the non-Catholic confessions. Thus articles of faith that were not distorted by translation formed the basis on which the Lutherans were accepted by the state.[13]

In the case of ethnic Slovak Lutherans, emphasis on the absence of change meant renouncing the translation of their basic texts (the Augsburg Confession, the Formula or Book of Concord) into their own language until the end of the eighteenth century. Translation of the basic 'identifying' texts of the confession into the spoken, but still basically uncodified, language, which lacked a precise religious and political terminology, might have been a source of significant changes and so a threat to the vulnerable political status of the Church. Inaccuracies in translation would have allowed political opponents to cast doubt on the legality of the confessional community and deny it the right to exist. In the case of the Kingdom of Hungary, this meant the possibility that laws decreeing the

---

[10] The result was that Latin continued to be spoken and remained one of the official languages in Hungary until the late eighteenth century: Tóth (1996), 130–45.

[11] The towns in Upper Hungary/Slovakia were language islands where German developed independently from the core German regions.

[12] Suda (1996); Bodnárová (1999).

[13] Daniel (1980). On the discourse concerning the use of different languages within the Catholic environment, Smolinsky (1998); Köster (1995).

physical liquidation of adherents of the Reformation might be applied once more.[14]

The later acceptance by the Slovaks of Czech as the language of the liturgy, Bible and written communication brought no change in this perception of the importance of preserving the basic confessional texts in the language in which they were conceived and accepted by the state authorities. On the contrary, this version of the Bible became obligatory, especially if it was used as the ultimate and exclusive argument supporting the identity of the Lutherans at the beginnings of the massive re-Catholicization in Hungary (the 1670s and 1680s).[15] However, it was not only politics that influenced the possibility or impossibility of translation in the late seventeenth and early eighteenth centuries. Religious orthodoxy and traditionalism also played a part in maintaining the existing situation.

In any case, the use of the printed word was not a main feature of the spread of the Reformation in the Kingdom of Hungary. The absence of printing presses there until the second half of the sixteenth century was compensated by extensive imports of books.[16] These imports included not only scholarly works in Latin, but also books in German and Czech, which were easily intelligible in the urban environment: in the first case thanks to the coexistence of Slovaks and Germans in the majority of towns, in the second thanks to the related character and comprehensibility of Czech. The use of Czech among the Slovaks was already established in the Middle Ages, thanks to the use of legal texts, for example. However, some legal terms changed meaning compared to the German original, the result of differences in attitudes or simply to the linguistic incompetence of some translators or users of these texts. An example is the inaccurate translation from German into Slovakized Czech of some parts and terms of Magdeburg law, which was a model for the free royal cities in Hungary. Its terminology was not very clear to lay users.[17]

On the other hand, the Czech language had already been codified (it was one of the first European languages to be standardized in this way) and so it could be used as the medium of translations.[18] Its position in the Reformation period is revealed by the reception of the translation of the Wittenberg Agenda and the use of Czech hymnbooks, whether produced

---

[14] Mrva (1995).

[15] Daniel Klesch (1679) told the laity how to use the Bible in disputes with Catholic missionaries. Lay Protestants should stress that Lutherans do not argue from tradition like Catholics, or from reason like Calvinists. Although Klesch's recommendations concerned German-speaking Lutherans they were generally accepted.

[16] Daniel (1998).   [17] Ryšánek (1954), 15–25.   [18] Veselý (2002).

by the Utraquists (1522, 1531) or by the Czech Brethren (1541), which allowed the identification of the confessional position of individual church synods.

The transformation of church services was the first visible manifestation of the Reformation, with clear definitions of belief coming only later. The Bible was already accessible in Czech before the Reformation, for example the so-called Venice Bible of 1506. So the oldest texts concerned with religious belief produced in the Kingdom of Hungary in the 'vernacular' (actually the Czech language) appeared only in the second half of the sixteenth century. They arose from the need for the clear definition of orthodox Lutheran positions in the controversies with crypto-Calvinism. Czech was used as a medium of communication because it was easy for Slovaks to understand, while it had already developed a precise religious terminology.

This fact is extraordinarily important, since only by the use of unambiguous terms was it possible to avoid being suspected of the 'Calvinist heresy' or actually falling into it. This hypothesis is confirmed by the fact that the dispute about the theological orientation of the urban communities of eastern Slovakia, expressed in polemical works written in Latin, accompanied the publication of the Martin Luther's *Little Catechism*, the first book published in Slovakized Czech in this region (Bardejov, 1581). Through this book the 'codified' pure teaching of Martin Luther became the doctrinal standard for the ethnic Slovak Lutherans of the period. General acceptance of the Formula and the Book of Concord as the basic doctrine of Lutheranism followed only three decades later at the Synod of Žilina (1610) after many years of debate.[19]

Through the catechism, the faithful who did not otherwise come into contact with the printed word first became acquainted with basic theological expressions in an easily comprehensible language.[20] However, the publication of the catechism was only a first step towards the strengthening of the confessional identity of believers.[21] The text of the Bible as a starting point for teaching was an important medium for the formation of the life and identity of the confessional community.

Various translations were used to make the Bible accessible to the Protestant communities of the different ethnic groups in the Kingdom of Hungary. The translation of the Bible into German was available to German Lutherans immediately after its publication. This was reflected,

[19] Daniel (1979). On the synod in Žilina (Silein) see Kvačala (1935), 293–303.
[20] Zach (2002).   [21] Crăciun et al. (2002), 1–30.

for example, in the increased frequency of Bibles in town libraries in the sixteenth and seventeenth centuries.[22] In the case of the Hungarians (Magyars), who were the dominant ethnic group, a situation favourable to the rapid translation of the Bible into their own language developed. The cultural needs of the Hungarian social elite had already stimulated the development of fine literature, so a highly cultivated language already existed and could be used for translation of the Bible into Hungarian.[23]

In towns with an ethnically heterogeneous population, mastery of several languages was natural, and so it is not surprising that for many years the theological leaders of the Slovak Lutherans carried on disputes about crypto-Calvinism and the problem of images in Latin and German.[24] Considering the urgency of solving these theological problems for the character of the whole confession, it is only natural that Latin remained the medium of communication for intellectuals of Slovak origin.

However, where it was necessary to use the spoken language, they did not choose the 'Hungarian route' of the cultivation of the local spoken language, which was demanding in time and expertise. The cultivated language of the nearest ethnic group, the Czechs, was available. It fulfilled the role of communication perfectly, and even in the fifteenth century there was already a tradition of using Czech in some town offices and at the courts of some noblemen.[25]

Since ethnic Slovak scholars formed only a very small group and one fully engaged in solving religious disputes, no appropriate personalities emerged among them to carry out a translation project that would have been extremely demanding. It was more convenient to use the already available Kralice Bible, published in Bohemia in 1579–94, for the needs of the Slovak Lutheran community in the Kingdom of Hungary. For a long time it was simply imported into the territory of today's Slovakia as a finished product. Although it was prepared by theologians of the Union of Brothers (*Unitas fratrum*), who inclined to Calvinism, this was not a problem in the period when the Lutherans in Hungary were still seeking a doctrinal standard. What was considered important was to make a comprehensible text of the Scriptures available to the general public.

The highest theological authority, the Synod of Žilina of 1610, confirmed the validity of the Kralice Bible for the Slovak Lutherans, and so it also confirmed the use as the liturgical language of the form of Czech found in it. At the time of the synod, the Church was mainly concerned with the stabilization of doctrine on the basis of the possibilities provided by the first

---

[22] Čičaj (1996).   [23] Kósa (1999), 249–56.   [24] Daniel (1995).   [25] Skladaná (2002).

law on the equality of confessions in Hungary (1608).[26] For this reason, as well as accepting the Kralice Bible, the synod also adopted a resolution that the Formula and the Book of Concord were binding.

In the following period, the political situation developed in an ever more unfavourable way for the Lutherans. The material possibilities of the Lutheran Church, which declined with the gradual re-Catholicization of the rich noble and formerly Lutheran families, did not enable the preparation of a Bible in the local spoken language or in a theologically revised form. The position of Czech was also strengthened by the great wave of emigration of Protestants from Bohemia and Moravia to Upper Hungary after the Battle of the White Mountain and the introduction of re-Catholicization laws in the Austrian and Czech part of the Habsburg Monarchy.[27] Czech preachers produced popular editions of religious texts, for example the hymnbook *Cithara sanctorum* of Juraj Tranovský from 1636. They were quickly integrated into the community and became patriots for the country which had given them new homes.[28]

These socio-political circumstances were more important than the actual development of the spoken language of the Slovak Lutherans, which occurred independently. In spite of the tendency to include elements of their spoken, Slovak language in 'non-biblical' texts such as Passion plays and the formulations of agendas, this tendency did not become dominant and it was not applied to the publication of biblical texts. On the contrary, the language of the Bible, the so-called *Bibličtina*, began to penetrate all printed texts and acquired the status of a literary language. Hymns were the most important category of literature. In the *Cithara sanctorum* collection, they formed a summary of theological ideas intended for the general public and more accessible in price for them than other texts.

This medium also preserved the confessional and cultural identity of the people, who were deprived of direct contact with preachers because of re-Catholicization. In many counties they had few opportunities to attend their own church. Non-Catholic publications were drastically limited and more or less came to an end in the 1730s. In this way, the hymnbook and the catechism became the exclusive sources of knowledge of the teachings of the Lutheran Church. Their symbolic value increased because they were the only resources approved for the so-called private practice of religion. Wherever the Lutheran faithful had limited access to churches and schools,

---

[26] On this important law see Péter (1991).   [27] Mrva (1999).   [28] Franková (1993).

communal hymn singing, usually without printed aids, replaced the other ceremonies.

For these reasons it was not only the Bible that symbolized the unity and integrity of the Lutherans. The language in which it was printed acquired the same 'canonical' value. However, it is also necessary to note that by the seventeenth century, this form of language was no longer the living, spoken language in the Czech ethnic environment.[29] A development was occurring which confirmed the existence of two different ethnic groups – the Czechs and the Slovaks.

By means of the Czech language, the Slovak Protestants of the sixteenth–seventeenth centuries appropriated not only a consciousness of community with the Czech ethnic group, but also a theological and confessional connection with Hussitism or the 'Czech Reformation'. Its supporters, in reality only the remnants of armed forces serving as mercenaries for local magnates, found refuge in Slovakia in the course of the fifteenth century and allegedly spread the ideas of Hussitism. The direct line of development of the Reformation from Jan Hus to Martin Luther was emphasized. In the course of the eighteenth century in particular, this idea of development was used as a theological argument confirming the 'exceptional' character of Slovak Lutheranism.

Identification with this inauthentic, but theologically impressive tradition brought its bearers, who had a subordinate position in the structure of the population of the Kingdom of Hungary, the possibility of achieving acceptance and recognition within the framework of the multi-ethnic church community. On the other hand, this tradition and the self-stereotype built on it, of the Slovak Lutherans as preservers of the tradition of the Czech Reformation, was an apologetic instrument and a source of pride in the maturity of the whole 'Slavonic nation', which had participated in shaping the spiritual life of Europe. This fiction was created precisely in this period among various Slavonic ethnic groups.

The confessional element, which still played a substantial part in culture, contributed to the emphasizing of other historical traditions. Slovak Protestants were clearly not attracted to the combination of the traditions of Great Moravia and St Stephen on which the presentation of Hungary as the Kingdom of Mary (*Regnum Marianum*) was built. The invented tradition of Hussite influence on Slovakia, connecting the Slovaks with a spiritual movement to which Martin Luther himself appealed, was naturally more acceptable to them.

---

[29] On the special development of the Czech used by Slovaks see Ďurovič (1998, 2004).

The fact that Great Moravia was not directly connected with the destiny of the Czech nation, in which Slovak Protestants saw a natural ally and support in their cultural and national development, thanks to linguistic and cultural links, undoubtedly played a significant role in this acceptance. The activity of Cyril and Methodius as Christian missionaries among the Slavs received attention only with the acceptance of the concept of Baroque Slavism, which emphasized the important contributions of individual Slavonic ethnic groups to the development of culture and civilization. Their 'adoption' in the non-Catholic environment came only at the beginning of the eighteenth century, when respect for the two saints could already be justified in an 'academic' manner. The publication of documents from the Vatican Archives concerning the earliest history of the Central European region started at the end of the seventeenth century.

By appropriating and further cultivating Czech in its biblical form as their vernacular with its grammar fixed and printed (by Tobias Masník or Masnicius, for example, in 1696), the Slovak Lutherans symbolically took over the mission of preserving the confessional consciousness of the Czech Protestants, which survived only in exile or in the form of small communities of secret and persecuted Protestants.

However, the intellectual elites of Slovak Lutheranism (pastors and teachers) were forced to leave their homeland in 1674. They found their first refuge in Czech church communities in various parts of Germany. Even though only a few of them could obtain the position of pastor, many exiles from Hungary were active as guest preachers or they published sermons and religious literature.[30] These texts appeared in traditional biblical Czech and, thanks to this, religious literature from the pens of numerous Slovak Lutheran authors was also acceptable in the environment of Utraquist and even Czech Brother exiles and helped to maintain their confessional identity.

The consistent use of biblical Czech in non-biblical theological texts, often combined with some elements of spoken Slovak, was strengthened after the establishment of the Biblical Institute at Halle. The Institute systematically published works intended for a wider community than the Slovak Lutherans alone.[31] The Bible published for the Slovaks in 1722 was produced in harmony with grammatically codified biblical Czech. Thus a sense of community with their Czech fellow believers and of responsibility for their destiny was created in the consciousness of the

---

[30] An overview in Ďurovič (1940), 80–6.   [31] Rösel (1961).

Slovak Lutherans. Later, after the issuing of the Toleration Patent (1781), this sense of community was expressed in extensive missionary activity.[32]

The perception of language as a symbol of belief was also strengthened in the course of re-Catholicization. The university press in Trnava (Tyrnau, Nagyszombat), which was in the hands of the Jesuits, was especially concerned with cultivation of native, spoken Slovak. The texts of books and of surviving manuscript sermons by Franciscans or other preachers show a conscious use of language as a sign distinguishing the Catholics from the 'heretics'.

However, the ethnic consciousness of Catholic Slovaks was not connected to an unambiguous means of declaring their confessional allegiance – a Slovak translation of the Bible. The educated, who had the right (in accordance with the decrees of the Council of Trent), to ask for permission to read the Bible, were satisfied with the Latin text of the Vulgate and did not need a translation. There was therefore no attempt to translate the whole Bible into Slovak until the first half of the eighteenth century, and even then it remained unpublished.[33]

Religious literature was printed in large editions.[34] All the same, the absence of the books which tended to create norms, that is, of a widely accepted hymnbook and especially of a Catholic translation of the Bible into the spoken language, undoubtedly influenced the formation of the type of language used in the environment of Catholic intellectuals. Their language usage was more variable than that of the Protestant intellectuals, and only gradually became more fixed.

However, by becoming more distant from Czech, the language strengthened the consciousness of the linguistic and ethnic distinctiveness of the Slovaks and facilitated their separation from the broad framework of Slavism. The stabilization of Slovak was supported by the publishing of various legal or political texts which were issued by more and more active government institutions. The textbooks introduced into the schools during the first period of school reforms in Hungary (1777–90) also helped to fix the form of language.[35]

---

[32] Kowalská (2001), 145–7.

[33] It is not clear why the first translation of the Bible into cultivated spoken Slovak (the so-called Bible of the Camaldul monks, prepared for the press in 1758) was forbidden to be published. The church archives in Slovakia are still not well organized and opened and this question has not yet been answered by specialists on church history. The Bible was first published by Rothe, Scholz and Doruľa (2002).

[34] On the products of the university press in Trnava (Tyrnau, Nagyszombat) see Čaplovič (1972–84); Mišianik (1971).

[35] Keipert (1993).

However, the interconnection between the type of language used by an individual and his or her confession can be observed even in the 1790s, in the context of the textbooks published by and used in the state elementary schools, especially the Reading-Book (*Lesebuch*) which included the principles of Christian ethics and religion as well as instruction about the behaviour of children and especially altar boys in church during religious ceremonies. One of the reviewers of these textbooks recommended the use of a form of language that would not encourage doubts about the Catholic religion by using curious (Czech) terms. On the other hand, accurate expressions in the vernacular might bring the 'heretics' back into the Catholic Church.[36]

The shaping of historical consciousness among the Catholics was more complicated. It did not rely on any inherited or adopted tradition. The legends and chronicles that first passed on historical knowledge in the Kingdom of Hungary did not provide sufficient stimuli. They were written by medieval scholars from the circle of the kings of the House of Arpád, and emphasized the tradition of the taking of land by means of war. The most important medieval chronicle spoke directly of the dishonour of the original native Slavonic inhabitants – the ancestors of the Slovaks.

Until the beginning of the eighteenth century, members of the Hungarian political Estate did not feel themselves committed to an ethnic identity. Linguistic identification did not play a very important role. In the eighteenth century, those who accepted the importance of ethnic adherence as well as the concept of a political nation or Estate discovered the importance of the Great Moravian Empire. They even combined the concept of the statehood of Great Moravia with that of Hungary. The ultimate localization of the 'first state of the Slovaks' in the territory of Pannonia and Upper Hungary as well as the stressing of the contribution of Slovaks to the civilizing process in the early stages of the Hungarian Kingdom provided the basis for arguments for the equality of the whole ethnic group within Hungary.[37]

The Lutherans also agreed with this idea. They accepted the Great Moravian state as the point of departure for the history of the Slovaks. However, they also emphasized the connection with the Czech lands

---

[36] Comment by canon Johann Ludwig Schwartz from Nitra (Nyitra), in the Hungarian State Archives in Budapest, C 69, 1780, Scholae Nationales, Miscellanea, fons 3, pos. 54, fol. 97.

[37] This concept was formulated as a scientific hypothesis only in the eighteenth century by Juraj Papánek in *Historia gentis Slavae: de regno, regibusque Slavorum* (Pécs, 1780). See Tibenský (1992).

(especially with Moravia) and the preservation of the Slavonic (or Great Moravian) culture in Bohemia.

Since the Lutherans were deprived of the possibility of declaring their confessional allegiance by active participation in church services at most places in Hungary, the symbols of their identity acquired more importance. The identification of Slovak Lutherans with a language which was actually foreign or at least common with a different ethnic group, and functioned on various levels of communication in parallel with the local spoken language, was so strong that massive assimilation of Slovak migrants into the surrounding environment did not occur in ethnically and confessionally mixed regions such as the Lowlands in the south of the Kingdom of Hungary.

On the other hand, Catholics did not have to present themselves as anything but members of the dominant Church. This act in itself secured them full participation in public life, for example the rights of a town burgher, guild membership or the right to hold a public office. Manifesting their identity in a programme or in texts did not have great importance for them, and the form of the language of such texts was even less important.

Interconfessional relations were therefore a determining factor in the process of the integration of the Slovak ethnic group and its development into the form of a modern nation. It is certainly no accident that the codification of a common written language came only after a period of stabilization of interconfessional relations in the course of the first half of the nineteenth century. However, the translation of the Bible into archaic Czech did not cease to have symbolic value: it continued to be used in the Slovak Lutheran community until the middle of the twentieth century.

CHAPTER 4

Translations into Latin in early modern Europe

Peter Burke[1]

It is well known that both spoken and written Latin were regularly employed in early modern Europe not only in the Catholic Church but also in the world of scholarship, diplomacy, the law and elsewhere.[2] The importance of early modern translations from Latin into the vernacular languages of Europe has also been recognized. So has the importance of translations from ancient Greek into Latin.

On the other hand, translations from the vernacular into Latin have been relatively neglected.[3] The reason for this neglect may be that the phenomenon seems to be counter-intuitive. After all, why should anyone want to make translations in the 'wrong' direction, from a modern language into an ancient one? Insofar as they have been studied at all, these texts, in particular the translations of literary classics such as Dante, Ariosto, Tasso, Cervantes, Camões or Milton, have been treated as curiosities, simple exercises of ingenuity.

However, I have discovered no fewer than 1,140 published translations of substantial texts by known authors between the invention of printing and the year 1799, and there may well be many more, especially of books published in Central Europe and not available in libraries further west. One day, when an on-line catalogue of all early modern European publications becomes available, these omissions will come to light.

The number of these translations testifies not only to the widespread knowledge of Latin at this time, but also to the fact that many educated people outside frontier regions found foreign vernaculars difficult if not impossible to read. Compared to what was available for the teaching of

---

[1] In the course of this investigation, begun in 1991, I have received encouragement and assistance from many people, but particular thanks are due to Rino Avesani, Dietrich Briesemeister, Zweeder von Santen and Thomas Worcester.

[2] Burke (2004), 43–60.

[3] The rare general studies include Grant (1954) and Binns (1990). More specialized studies will be cited below where appropriate.

Latin, facilities for the teaching of Italian, Spanish and French in schools, colleges and universities were extremely limited, while they were virtually non-existent for the teaching of other languages. English, for example, was rarely taught before the eighteenth century.[4]

I

Most of the texts translated were what librarians today call 'non-fiction', making a major contribution to the spread of information at this time. Such a large number of translated texts suggests the value of asking the following questions, on the model of chapter 1 above. What was translated into Latin in this period? From what languages? By whom, for whom, where and when? What were the main linguistic problems which the translators confronted?

Given the lack of any bibliography of translations into Latin, or indeed any complete catalogue of publications in any European country in this period (apart from Britain, Belgium and the Netherlands), all general-izations offered here must be taken as extremely provisional, and the figures quoted as no more than indications of relative importance.[5] Nevertheless, the chronology and geography of the translations are extremely striking, and suggest that the main conclusions of this chapter will survive the discovery of more material.

The main criteria for inclusion in the list of 1,140 translations are as follows:

1. The text must have a known author. That means omitting discussions of translations of the Bible, from the version of Sébastien Castellion (criticized at the time as too ornate) to that of Arias Montano (criticized as too literal). It is a pity to exclude such works as the translations of *Pathelin*, *Lazarillo de Tormes*, *Reineke Fuchs* and *Till Eulenspiegel*, or the *Eikon basilike*, or the first few years of the *Transactions of the Royal Society of London*, or the decision of the Parlement of Toulouse in the case of Martin Guerre (published in Latin by Suraeus in 1576), or the two anonymous accounts of the death of the Jesuit Edmund Campion. However, consistency would require the inclusion of a mass of occasional writings (descriptions of royal entries, coronations, missions and trials, the texts of treaties, liturgies, instructions to officials and so on), and it

---

[4] Burke (2004), 113–17.
[5] The main sources used for this list are the catalogues of the British Library, London; the Bibliothèque Nationale, Paris (now the Bibliothèque de France); the Bodleian, Oxford; and the University Library, Cambridge. Wherever possible I have consulted the editions listed. For Spanish books I have also used Palau y Dulcet (1948–77), and for Dutch and German books the new on-line catalogues, Short Title Catalogue Netherlands and www.vd.17de.

is even more difficult to make a complete list of such texts than of works by known authors.

2. The text must be a printed translation of a text previously published in the vernacular. Therefore the five manuscript translations of *Os Lusíadas* produced in this period are omitted. In similar fashion it excludes manuscript translations of poems by Dante, Petrarch, Jorge Manrique, Spenser and Tasso, of the Koran (by Widmanstetter), of a play by Scipione Maffei, of Mandeville's *Travels*, and of treatises such as Filarete on architecture or Rousseau's *Contrat social*.[6] Texts first published in Latin which may have been translations from a manuscript in the vernacular are also omitted (for example Huldreich Mutius's *De Germanorum origine*, Pietro Aron's *De institutione harmonica*, Anthony Wood's *History of Oxford* and Johann Brucker's *Historia critica philosophiae*).

On the other hand, the rare cases of books published in the same year in Latin and the vernacular (such as Scalvo's treatise on the rosary) are included, as well as the unusual case of a Latin translation of a Dutch translation of an originally Latin text (by Scribanius). Different translations of the same work (including the four translations of the *Semaine* of Du Bartas, and the eight translations of Pibrac's moral quatrains) are counted separately.

3. Defining a 'vernacular' is not as easy as it might seem. The substantial number of translations from ancient Greek into Latin have been omitted, but the much rarer translations from Arabic, Byzantine Greek, Chinese, Hebrew and Persian have been included (Jerónimo Xavier's life of Christ in Persian, for instance, or the history of the decline of Byzantium by Laonikos Chalkokondyles) although these were made from 'classical' forms of written language.

4. It is difficult to be specific about length. Very short poems, and fragments like Sainte-Marthe's translation of part of Ronsard's *Franciade* are not included. On the other hand, the three Latin versions of Gray's *Elegy* do figure in the list, together with odes by Boileau and Dryden.

5. It is even more difficult to be specific about what exactly constitutes a 'translation' (as noted above, p. 30). The 1,140 items include selections (among them the first books of Castiglione's *Cortegiano* and Machiavelli's *Istorie Fiorentine*, and five stories from the *Decamerone*); abridgements (such as Sleidan's version of Froissart's *Chronique*, the anonymous translation of Bossuet's *Variations* and the historical works of Maimbourg); and paraphrases or adaptations (including free versions of Aretino, Della Porta and Milton).

6. It is not always clear when a work was first published; whether it was translated from the vernacular into Latin, or vice versa; or even whether certain Latin texts really exist or not. Among the 'ghosts' (in other words, works referred to in the secondary literature, which I have so far been unable to trace in library catalogues, though they may possibly exist somewhere) are Latin versions of Aretino's *Letters*, Mexia's *Historia Caesarea*, Guarini's *Pastor fido*, D'Urfé's pastoral romance *L'Astrée* and *Don Quixote* (of which a translation into macaronic Latin by Ignacio Calvo was published in 1905).

---

[6] On Mandeville, Vogels (1885).

II

To analyse the chronology of the translations it is convenient to divide the early modern period into fifty-year sections. The distribution of texts turns out to have been extremely uneven. Only five texts were published in the period before 1500. The number rises to 61 texts from the period 1500–49, increasing to 220 texts 1550–99; continuing to rise to a peak of 387 texts 1600–49, in other words over seven a year on average; declines to 249 texts 1650–99, falling to 157 texts 1700–49 and 50 texts 1750–99 (total 1,127, the remaining texts being impossible to date precisely). The absolute figures should not be taken very seriously, in the sense that they are necessarily incomplete, but the trend seems clear enough.

It should also be noted that a considerable difference to the figures for 1700–49 is made by a single enterprise undertaken in the Dutch Republic, originally planned by the German scholar Johann Georg Graevius, professor at Utrecht, and carried on by his former student Pieter Burmann the Elder, professor at Leiden. Thanks to this initiative, over thirty antiquarian studies were translated from Italian and published in Leiden in the 1720s as part of a series called the 'treasury of Italian antiquities' (*Thesaurus anti-quitatum Italiae*).

Translations from the vernacular into Latin did not of course disappear after 1800. *Hiawatha, Robinson Crusoe* and works by Goethe and Schiller, not to mention children's books such as *Max und Moritz, Pinocchio* and *Winnie the Pooh*, have been translated since that time. The tradition is not yet dead, witness Peter Needham's version of Harry Potter, *Harrius Potterus et philosophi lapis* (1997). However, the crucial period was the one from 1550 to 1700.

One can only speculate about the reasons for this distribution over time. Two explanations may be offered, and curiously enough they are almost exactly the inverse of each other. In the first place, the lack of translations in the early sixteenth century might be explained by the strength of the prejudice of many scholars against the vernacular languages. On the other hand, the slow decline of translations from the later seventeenth century corresponds to the declining use of Latin.

The chronology of the original texts also deserves a mention. In a number of cases they date from the Middle Ages, while a few sixteenth-century texts were not translated into Latin for a hundred years or more. In the majority of cases, however, the time-lag between the first publication of the text and the publication of its Latin translation was relatively short, as low as a year in the case of Paolo Sarpi's *Historia concilii tridentini* for example, or Blaise Pascal's *Litterae provinciales*.

A third point concerns the vernaculars from which texts were translated into Latin, in the order of their relative importance. Italian (with 321 texts) and French (276) were ahead of all competitors, with Italian dominating the earlier part of our period and French the later part (51 translations from French were published between 1650 and 1699, as compared to 42 from Italian). Next came English (159) and Spanish (133).[7] Other languages lagged a long way behind: German (77, dominated by Luther); Dutch; Portuguese; Arabic; Persian; Chinese; Hebrew; Polish; Catalan; Swedish; Byzantine Greek; Czech; Danish; Croat and Turkish (if translations of anonymous works were added, the list would also include Ethiopian and Icelandic). It should also be noted that – as was not infrequently the case in this period – a number of translations were not made from the original language.

III

By whom were the translations made? A few translations are anonymous or pseudonymous – Pascal's translator 'Wendrock', for example, or Bodin's translator 'Philoponus', or Huarte's translator 'Aeschacius Major' – or they are signed with mysterious initials, such as the T. G. who translated Addison, the T. D. M. who translated Boileau, the J. W. who translated Boyle, or the P. I. L. M. who translated Naudé.

However, 557 translators have been identified. From the sociological point of view we find a group dominated, unsurprisingly, by the clergy, especially the Catholic clergy and above all the Jesuits, who contributed over eighty translators. Then came Protestant pastors, teachers (in schools and universities), writers and physicians. The few semi-professional translators (above, p. 13) included Aegidius Albertinus (a Dutchman who lived in Munich), Caspar Barth, Caspar Ens, Andreas Schottius and Adam Schirmbeck.[8] Other prolific translators were the German Kerbekius, professor of theology at Mainz, and the Netherlanders Anton Dulcken, Sigebert Havercamp, Michael Isselt, Theodore Petreius and Mateo Martinez Waucquier, who came (contrary to what his name might suggest) from Middelburg. Havercamp translated no fewer than eighteen texts for the *Thesaurus antiquitatum* project mentioned above, while Waucquier specialized in works of piety.

[7] On French, Briesemeister (1985); on Spanish, Briesemeister (1978).
[8] On Albertinus, Gemert (1979); on Barth, Bataillon (1957) and Briesemeister (1990); on Ens, Fitzmaurice-Kelly (1906).

A geographical analysis offers more surprises than a sociological one. The German speakers contribute at least 164 known translators. The French speakers (including inhabitants of the Netherlands, Luxembourg and French Switzerland) contribute 100, while English speakers (including Irish, Scots and Welsh) contribute 60. The Dutch and Flemish speakers, not always easy to identify, contribute at least 48, a high figure given the relatively small size of that population.

On the other hand, the Italians contribute only 46 translators, among whom should be noted Protestants such as Celio Secundo Curione, Elio Diodati, Scipione Gentile, Francesco Negri, Silvestro Teglio and Giovanni Niccolò Stoppani, all exiles and mediators between their two cultures. Gentile lived in Germany, while Curione, Negri, Stoppani and Teglio were all refugees in Switzerland. Among the secular texts they translated were works by Machiavelli, Guicciardini and Tasso.[9]

The Spanish and Portuguese together contribute only 17 or 18 translators (including the famous humanists Antonio Nebrija and Benito Arias Montano), the Poles 7, the Czechs 4, the Hungarians 3, and the Slovenes, Finns and Swedes 1 each. It should be added that the British, French and Italians almost always translated works from their own languages, leaving the Germans and the Netherlanders to translate the Spanish texts and many of the Italian ones as well.

IV

For whom were the translations made? Obviously for the minority of Europeans who were able to read Latin. The use of Latin ensured a wide geographical distribution at the price of appealing to a cultural minority. This price was sometimes considered to be worth paying: the authorities of the Catholic Church allowed Bodin's book on demons to appear in Latin, but vetoed a proposal for an Italian translation.[10]

However, translations into Latin seem to have been made for a minority within the minority of Latinophones. Once again, a geographical analysis is revealing. One way to approach the problem of the audience is by examining the place of first publication of translations, 121 cities altogether, from Altdorf to Zürich, of which 120 were in Europe (a translation of a work by a Jesuit missionary was published in Macau).

---

[9] On Negri, Zonta (1916); cf. Körner (1988).   [10] Tippelskirch (2003), 341.

There were 496 texts first printed in the German-speaking world (including Basel, Danzig, Strassburg and Vienna); 171 in the Netherlands, north and south; 112 in the French-speaking world (including Geneva); 74 in Britain; only 56 in Italy, despite the importance of Venice as a printing centre; and a mere 9 in Spain and Portugal. The role of particular cities may be worth a mention. The five leaders are Cologne (115 texts), Leiden (68), London (54), Amsterdam (52) and Antwerp (45). Four of these cities are well-known centres of publication (Leiden's score being augmented by 31 items from the Graevius enterprise mentioned above), while the special case of Cologne will be discussed below.

In short, the evidence points to the main demand for translations into Latin as coming from northern Europe (including Poland), and more especially from the German-speaking world. Latin was perhaps most useful in 'popularizing' – if such a word may be used in this context – books originally written in romance languages, especially works of piety.[11] Its importance for the reception of English culture in Germany in the later seventeenth century has also been pointed out.[12]

V

What kinds of book were translated? To answer this question it is tempting to use the categories of sixteenth- and seventeenth-century librarians (theology, canon law, civil law, moral philosophy, natural philosophy etc.). However, it is probably more useful to employ modern categories. The six major categories were religion, science, fiction, history, politics and travel, in that order.

In the first place, by a very long way, came religion, with 422 titles, including works of theology, works of controversy, works of devotion, prophecies and sermons (at least 24 items, the authors including Andrewes, Bullinger, Calvin, Camus, Coton, Gerson, Luís de Granada, Panigarola, Richeome, Savonarola, Segneri, Skarga and Vieira). The total of religious works would be even larger (470) if ecclesiastical history (15 texts, including works by Bartoli, Bossuet, Burnet, Florimond de Raemond, Maimbourg, Sarpi and Sforza Pallavicino), and the lives of saints and other religious leaders (33 texts, including lives of Christ, Luther, Calvin, Ignatius Loyola, Francis Xavier and Teresa of Avila) were included here. These texts will be considered below as history.

---

[11] Briesemeister (1983).   [12] Fabian (1992), 181.

Of the 422 religious texts, 6 are Jewish, 1 (Feofan) is Orthodox and 101, or less than a quarter, are Protestant, including 8 works by Martin Luther, 4 by Jean Calvin and 6 by the English puritan William Perkins. The translation of Anglican theologians by Germans is worth noting as evidence of contact and sympathy between different Protestant Churches. All the same, the fragmentation of the Protestants into Lutherans, Calvinists, Zwinglians and so on together with their stress on the vernacular should be sufficient to explain why they fell so far behind the Catholics. On the Catholic side, the 314 texts include no fewer than 5 works devoted to the controversial issue of frequent communion. However, works of devotion rather than works of controversy account for the bulk of the translations. They include Lorenzo Scupoli's *Combattimento spirituale*, which was translated twice, and the *Introduction à la vie dévote* by St François de Sales (cf. Eire's chapter below).

Spanish devotional writers in particular were current in Latin, including Pedro de Alcantara, Alfonso Rodriguez, St Teresa of Avila, San Juan de la Cruz (John of the Cross), Juan de Jesús, Luis de la Puente and above all Luís de Granada (with 11 different texts). The Latin translation of these devotional texts is one sign among others of the cultural hegemony that Spain exercised over much of Europe around the year 1600. It coincides with what has been called the 'mystical invasion' of France by Spain in the seventeenth century, in other words the translation of Spanish devotional writers into French.[13]

These authors were read outside Spain in Latin translations which were for the most part produced and published in the German-speaking world, in Mainz, for instance (22 texts), Munich (24) and especially in Cologne (104), where certain publishers, such as Kinck, Mylius and Crithius seem to have specialized in works of devotion. They were doubtless intended for readers in Central and East-Central Europe in particular (the 1626–7 version of the *Opera* of St Teresa was dedicated by the publisher to a Polish nobleman, Stanislas Lubomirski, while Bellarmino was translated by Prince Władislaw, or Ladislaus). Cologne was a notorious false place of publication in this period, but only one of the Latin translations using this name looks like a fake, Jouvancy's translation of Daniel's *Cleandre et Eudoxus* 'typis Petri Marteau'.

Interesting exceptions to the rule of Catholics translating Catholics are the translation of Francis Xavier by the Dutch professor Louis de Dieu and

---

[13] Bremond (1916–33).

that of Miguel de Molinos by the leading Pietist August Hermann Francke, published in Protestant Halle.

In the second place, a long way behind religion, we find works of history: 152 works altogether, including 21 works of ecclesiastical history, 33 biographies of religious leaders, 5 biographies of political and military leaders (2 of Philip II, together with Castruccio Castracani, Wallenstein and the Duke of Newcastle) and 56 antiquarian treatises (31 of them from the Graevius project), including Guillaume Du Choul's study of the Roman army and Charles Patin's study of coins.

The works translated also include the most famous Italian vernacular histories of the period – Machiavelli, Guicciardini, Sarpi and Davila (even though Davila had to wait for more than a century to find a translator). Works by relatively minor Italians such as Pietro Bizzarri, Pandolfo Collenuccio, Gianpietro Contarini, Pompeo Giustinian, Galeazzo Gualdo Priorato and Giovanni Tommaso Minadoi were also translated, a sign of the prestige of the Italian model of historical writing from the Renaissance to the Baroque.

Far fewer texts were translated from French, notably Froissart's *Chroniques* and the memoirs of Philippe de Commynes, both of them translated on the initiative of the Protestant humanist Johann Sleidan, himself no mean historian.[14] Commynes was actually the work which sold best in Latin (with two translations and at least fifteen editions) as he did in other languages (below, p. 129). Iberian texts are also few – Correa, Herrera, Mendoza, Pulgar, Sandoval – and English texts still fewer: there is only Francis Bacon's *Henry VII* and the history of the Reformation in England by the Scottish divine Gilbert Burnet, translated into Latin by a German at a time when the knowledge of English was just beginning to spread, and published in Geneva in order to reach an international Protestant public.

In the third place, natural philosophy (from mathematics to medicine and including magic) with 135 items (cf. Pantin, below, p. 163). The Scientific Revolution was an international movement which came at a time when scholars were beginning to abandon the traditional language of the Republic of Letters. The number of translations increased during the early modern period as increasing numbers of natural philosophers decided to write in the vernacular.

Paracelsus, who insisted on writing and even delivering university lectures in German, was a pioneer in this respect, and – since German was not a language many foreigners knew – he owed a good part of his international

---

[14] On Sleidan, Vekene (1996).

reputation to the various translations of his work into Latin. Galileo began by writing in Latin, the *Sidereus nuncius* (Starry Messenger) for example, but switched to Italian in order to widen his domestic audience, provoking a protest from one of his German friends, Mark Welser. It was necessary for Bernegger and Diodati to translate him into Latin before his ideas could continue to circulate outside Italy. At the end of the century, Newton – who himself read Galileo in Latin – made a similar decision, shifting from his Latin *Principia* to his English *Optics*, translated by his disciple Samuel Clarke.[15]

The most translated European scientist was Robert Boyle, with twenty-six separate works, thanks not only to his reputation as a natural philosopher but also to his reluctance to write in Latin coupled with the general ignorance of English in the learned world.[16] The problem of English surfaces in the correspondence of the secretary of the Royal Society, Henry Oldenburg, who received letters from Venice and the Dutch Republic hoping for a Latin translation of Thomas Sprat's history of the Society. Although Louis de Moulin agreed to make the translation, it never materialized, and readers without English had to turn to a French version.[17]

Other well-known figures in the world of natural philosophy whose works were translated include Francesco Redi, Simon Stevin and Jan Swammerdam. The number of medical and pharmacological books translated, even those by lesser-known authors, also deserves emphasis: Bauderon, for example, Cheyne, Fizes, Freind, Gérin, Havers, Joubert, Du Laurens, Monardes. The existence of these translations suggests that there was an international demand for guides to practice as well as for theoretical works.

To meet this kind of demand, works on technology were also translated on occasion; treatises on architecture (discussed below under 'art'); Biringuccio's *Pyrotechnica* on fireworks, Boeckler's *Theatrum machinarum* on machines, Wagenaer's *Speculum nauticum* on navigation or Neri's *De arte vitraria* on glassmaking. All the same, the relative rarity of this type of book suggests a lack of overlap between the members of the public who were able to read Latin and those who wanted (say) to learn how to make glass.

In the fourth place, eighty-four books concerned with geography or 'travel', a subject which it is not always easy to distinguish from history, as in the case of Benzoni's and Herrera's accounts of the New World, which are therefore included – like accounts of missions outside Europe – in both

[15] What Newton owned, at least, was Galileo in Latin: Harrison (1978).
[16] Fulton (1961).   [17] Oldenburg (1965–77), vol. IV, 69, 255n, 281, 326.

sections. General works included Botero's *Relazioni*, Sebastian Münster's cosmography and the atlases of John Speed and Joan Blaeu.

Most of the best-known accounts of explorations and discoveries in the Americas circulated in Latin, beginning with those of Columbus, Vespucci and Cortés. The Englishmen Francis Drake, Thomas Hariot and Walter Raleigh also appeared in Latin dress, alongside the Frenchmen Léry and Laudonnière, the Spaniard Las Casas and the German Heinrich von Staden, who claimed to have narrowly escaped being eaten by cannibals in Brazil. A number of translations of these accounts of exotic lands appear to have been commissioned by a single publisher, the engraver Theodore De Bry, at the end of the sixteenth century, in order to form part of a series on America.

Asia too received a good deal of attention. The Turks in particular were an object of concern, but there were also the accounts of India by Balbi, Peruschi, Pimenta, Pinner and Varthema, of Japan by Carvalho, Frois and Kaempfer, and of China by Marco Polo (translated twice), Mendoza and Pantoja, together with the account of the Dutch embassy to China in 1655–7 published by the steward to the ambassadors, Jan Nieuhof. Africa, on the other hand, was scarcely represented, with the exception of Leo Africanus on the whole continent, Cadamosto on West Africa and Lopes on the Congo.

In the fifth place, fiction, seventy-two works in different genres. There were plays, such as Ariosto's *Suppositi* and *Negromante*, the *Celestina* of Fernando de Rojas, Birk's *Susanna*, Tasso's *Aminta* and Giambattista Della Porta's *Astrologo*. There were epics, such as *Orlando furioso, Gerusalemme liberata, Os Lusíadas, Paradise Lost*, the *Semaine* of Du Bartas, Voltaire's *Henriade* and Klopstock's *Messiah*. There were other long poems, from Dante's *Divina commedia* and Brant's *Narrenschiff* to Spenser's *Shepherd's Calendar*, Dryden's *Absalom and Achitophel* and Pope's *Essay on Man*.[18] Shorter poems included the lyrics of the Persian poet Saadi and the Catalan Ausias March, works by Ronsard, Pibrac's moralizing verses, Boileau's ode on the taking of Namur, Corneille's on the victories of Louis XIV, Montgomerie's *The Cherry and the Plum*, La Fontaine's *Fables* (three translations) and Gray's *Elegy in a Country Churchyard* (which was also translated three times).[19]

In prose there were stories taken from Boccaccio and Cervantes ('Homo vitreus', in other words *El licenciado vidriero*), as well as Gil Polo's pastoral

---

[18] On *Os Lusíadas*, Fonda (1979), Briesemeister (1984); on *Paradise Lost*, Feder (1955); on Klopstock, Wallner (1982).
[19] On Ronsard, McFarlane (1978), Smith (1988); on La Fontaine, Desmed (1964).

romance *Diana*, Mateo Alemán's picaresque novel *Guzmán de Alfarache* and Fénelon's novel *Télémaque* (translated three times).[20] It is likely that Fénelon's romance was read as a political work, just as the epic of Du Bartas was read as a scientific work; classification systems are rarely watertight.

In the sixth place, sixty-four books on politics, again dominated by the Italians (cf. Baldwin, below). No one will be surprised to find famous Renaissance texts such as Machiavelli's *Principe* and *Discorsi*, for example, Giannotti's dialogues on Venice, Botero's *Ragione di stato* and other works, Campanella's *Città del sole*, or even Ammirato's *Discorsi sopra Cornelio Tacito*.[21] Guicciardini owes his place here to the political maxims extracted from his history, since his political writings were not yet in print. The presence of the seventeenth-century political writers Traiano Boccalini and Virgilio Malvezzi (no less than four of whose works appeared in Latin) is worth emphasis, like that of Raimondo de Montecuccoli on war.[22]

French texts include Seyssel's *French Commonwealth*, Bodin's *Republic*, Gentillet's attack on Machiavelli, La Noue's political and military discourses and Rohan's pioneering study of international relations. From Spanish comes the much reprinted *Reloj de príncipes* by the Spanish court preacher Antonio Guevara, together with Furio Ceriol on councillors, Rivadeneira's *Christian Prince*, Quevedo's commentary on Plutarch's *Brutus* and Saavedra's *Idea of a Prince* (which went through at least eleven Latin editions in the seventeenth century). Once again, the importance of Spain deserves to be noted. As for English, Hobbes's *Leviathan* was translated soon after its publication, but Locke's equally famous *Treatise on Government* was not.[23]

Most of these books might be described as 'political philosophy', but a few were more topical. Some were works of propaganda, like the pamphlets by La Chapelle, who defended Louis XIV during the War of the Spanish Succession in his *Helvetii epistolae*, or Caramuel's attack on the legitimacy of King João IV of Portugal. On the margin between politics and travel (and so counted in both sections) are some analyses of the Ottoman Empire and its military forces, five in particular – by Giovio, Geuffroy, Lucinge, Soranzo and Tarducci.

A few smaller categories deserve a brief comment. Conduct books, for example, ranging from moral philosophy to advice on table manners, include not only the three famous Italian treatises by Castiglione, Della

---

[20] On Boccaccio, Tournay (1981); on Cervantes, Fitzmaurice-Kelly (1897).

[21] On Machiavelli, Gerber (1911–13), 60–92; Anglo (2005).   [22] On Boccalini, Firpo (1965), 59–66.

[23] On Hobbes, Tricaud (1969); Löfstedt (1989).

Casa and Guazzo, but also the discussions of the court by Guevara, Faret and Du Réfuge, two treatises by Gracián, Courtin's manual of civility, and the essays of Francis Bacon, translated under the title 'Sermones fideles'. In this domain we find more Protestant translators of texts by Catholics: Chytraeus, for example, who translated Della Casa, Salmuth, who translated Guazzo, or Wanckel, who translated Guevara. Ideals of good conduct seem to have been independent from theology.

Philosophy in its relatively narrow modern sense has only a small place in this list: eighteen items. Given the importance of Latin as a language in which to write on philosophy, it is perhaps surprising to find that Latin translations were needed at all. All the same, Descartes on method, Kant on reason, Leibniz on theodicy, Malebranche on truth, Pascal's *Pensées* and Locke on human understanding were all turned into Latin in this period (Hume is represented only by his autobiography). The so-called 'Logic of Port-Royal', by Arnauld and others, Cudworth's *True Intellectual System of the Universe* and Wolff's *Cogitationes rationales* should also be included here, together with three works by Bouhours, the Neoplatonists Leone Ebreo and Francesco Patrizzi, and of course Confucius, whose Latinized name still testifies to the language in which his ideas reached the West.

Only a handful of books are to be found in other categories. Art, for example (Dürer, Sandrart, Serlio, Menestrier); literary criticism (Bartoli, Huet, Sforza Pallavicino, Tesauro); emblems (Borja, Coornhert, Montenay); a Spanish grammar (Oudin); and a study of prices (Bodin). Even law is poorly represented, despite Azpilcueta, Hotman, Sarpi and Selden; in this period – outside England, which had a common law system of little interest on the Continent – it was still rare to write on law in the vernacular. In a class by itself is Naudé's advice on forming a library (appropriately enough, a text concerned with the problem of classification).

In short, the great intellectual movements of the period – until the Enlightenment – are well represented in Latin translation. The Renaissance is represented in the form of Italian historians and political writers if not artists. The great discoveries, the Reformation, the Counter-Reformation and the Scientific Revolution are also obviously present in this list. On the other hand, the list as a whole is not a simple mirror of the taste of the time. It was influenced by a few individuals in a position to turn their personal interests into publications. Without Theodore de Bry, fewer translations of accounts of the New World would have appeared. Without Samuel de Tournes, Geneva's place in the history of scientific publications would have been much smaller. Without Graevius and Burmann, a number of Italian antiquarians would not have been known abroad.

VI

Translating modern works into Latin posed the problem of writing in a Latin that humanists would regard as classical about phenomena unknown to the ancient Romans. The humanists themselves were divided on this issue, the 'Ciceronians' being opposed to neologisms while Alberti, Valla, Erasmus and others considered some new Latin words to be necessary.[24] On one side, some translators of Machiavelli tried to classicize the text. Silvestro Teglio's version of *Il principe*, for example, refers not to cardinals but 'the college of priests' (*sacerdotum collegium*). In similar fashion, the anonymous translator of the *Arte della guerra* called the Swiss pikemen 'legio Helvetica' or 'hastatorum ordines'.

Guicciardini's fate in Latin was a similar one to Machiavelli's.[25] In his preface the translator, Celio Secundo Curione, explains the need for using modern words for modern places, offices and equipment (*locorum, officiorum, armorum et machinarum nova vocabula*), the reason being 'the great contrast between the ancient and modern worlds' (*tanta ... veterum à novis dissimilitudo*), making it necessary to write about *Ammiralii, Cardinales* and so on.

In practice, however, Curione did try quite hard to find classical equivalents for many modern objects or organizations. Thus *antiguardia*, 'vanguard', becomes *primum agmen*; *artiglierie*, 'artillery', lacking in antiquity, becomes *tormenta*, a term originally referring to Roman catapults; *bastione*, 'bastion' (a new Italian invention) becomes *vallum*, 'fortification', losing its specificity; *ducati* similarly become *aureorum numum*, 'gold coins'; *lancie*, 'lancers', turn into classical *cataphracti*; and *trombetta*, 'trumpet', into an ancient term for herald, *praeco*. Even the *stradiotti*, a distinctive form of Greek or Albanian cavalry in Venetian service, are given the vaguer name of 'Illyrian horsemen', *illyrici equites*. In the case of archers and crossbowmen (*arcieri, balestieri*), Curione produces a compromise, 'those whom they call *arcieri* and the Romans *sagittarii*'.

On the other side, we might take the case of Paolo Sarpi's *History of the Council of Trent*, turned from Italian into Latin by Adam Newton in 1620. Newton occasionally classicized, referring to the Council as *conventus* and to universities as *academiae*. Generally speaking, however, he preferred to keep technical terms in their original medieval or later Latin: *bulla*, for instance, *cardinales, curia romana, episcopi, jesuitae, indulgentiae, nuncii, scholastici* and so on. In similar fashion the translators of Sarpi's treatises on

---

[24] On Alberti, Grafton (2001), 283ff.   [25] Luciani (1936), 27ff., 35ff.

the Inquisition and the Interdict used the non-classical terms *inquisitio* and *interdictus*.

In the case of translations of Castiglione's *Cortegiano* into Latin, of which there were three in the period (by Bartholomew Clerke, Johannes Ricius and Johannes Turler), problems arose more rarely, but they were even more serious. The translators generally tried to write classical Latin. On the other hand, Castiglione was discussing behaviour in a milieu unknown to Cicero, the court. Linguistic problems inevitably arose, notably in the case of the renderings of the keywords *cortegianía* and *sprezzatura*.[26]

The first term, *cortegianía*, which the translator of Castiglione into English had rendered as 'courtiership', gave Clerke so much trouble that he discussed it in his preface to the reader. 'What shall I call what the English describe as courtiership and the Italians as *cortegianía*? *Aulicalitas* does not sound well ... I am forced to use the term *curialitas*, which is closer to the original even if it is less pure Latin.' (*Quid enim appellem id quod Angli* Courtiership, *Itali Cortegianiam nominant? Aulicalitatem dicere non placet ... Curialitatem cogor appellare, quod verbum etsi minus purè Latinum sit, latinitati tamen propius accedit.*) Ricius avoided the problem by omitting altogether the phrase including *cortegianía*.

Sprezzatura also gave trouble. Clerke's solution to the problem was to paraphrase Castiglione, referring to the need to behave 'negligently and (as is commonly said) in a careless manner' (*negligenter et (ut vulgo dicitur) dissolute*), the latter term being his attempt to render Castiglione's neologism. He also used the term *incuria*. As for Ricius, he rendered the famous phrase *usare in ogni cosa una certa sprezzatura* as 'use in everything a certain kind of something like contempt' (*inque omni re usurpetur certa quaedam veluti contemptio*). That *certa quaedam veluti* surely betrays a certain hesitation or discomfort with the translator's neologism *contemptio*.

A still more dramatic illustration of the problem of choice between 'foreignizing' (above, p. 26) and classicizing is the case of books about the Ottoman Empire, which was unknown to the ancients as well as organized in a different manner from the contemporary West.[27] How should terms for culturally specific items be rendered?

On one side, the history of Venice written by the Ciceronian humanist Pietro Bembo classicized the Turks, giving up specificity in order to be elegant. Bembo called the galleys *biremes*, the spahis *equites*, the admiral of the Turkish fleet *prefectus classis Thraciae* and the sultan 'the King of Thrace', *Regem Thracium*. Again, in his history of his own time, Paolo Giovio,

[26] Burke (1995).   [27] This was also a problem for vernacular writers and translators (Burke, 2007).

another humanist, called Sultan Selim 'Selymus Turcarum imperator', while the janissaries, at least on occasion, become 'praetoriani milites'.

   On the other hand, when the German humanist Johannes Leunclavius translated the Ottoman annals into Latin, he decided to be useful rather than elegant, and so to take over Turkish terms like *Bassa, Genizari, Sangiacus* or *Vezir* (pasha, janissaries, sanjak, vizier). A similar solution was adopted by Jacob Geuder when he translated Minadoi's history of the war between the Turks and the Persians. After hesitating over place names such as 'Babilonia (quae hodie Bagadat dicitur)', he opted for keeping technical terms like *Caddi, Calif, Defiadar* and so on. Translating Geuffroy's account of the Turkish court, Geuder followed a similar principle, although he did give some Turkish words such as *odabashi* or timariot Latin inflections – *Odabasii, Tymariolzi*, etc.

   We are accustomed to think that the well-known dilemma between two styles of translation, 'domestication' – in other words, cultural translation – versus 'foreignizing', goes back to the nineteenth century or at the earliest to the eighteenth.[28] These examples from the Renaissance reveal an earlier awareness of the problem, complicated by the existence of a third possible solution, classicizing.

   The classicizing option might be described as a kind of cultural translation in reverse. We are accustomed to the translation of the language of the past into that of the present. After all, that is one of the major functions of historians. Here, however, we find the opposite phenomenon, the translation of the language of the present into that of the past, justified by the Renaissance project of reviving antiquity.

   The practice of classicizing, precisely because it is alien to our own culture, offers a vivid reminder of the fact that language is neither neutral nor free-floating. It is always encumbered by cultural baggage. Here as elsewhere in this volume, the choices made by early modern translators reveal a good deal about their culture.

---

[28] Venuti (1995).

PART II

Translation and culture

CHAPTER 5

Early modern Catholic piety in translation

Carlos M. N. Eire

Translations matter so much in the history of early modern Catholicism that one might easily argue 'no translations, no spiritual renewal, no Catholic Reformation' – at least not the kind of Reformation that historians now seem to take for granted. One counterfactual exercise alone should suffice to prove this point. Imagine a different St Ignatius Loyola: a wounded Basque nobleman named Iñigo who remained untouched by religious fervour after his encounter with a cannonball at the Battle of Pamplona in 1521. What if this crippled Iñigo had dedicated his life to co-ordinating the local *fiesta* of San Fermín every July? What if he had looked forward more to the running of the bulls than to prayer and the service of God and the Catholic Church? How would Catholicism have evolved in the sixteenth and seventeenth centuries without St Ignatius and the Society of Jesus?

Everyone knows that history would have taken a very different turn if the convalescing Iñigo had not been confined to a room with nothing else to read but two devotional texts in translation: the *Legenda aurea* of Jacob Voragine and the *Life of Christ* of Ludolph of Saxony. Later in life, as Ignatius and others around him reconstructed the sequence of events that led to his religious conversion, these two translations would be given the credit – along with God Himself – for having changed the wounded soldier into a saint. Those texts, and many others like them (some written or translated by Jesuits), would also be given credit for animating a wholesale renewal of the Catholic faith. Is such an assessment of the power of translated texts an exaggeration? Can one ascribe too much influence to a pair of translated texts?

Yes, undoubtedly, one might argue: Iñigo could have still turned into St Ignatius without those two translations, but it is hard to imagine how, exactly. Yes, undoubtedly, one might argue too: Catholicism would have been renewed without Ignatius and his Jesuits, but it is difficult to imagine the contours of that renewal without them. In the same way, it is difficult to imagine the landscape of Catholic piety in this period without translated devotional texts.

Translations often assume a central place in many a survey of Catholic spiritual life because the history of devotion or piety or spirituality – or whatever one decides to call the *living out* of religion – is inseparably linked to texts, especially after the invention of the printing press.[1] Texts played a key role in the transmission of ideas, attitudes and patterns of behaviour among early modern Catholics on two interdependent levels: among the clergy who gave shape to the faith and among the laity they shepherded. Those who wrote devotional texts in Catholic culture were most often the professional 'experts' on piety and on the supernatural: men and women who devoted their lives to the pursuit of holiness.

This class of religious elites not only authored the vast majority of devotional texts, but also constituted a well-informed critical audience that controlled the flow of information and gave shape to the devotional life of the Church as a whole. This audience consumed texts in Latin and also in the vernacular. It was this class, especially the priests and friars involved in public ministry, that distilled and passed on to the literate and illiterate laity the piety that the texts embodied. The laity, while not entirely passive, tended to be consumers rather than producers, and also tended to read vernacular rather than Latin texts, even though a fair number of those who were literate could read Latin.

Translations were essential for both audiences. Texts written in Latin by the 'experts' – if deemed significant enough – needed to be translated into vernaculars for a broader lay audience. Significant texts written in the vernacular, in turn, needed to be translated into Latin for international distribution, since Latin was the common tongue of the elite throughout Europe, especially among the 'experts' in religion. Naturally, significant texts written in one vernacular also needed to be translated into other vernaculars. Clergy and laity alike, then, shared in the need for translations. In all of this, at nearly every level save that of the manual labour in the print shops and the actual promotion and sale of books, the clerical elites assumed control of the process, both in the writing and translating of texts, and in the judging of what was significant. The fact that some of the authors of key devotional texts also turn out to be translators of other significant titles is no coincidence: it is due to the leading role played by clerics in the whole process.

---

[1] Rennhofer (1961), v.

Clerical domination of the process is undeniable. For instance: take the case of one of the most significant texts of all, the *Imitation of Christ* attributed to Thomas Kempis, an Augustinian canon, and let us limit our scope to Spain alone. The first Spanish edition is in Catalan, *Imitacio de Jesu Crist*, published in Barcelona in 1482. The translator, a cleric named Miguel Perez, attributes the book to Jean Gerson, a very prominent cleric and theologian, also chancellor of the University of Paris. This causes subsequent editions to name Gerson as the author and to give the book the name *el Gerçonzito* ('small Gerson'). We do not know who made the first Castilian translation (Zaragoza, 1490), but chances are that the work was done by a cleric. This translation, which also assumed Gerson's authorship, was published seven times between 1493 and 1526. Then, in 1536, the *Imitation* was translated into Castilian once again by none other than Luís de Granada, one of the leading spiritual authors of the day, a Dominican friar whose own works would be translated numerous times into Latin and other European vernaculars. After going through at least thirty editions, under the title *Contemptus mundi o menosprecio del mundo y imitacion de Cristo*, attributed to Thomas Kempis, this devotional classic was again translated in the seventeenth century by Juan Eusebio Nieremberg, a Jesuit priest whose own devotional works enjoy great popularity and are themselves translated into other European vernaculars by other clerics.

Dealing with the history of devotional texts entails dealing with a closely controlled process of cultural transmission and a social structure in which monks, nuns and priests play a very prominent role. Consequently, much of the scholarship on devotional texts focuses on this elite class, and much of it is devoted to tracing the lives of these clerical authors and the routes by means of which texts made their way from one person to another. Much of the scholarship also tends to be highly genealogical and obsessed with tracing lineages through texts and therefore also through translations. This means that most of the scholarship on this subject, up to the present, tends to fall under the category of the history of spirituality or mysticism and that it is overwhelmingly focused on a relatively narrow range of texts and authors – the 'classics', as it were – those texts that the elite spiritual 'experts' themselves have deemed most significant.

This naturally brings us to the question: 'what is a devotional text?' In this essay, I shall consider a very broad range of literature as 'devotional'. In essence, any text that could be viewed or used as a means of stirring religious fervour or of shaping the faith of its readers will be considered 'devotional'. This means that many different kinds of text can be included: prayer books, instruction manuals, printed sermons, mystical treatises, hagiographies, catechisms, polemical tracts, some theological tomes and, ultimately, the Bible itself.

Nonetheless, while it is absolutely necessary to keep in mind that the range of texts that can be called 'devotional' is broad indeed and that many formerly significant devotional texts have slipped into obscurity – hagiographies such as Jacobus de Voragine's *Legenda aurea* (Golden Legend), once the most popular collection of lives of the saints, with over a dozen editions and many translations in the early age of printing, or Gracián's *Summary of the Virtues of St Joseph* and manuals such as Achille Gagliardi's *Brief Summary of Christian Perfection* – it is just as necessary to admit the limitations of a very brief survey on the subject, such as this one. At best, it can aim to provide only an overview of the most significant texts and translations, and its main focus will have to be more narrative than analytical. Its structure will follow the pattern set in most of the secondary literature, tracing the circulation of texts and translations in three centres of origin from the late fifteenth to the late seventeenth century – centres that had an undeniable dominance in Catholic culture during this period, in chronological order: first Germany and the Low Countries, then Spain and finally France, with some inevitable sidelong glances at Italy along the way. Identifying lacunae, critiquing the scholarship and suggesting new avenues for research will have to be reserved for a brief conclusion.

THE NORTHERN EPICENTRE

Nearly every survey of early modern devotional literature begins its narrative in one relatively small corner of northern Europe, along the lower Rhine. Two major spiritual traditions merged there in the late Middle Ages, giving birth to devotional currents that would dominate the sixteenth and seventeenth centuries: the so-called Rheno-Flemish mystical tradition, which went back to the fourteenth century, with its roots in Meister Eckhart and his disciples, and the *Devotio moderna*, flowing from it, but also rooted in the Brethren of the Common Life and the Canons Regular of Windesheim.[2] This merging produced a number of texts, but none more important than the *Imitation of Christ*, now attributed to Thomas Kempis (1380–1471), but for quite some time ascribed to Jean Gerson (1363–1429). Its focus is the development of a rich inner life of the spirit, detachment from the world, a keen awareness of one's states of mind and wholesale

---

[2] Fuller (1995); Hyma (1965); Cognet (1968); Lücker (1950).

immersion of one's self in Christ. This text would eventually become one of the most-published and translated devotional classics.[3]

The *Imitation of Christ* was only one of many influential texts that flowed from the newly devised printing presses of Germany and the Low Countries. Another one of these was the *Life of Christ* by Ludolph of Saxony, better known as Ludolph the Carthusian (d. 1378). Ignatius Loyola was but one of the readers of this text (in translation) who were deeply affected by what it had to say. Ludolph's *Meditationis vita Christi* was first printed in 1474 at Strassburg and Cologne, in Latin. It was not a narrative of the Life of Jesus, as found in the Gospels, but rather an extended meditation on it, heavily laced with patristic citations, moral and doctrinal lessons, and many prayers.[4]

Texts by the disciples of Meister Eckhart (1260–1327) also figured prominently in the first few decades of printing: Johannes Tauler (1300–61), Heinrich Suso (1295–1366) and Jan van Ruysbroeck (1293–1381). All of their texts were linked by a common bond: the belief that at the very core of the human person, a divine spark dwells – a point of ontological oneness with God that can only be discerned and experienced through detachment from the world. The teachings of these three disciples of Eckhart were further popularized by a talented synthesizer, Hendrik Herp, or Harphius (d. 1477), whose works became immensely popular in various European vernaculars, as well as in Latin. Much credit is also given to Denis Rijckel (1394–1471), better known as Denis the Carthusian, for distilling and passing on this tradition. Denis was a prolific and popular author of devotional texts, with no fewer than seven major treatises to his credit, including one entitled *The Four Last Things*,[5] which had considerable influence in the popular genre of the art of dying well, commonly known as the *ars moriendi*.

But the roots of late medieval devotional literature went much deeper than the fourteenth century, and were much broader in their reach than the lower Rhine. The taproot itself, deepest of all, led to the Bible. Around the time that Harphius and Denis the Carthusian died, biblical studies began to undergo a rebirth. Not surprisingly, a student of the Brethren of the Common Life who was deeply influenced by the *Devotio moderna* would emerge as the leading biblical scholar of his day: Erasmus of Rotterdam (1469–1536).

[3] Iserloh (1971).
[4] García Mateo (2002); Shore (1998); Bodenstedt (1955); Baier (1977); Conway (1976).
[5] Wassermann (1996).

Erasmus blazed new trails, contributing substantially to the return *ad fontes*, to the original sources of the Christian faith. By far his most impressive achievement was his 1516 edition of the New Testament, based on the study of various ancient manuscripts, which also contained copious annotations and a new Latin translation that sought to improve upon Jerome's Vulgate. Erasmus's new translation provided alternate readings of some key texts, casting doubt on the validity of medieval interpretations of these passages, some of which had long served as proof texts for important doctrines.

A good example is the text of Matthew 4:17, which in the Vulgate reads 'Do penance, for the Kingdom of Heaven is at hand' (*Poenitentiam agite*). This passage had been interpreted for centuries as proof of the fact that the sacrament of penance was clearly instituted by Christ himself. In 1516, Erasmus insisted that the correct translation from the Greek was not 'Do penance', but rather 'Repent' (*poeniteat vos*); in 1519, he insisted instead on 'change your mind' (*resipiscite*) – two very subtle, yet significant differences. Whereas *Poenitentiam agite* bolstered the legitimacy of the outward act of confessing one's sins to a priest, *poeniteat* and *resipiscite* pointed to an interior act, perhaps even to an inner disposition.

This questioning of the Vulgate text, along with his constant criticism of the late medieval Church and its piety, led many to say later that Erasmus had laid the egg hatched by Luther. Erasmus rejected such charges, but there is no denying that he had a lasting impact on Protestant piety through his translation of biblical texts. A few years after the publication of his New Testament, Protestant theologians would be centring some key aspects of their theology and piety on Erasmus's alternative translations. Additionally, the second edition of Erasmus's New Testament (1519) would end up serving as the basis for the first translations into German, French and English – the translations used to establish Protestant Christianity in northern Europe.

Erasmus and many of his fellow humanists also sought out the writings of the early Christian Fathers, with an eye on the renewal of Christendom. Many of the greatest scholars of the age, and some of the lesser ones too, devoted great time and effort to collating Greek manuscripts and translating them into Latin. Sometimes, the spirit of collaboration transcended the personal quest for fame. Erasmus, for instance, published the German humanist Wilibald Pirckheimer's translation of the *Orationes* of Gregory Nazianzus in 1531, with a preface that praised Pirckheimer's Latin rendering, arguing that it was so wonderful that no one would ever have to turn to the Greek original ever again. Strange praise from a humanist who dedicated his life to returning *ad fontes*, but nonetheless very revealing, for capturing the essence of a text and disseminating its translation could be as important a task for a humanist as arriving at a definitive rendering of the original text.[6]

Erasmus poured much of his energy into editing and publishing patristic texts, and to translating the Greek Fathers into Latin. At bottom, what mattered most to Erasmus and many other humanist editors and translators was the recovery of the devotional life of the early Church, not the search for theological precision. Above all, the return to the Fathers was a search for the best possible devotional literature.[7]

Chief among those who received attention were Origen, Jerome and Augustine. Along with these came the sixth-century pseudonymous Father, Dionysius the Areopagite. The fact that Lorenzo Valla (1406–57) had convincingly cast doubt on Dionysius's identity – turning 'the Areopagite' into 'the *Pseudo*-Areopagite' – did little to lessen the ancient author's influence. The deeply Platonic texts of Dionysius and his apophatic spirituality, championed by Marsilio Ficino (1433–99) and the Florentine Platonic Academy, found a great promoter in the French humanist Jacques Lefèvre d'Étaples (1455–1536), who in 1502 began to edit and publish Dionysius's texts, along with other early Christian documents. Making Dionysius available to a wider reading public was a crucial step in the forging of early modern spirituality and imbuing it with Neoplatonic tendencies in its metaphysics and epistemology.

Lefèvre was also keenly interested in the Bible. His biblical scholarship had as its main aim the search for 'true' texts and the development of faithful translations so that the Scriptures could become more accessible to everyone. In 1509 Lefèvre published a pioneering book, the *Psalterium quintuplex*, in which he laid out for comparison five different Latin versions of the Psalms, side by side. For centuries, all that had been available was the Vulgate Latin translation of St Jerome. In 1512 Lefèvre broke new ground once again by publishing a French translation of Paul's *Letter to the Romans* based on the Greek original, with a commentary, and also with the Latin Vulgate text alongside for comparison. In the commentary, Lefèvre questioned the Vulgate text and other venerable authorities in various ways, arguing, among other things, that the Bible was the ultimate authority in the Christian religion – a position he never tired of defending, and which was further elaborated upon in 1522, when he published a commentary on the four Gospels.

---

[6] Spitz (1963). [7] Walter (1991); Backus (1995); Peters (1967).

Though he drew fire for his opinions, and had some writings condemned by the theologians at the Sorbonne, Lefèvre pushed ahead with
his biblical scholarship and his translating, undaunted. In part, his confidence stemmed from the support that he received from King Francis I
and his sister Marguerite of Navarre, who were so pleased by his work that
they asked him to translate the entire Bible into French. Lefèvre's translation would appear in instalments: the New Testament in 1523, the Psalms
in 1525 and the entire Bible in 1530. Lefèvre would earn a reputation as a
crypto-Protestant and even as a Protestant ideologue, but he also had a
deep interest in more recent authors and texts that Protestants shunned.
The very same Lefèvre, the reputed godfather of French Protestantism,
lauded by Theodore Bèze in his *Icones* (a book containing portraits and
capsule biographies of all of the men who had led the Protestant
Reformation), also took it upon himself to translate into Latin and to
publish Ruysbroeck's *Spiritual Espousals* in 1512 – a text that all of the
magisterial Protestant reformers would reject or even despise.

When it came to some medieval mystics, Lefèvre was no crypto-
Protestant, but rather very much in step with some of his devoutly
Catholic brethren, and especially with some monks. The dissemination
of Rhineland mystical texts throughout Europe was chiefly the work of one
German monastic community: the Carthusians of Cologne, better known
in English as the Charterhouse of Cologne.[8] It was there that many of the
great texts of the Rhineland mystics were translated into Latin, the lingua
franca of the intellectual and spiritual elites. And it was not just
Ruysbroeck, Tauler and Suso who were made available to all of learned
Europe by the Cologne Carthusians. They also translated and helped
publish a wide array of devotional texts, ranging from the relatively recent
Mirror of Perfection by Harphius (1474) to the letters of Catherine of Siena
(1347–80).

Though Carthusians shied away from revealing their identities, we know
that one of the most important translators at the Cologne community was
Laurence Surius (1522–78), who translated Tauler, Ruysbroeck and Suso
into Latin.[9] One of his most important Latin translations was that of an
anonymous Dutch text, *The Pearl of the Gospel* (1545). The *Pearl* was a great
summation of Rhineland mysticism and also an anthology. Whole sections
from the works of other authors, especially from Ruysbroeck and from the
more contemporary Harphius were inserted into it. Surius himself

---

[8] Chaix (1981); Marks (1974); Schäfke (1991).   [9] Hebenstreit-Wilfert (1975).

acquired a reputation for spiritual wisdom and came to be revered in learned Catholic circles throughout Europe.

The Cologne Carthusians did more than translate: some wrote their own treatises, which were also later translated. Among them, one of the most significant is Johannes Justus Lansperger (1489–1539), better known as Lanspergius, whose writings were wholly conscious of the threat posed by Protestantism. His *Discourse of Jesus Christ to the Faithful* and his *Manual of the Christian Army* (a title that is an all too obvious allusion to Erasmus's most famous book), much published and translated, self-consciously sought to defend the freedom of the will, the necessity of self-denial and the possibility of union with God, in opposition to Protestant teachings.

Another devotional writer whose work was promoted by the Cologne Carthusians was even more popular than Lanspergius. This was Louis de Blois (1506–66), abbot of Lessies, better known as Blosius, a great Renaissance synthesizer who not only assimilated the writings of the Rhineland mystics, but also incorporated texts from great spiritual masters such as Augustine, Gregory the Great, Mechtilde of Magdeburg, Tauler, Suso and Ruysbroeck into his own works.[10] Blosius wrote initially for the monks at Lessies, but his texts eventually found their way outside the cloister walls to a very wide reading public, thanks largely to translations, and thanks largely to the Cologne Carthusians who published and promoted them. His *Book of Spiritual Instruction*, in particular, sold for several generations in many languages.[11] His complete works, first published at Louvain in 1568, were reprinted and translated many times, and for long he had few rivals in popularity. His influence should not be underestimated. In 1598, King Philip II – arguably the most powerful monarch in the world, and the most ardently devoted to defending the Catholic faith – would ask for Blosius to be read to him continually as he lay dying at the Escorial. Though King Philip could have understood Blosius in Latin, it is quite likely that he heard the Castilian translation of the *Spiritual Instruction* by Juan Vazquez del Marmol.

SPAIN'S GOLDEN AGE

In the sixteenth century, Spain gradually assumed an ever larger role in the publication and dissemination of devotional literature. Much of the credit is given to Cardinal Francisco Jiménez (Ximenes) de Cisneros (1436–1510), who, as Archbishop of Toledo and Confessor to Queen Isabella sponsored

---

[10] Blois (1875).   [11] Vos (1992), esp. 191–201.

the translation of numerous devotional texts into Castilian, especially John Climacus (570–649), Angela of Foligno (1248–1309), Catherine of Siena, Girolamo Savonarola (1452–98) and Ludolph the Carthusian. Jiménez also sponsored the publication of some Latin devotional texts – most notably from Raymond Lull (1232–1316) – and the translation of some Greek texts into Latin, including once again John Climacus's *Scala spiritualis* (Toledo, 1505) and the *Erotemata* (Alcalá, 1514) of Emanuel Chrysoloras (1350–1415). From these mystical 'plantings', some experts argue, Jiménez de Cisneros helped to produce an abundant harvest a generation later.[12]

At roughly the same time, other Spanish translators and publishers brought out texts from the Rhineland tradition, and their translations are directly linked to the relatively sudden outpouring of mystical fervour and mystical texts in Spain. Among the first in Spain to publish an influential treatise was García de Cisneros (1455–1510), abbot of the Benedictine monastery of Montserrat and a cousin of Cardinal Jiménez. Experts agree that his *Book of Exercises for the Spiritual Life*, which was deeply influenced by the *Devotio moderna*, marks the beginning of a century of Spanish predominance in the field of devotional literature.

By the 1520s, a good number of devotional texts began to appear in Spain, all of them influenced by the northern spiritual traditions: Alonso de Madrid's *Art of Serving God* (1521); Francisco de Osuna's *Third Spiritual Alphabet* (1527); Bernardino de Laredo's *Ascent of Mount Sion* (1535); Luís de Granada's *The Sinner's Guide* (1542) and *Book of Prayer and Meditation* (1554); and Juan de Avila's *Audi filia* (1556). These authors were followed in turn by the two towering giants of the golden age of Spanish mysticism, the Carmelites Teresa of Avila (1515–82) and John of the Cross (1542–91).[13] Almost a century ago, scholars recognized that St Teresa and St John were direct heirs of the northern traditions.[14] Most specialists nowadays would probably also agree with this proposition: no translations, no Teresa, no John of the Cross – at least not the Teresa and John who scaled the mystical heights with such grace and authority.[15]

But some of the harvest from this northern seed proved heterodox, or close to it. Alongside the well-accepted spiritual masters there also sprang up a host of men and women who ran afoul of church authorities. The passivity or detachment that was so central to the northern mystics took on a different meaning in Spain, giving rise to a movement that was deemed

---

[12] Sainz Rodriguez (1979).   [13] Groult (1927); Alventosa Sanchis (1963).
[14] Hoornaert (1922); Etchegoyen (1923).   [15] Orcibal (1966).

heretical: the *Alumbrados*, or 'Illumined', who began to be persecuted in 1525. In part, the misfortune of the so-called *Alumbrados* can be blamed on the translation of a single word from the Rhineland mystics, *inwerken*, which referred to the way in which the divine worked inwardly within the human self. Latin translations awkwardly rendered *inwerken* into *inactio*, giving the concept an even more heightened passivity. The translation of this word also had an impact on French spirituality.[16]

But that was not all. This so-called Illuminism also joined hands with another strong current flowing from the north, that of Erasmian spirituality.[17] An heir himself to the Rhineland traditions and to the *Devotio moderna*, Erasmus became immensely popular in some circles in Spain before he was ever translated into Castilian. Erasmus wrote many treatises that could be called 'devotional' and he gained a following throughout all of Europe thanks to these works rather than to his biblical scholarship. By far the most significant of these devotional texts was the *Enchiridion*, or *Manual of the Christian Soldier* (1503), a manifesto of the inward piety favoured by the *Devotio moderna* and the Neoplatonism of Ficino.

The *Enchiridion* was one of the most widely translated texts of the sixteenth century, appearing in English (1518), Czech (1519), German (1520), Spanish (1524), French (1529), Dutch (1542), Italian (1542) and Polish (1585).[18] The translation of the *Enchiridion* into Castilian in 1524, 1528, 1541 and 1555 enlarged his popularity further, beyond Spanish learned circles, but 'Erasmianism' eventually proved as unacceptable to church authorities as Illuminism. In the same way that the *Alumbrados* were crushed, so were the Erasmians. After 1559, when Erasmus's works began to be listed in the Church's *Index of Forbidden Books*, many of his texts would be difficult to find in Spain, even though some had been recently translated and published.[19] Some Erasmians, such as the brothers Juan and Alfonso de Valdés, would eventually be linked with Protestantism outside the Iberian peninsula. Juan de Valdés's *Dialogue of Christian Doctrine* (1529), deeply influenced by Erasmian ideas and Rheno-Flemish spirituality, would wind up on the Catholic Church's infamous *Index librorum prohibitorum.*[20]

---

[16] Van Schoote (1963), esp. 334–5.
[17] García Gutiérrez (1999); Hamilton (1992); Andrés Martín (1975).
[18] Haeghen (1897–1907). Van der Haeghen does not include every edition, however. Simply by checking the Eureka online database (eureka.rlg.org), I found twelve English editions and four Dutch editions not listed in this bibliography.
[19] Bataillon (1937); cf. Homza (2000).   [20] Nieto (1970); Bakhuizen (1969).

This was not the sole extent of controversy engendered by the mystical 'invasion' from the north. Among those who remained orthodox, the passive tendencies of the Rheno-Flemish tradition never vanished completely, and never ceased to invite criticism or charges of heresy. Even Teresa of Avila and John of the Cross had their critics, who linked them with the Illuminists. In the seventeenth century, within Spain itself and also in France – where translations of the texts of the great Spanish mystics had a profound impact – the very same passive traits would give rise to an even more intense controversy and another heresy, Quietism.

Sixteenth-century Spain was also the birthplace of another towering giant in the history of spirituality, Ignatius Loyola (1491–1556), founder of the Jesuits. Loyola was himself deeply affected by translated devotional literature, and by the publishing efforts of Cardinal Jiménez. As has already been mentioned, he attributed his conversion to the religious life in the early 1520s to two medieval texts, recently published in Castilian translations, Ludolph of Saxony's *Life of Christ* and Jacobus de Voragine's *Legenda aurea*.[21] Ignatius also learned much from the devotional manual penned by Cardinal Jiménez's cousin, García de Cisneros's *Exercitorio de la vida espiritual* (1500), which greatly influenced his own immensely significant *Spiritual Exercises*, the cornerstone of all Jesuit spirituality – the devotional manual *par excellence*, which is not meant so much to be read as to be experienced over a period of several weeks under the guidance of a skilled director. Ignatius's *Exercises* are still employed, re-examined and constantly retranslated in Catholic circles.[22]

Within Spain's orbit, but certainly independent of it – no matter how much of their land was ruled *de jure* from Madrid – some Italian spiritual writers also made their mark in the sixteenth century. Three Italians in particular were enormously popular and influential. In keeping with the Spanish predilection for *recogimiento*, or interior prayer, the Capuchin father Mattia Bellintani da Salò (1535–1611) published his *Practice of Mental Prayer* in 1588. Also popular and influential was the Jesuit priest Achille Gagliardi (1537–1607), whose *Brief Summary of Christian Perfection* ended up being translated into English, French, Dutch, German and Latin. The Theatine priest Lorenzo Scupoli (1530–1610) was even more popular and influential. His *Spiritual Combat* not only enjoyed numerous editions in Italian, but also many translations, including English, Latin, French, Castilian and German.

---

[21] Dunn-Lardeau (1986); Reames (1985); Rhein (1995).   [22] Palmer (1996).

THE FRENCH CENTURY

As the sixteenth century belongs largely to Spain in the history of spirituality, the seventeenth belongs to France. The genealogy of this so-called 'mystical invasion', painstakingly documented in three volumes by Henri Bremond,[23] takes one deeply into the history of translations. First, great credit is given to the translations of the Cologne Carthusians, which made their way to France, opening up the great patristic and medieval texts, as well as those of the Rheno-Flemish tradition. In addition, other translations began to appear, even as France was wracked by the Wars of Religion.[24] In 1549, it was Harphius; and beginning in 1553, several texts by Blosius. Then came some Spanish texts in translation: Luís de Granada in 1572; Juan de Avila in 1586. Near the end of the Wars of Religion came the Italian writers: Lorenzo Scupoli's *Spiritual Combat* in 1595 and the *Life and Works* of Catherine of Genoa in 1598.

After the Edict of Nantes ended the carnage in 1598, the translation of texts from the Rheno-Flemish tradition and from the more recent Spanish mystics and Italian devotional writers began to increase. From the north came *The Pearl of the Gospel* in 1602; Ruysbroeck's *Spiritual Espousals* in 1606; and all of Harphius in 1607. From the south came Matthias Bellintani da Salo's *Practice of Mental Prayer* in 1600; Teresa of Avila in 1601; and John of the Cross in 1621.[25] In addition, translations of patristic and medieval authors also began to increase: Gregory the Thaumaturge, Ambrose of Milan, Bonaventure, Catherine of Siena, Thomas Aquinas and Dionysius the Areopagite, to name but a few. This flood of translations has led one expert to conclude that 'between 1550 and 1610 spiritual literature in France lived on borrowings'.[26]

At the turn of the century, as the fratricide subsided, French spiritual experts began to make their own substantial contributions to devotional literature. First came the English exile, the Capuchin Benedictus or Benoît de Canfield (originally William Fitch), whose *Rule of Perfection* was translated into French in 1609. Despite infelicities in style, this text soon became immensely popular and influential. According to Louis Cognet, 'all the mysticism of the age was nurtured on it'. He adds: 'Canfield, although he was an Englishman, remains one of the great names of French spiritual history, and it is a thousand pities that he could not write.'[27] Then came the formidable Francis de Sales (1567–1622), with his juggernaut of a book,

[23] Bremond (1916–33); Cognet (1949).   [24] Van Schoote (1963).   [25] Dagens (1952b).
[26] Marocchi (1988).   [27] Cognet (1958), 60.

Introduction to the Devout Life (1608), a text that sought to distil the wisdom of the great spiritual experts for the Catholic laity and to set them on to their own pursuit of holiness. The publication history of this treatise is remarkable: by 1620, over forty editions of the French text had been published; by 1656, it was available in seventeen translations. This was followed in 1616 by his immensely popular *Treatise on the Love of God*.

Next in line came Cardinal Pierre de Bérulle (1575–1629), founder of the Oratory, who not only brought the Discalced Carmelite reform to France, but also spearheaded a renewal of the French clergy and a style of devotion that centred on the humanity of Christ, best summarized in his very popular *Glories of Jesus* (1626). It is not at all insignificant that those who write on Bérulle often try to trace his spirituality to the various translated texts.[28] One Italian treatise in particular stands out in all efforts to discern the sources of Bérulle's spirituality: Achille Gagliardi's *Brief Summary of Christian Perfection*. Bérulle acquired a large following, and was so popular that by 1644, a mere fifteen years after his death, most of his works had been gathered together in a single edition. His disciples produced many devotional texts of their own. One of the most influential of these was Jean Duvergier de Hauranne, abbot of Saint-Cyran, who would figure prominently in the development of Jansenism.[29]

An abundance of devotional texts, however, does not necessarily indicate an upsurge in piety. It can also be a symptom of tensions, or perhaps even their cause. Consequently, the flood of devotional texts published in seventeenth-century France must always be placed in the context of the great religious controversies of the period, especially that between the Jansenists and their mostly Jesuit opponents, and that between the school of Bérulle, with its focus on the incarnate Christ, and the so-called Abstract school, with its focus on the divine nature of Christ, which eventually erupted into the Quietist crisis of the late seventeenth century and its subsequent condemnations.[30] Neither can one overlook the conflict between Catholic and Protestant, which continued to be carried out in print throughout the seventeenth century. Even polemical treatises can sometimes count as devotional literature, and the number of such tracts published in France was tremendous.[31] Finally, one must also remember that by the end of the Thirty Years' War in 1648, other strong currents were sweeping through the spiritual landscape of Europe, and that some of the strongest were those of scepticism and doubt, leading up to the

[28] Dagens (1952a).   [29] Orcibal (1961, 1962).   [30] Orcibal (1959).
[31] Desgraves (1984). Vol. 1 alone has 3,595 entries.

Enlightenment, the Scientific Revolution and the ultimate demise of Christian hegemony in Europe. Much of the heat generated by these controversies was felt outside France, thanks largely to translations.

So much for the sweeping narrative. Let us now turn to its shortcomings.

LOOKING AHEAD

Reduced to its barest elements, almost to the point of caricature, twentieth-century surveys of early modern spirituality assume similar features, and the most common and prominent of these features is their genealogical obsession with the tracing of lineages through texts and translations. The basic narrative reads something like this: in the sixteenth century, medieval devotional literature from the Rheno-Flemish tradition caused a flowering of mysticism and devotional fervour in Spain, and the Spanish-Rheno-Flemish literature, in turn, gave rise to an even more dramatic outpouring of mystical fervour in seventeenth-century France. Then this French phenomenon gave shape to modern Catholic piety. Three assertions are thus taken for granted by most of these surveys – assertions engendered by an idealist kind of intellectual history.

First, it is assumed that the texts themselves and the themes found in them are transmitted from one culture to another and one generation to another, very much like chromosomes in living organisms, with distinct, readily identifiable characteristics that can be precisely traced as they make their way across national boundaries and over decades or centuries. Moreover, it is also assumed that these texts find their way to specific human beings who then interpret and recombine the basic elements and pass on the 'chromosomes' in new arrangements, as it were, by means of new texts. So, for instance, it becomes possible in this scheme of things to say that John of the Cross picked up one trait from Ruysbroeck, another from Tauler and yet another from Blosius, and that Bérulle, in turn, picked up this or that trait from John of the Cross, and another directly from Tauler. This entire process, naturally, depends on the translation of texts. And very seldom is the process of translation and all of its complexities analysed. It is always a given, as invisible and as unproblematic as the disembodied ideas that these surveys attempt to trace.

Second, it is also assumed that devotional literature is primarily mystical literature, that is, a collection of texts written by monastics for other monastics who seek undisturbed contemplation of God. Quite often, then, surveys of devotional literature limit themselves to a relatively narrow range of texts. Quite often, too, it is hard or impossible to find much of a relation between the devotional life of the cloistered and that of the laity. Innumerable questions immediately come to mind, such as the following: What about hagiographies? At what cost does one ignore the fact that hagiographies became ever more popular after the Council of Trent? For instance, in Spain one finds only 23 hagiographies published between 1500–59, but between 1600–30 the number climbs to 350, with 124 in the decade 1620–9 alone.[32] Many of these texts were translations.

And what about other sorts of devotional texts? What about translations of polemical texts for persecuted minorities, such as the English recusants?[33] What about Bibles, such as the English Douai translation? What about practical how-to manuals that dealt with ethical questions and everyday matters, such as Luis de León's *La perfecta casada* (The Perfect Wife, 1583)? These are just a few examples; the list of titles heretofore ignored by surveys of spirituality and devotional literature is so long that it has yet to be compiled.

Third, it is also assumed that Spain and France deserve the most attention in the early modern period because these two nations produced the greatest number of mystics and devotional texts – narrowly defined – in the sixteenth and seventeenth centuries. This assumption, while not wholly indefensible, has a doubly skewed perspective: it not only gives short shrift to texts published elsewhere in Europe, but also ignores the most prominent feature of the early modern world, the rise of Protestant cultures.

Much more work remains to be done in this area. Translation is the transmission of culture, the penetration of boundaries, the erosion of complacency, the explosion of localism. It involves translators, publishers, printers, distributors, travellers. It involves, above all, communication. And in the early modern period it involves technology and art. It is so much more than genealogy, mere texts and disembodied ideas.

In closing, as a means of summarizing and critiquing the subject at the same time, I would like to point out six rather large holes in the historiography of devotional texts, their translation and distribution – gaps in our knowledge that cry out for attention and will undoubtedly take some time to be filled, if anyone decides to take on the task.

1. We need a clearer definition of devotional literature and a systematic classification of texts. Up to now most of the focus has been placed on the 'classics' of the contemplative monastic tradition, those texts that give voice to the ascetic mystical quest. More attention needs to be paid to hagiographies, prayer books,

---

[32] Sanchez Lora (1988), 374, 448–50.   [33] Allison and Rogers (1989–94).

catechisms, practical manuals, apologetics and, in general, to texts that are directly aimed at the laity.

2. The impact of religious discord needs to be taken more into consideration, both in terms of internal and external controversies between competing factions within each denomination, and between competing churches. This essay has dealt with only Catholic devotional texts. Much more comparative work needs to be done for the early modern period as Catholics and Protestants develop their competing Reformations. Devotional life develops as much from discontinuities as from continuities, and identities are forged as much by antagonism and conflict as by axiomatic instruction. More needs to be done to sort out the similarities and differences among the religious traditions that emerged in the early modern period, especially in light of the fact that by the eighteenth century, all traditional religious belief came to be challenged ever more intensely by scepticism and the rise of the natural sciences.

3. The infrastructure and the personnel responsible for the actual work of translation itself need more attention, especially from the vantage point of social history. More research could be done on the identity of the translators and their place in the larger scheme of religious life. Centres such as the Charterhouse of Cologne, corporations such as the Society of Jesus, or individuals such as Juan Eusebio Nieremberg need to be approached as parts of a greater whole, in their social, political and economic context. Questions of sex and gender also need to be taken up, especially because devotional life is one of the very few areas in which women play a prominent and highly visible role in the early modern period, especially as authors and as paradigms of holiness.

4. The proselytizing spirit of the age should enter into the larger picture too, for this is a peak period in the Christianization of Europeans and non-Europeans alike. Within Europe itself, devotional literature has to be approached as part of the process of confessionalization, not just as one link in the chain of social disciplining and state formation, but also as an integral part of the forging of cultural and religious identities. Outside Europe, but also inseparably bound to it, devotional literature becomes part of the mission work in the Americas, Asia and Africa. Missions are not a one-way street: the encounter with non-Christian others produces perhaps as many changes within Europe itself as among the 'others' who are exposed to Christianization, whether by force or mere persuasion. All of the literature connected with mission activity, within and outside Europe, has a devotional dimension and an intimate connection to translation. It, too, awaits more research from various perspectives.

5. Translations in and of themselves also await further analysis from multiple perspectives: linguistic, epistemological, theological and social. The life of the texts themselves as they undergo translation is an area of research that needs further work by scholars of literature and social historians alike, not just as part of the history of ideas, but also as part of the history of the interaction and transmission of cultures. Texts that undergo multiple translations within one language or into several languages can shed all sorts of light on various questions. For example, what is one to make of the rendering of the Germanic

inwerken into the Latin *inactio* and of the consequences of this translation for the history of Spanish society and culture in the sixteenth century? Devotional texts can be volatile at times, and highly charged with the potential for controversy. At times the choices made by translators make a world of difference, literally as well as figuratively. At times, even the very fact that a text was chosen for translation into a particular language, either for the first or the fifth or sixth time, raises all sorts of questions about the history of a specific set of circumstances. Bible translations, in particular, open up nearly inexhaustible avenues of research for many different types of scholars.

6. Last, but certainly not least, we still need more bibliographical research. Arriving at a definitive and exhaustive bibliography of translations in this subject is probably impossible, due to the fluidity of the term 'devotional literature'. Nonetheless, we still need a more thorough bibliographical scrutiny of translated texts – one that aims for a more global inclusion of titles and a more detailed accounting of editions, printers, translators, places and dates of publication. Having a bibliography of translations would have made the writing of this essay much easier. It would also have allowed some sorely needed quantifying. Analysing this subject without a comprehensive bibliography is almost like trying to paint while blindfolded. The more complete the bibliography, the more solid the evidence we will have, the clearer the patterns that will emerge, the better equipped scholars will be to make sense of the ways in which Europeans crossed boundaries and established their identities, not just as Germans, Spaniards, Italians or whatever other nationality one might want to list, but as Christians – Catholic or Protestant or neither – and, most important, as Europeans and as men and women who knew they needed to adapt to an ever-changing, ever-shrinking, conflict-ridden world.

CHAPTER 6

The translation of political theory in early modern Europe

Geoffrey P. Baldwin

INTRODUCTION

The huge range of political ideas that circulated in early modern Europe can often seem bewildering, and bringing order and unity to this picture of diversity can be difficult. There were ideologies of monarchy, coming from both a Christian tradition and a Roman imperial one; theories of resistance against tyranny; republican political ideas from the Italian city states and the Netherlands; constitutional theories; approaches to politics stemming from epistemological or moral scepticism; political ideas based around the idea of the state; theories of natural law; and scientific approaches to political organization and moral truth. It is extremely difficult to say something intelligible about such a complex array of political ideas, despite their importance for understanding the early modern political world.

Methodologically, the study of such a range of political ideas presents a number of challenges. One recent approach has been to look at the texts concerned not just in terms of their contents and their logic, but also in terms of the context of their creation. This can be thought of either in terms of a particular political situation, or an intellectual tradition or, more fruitfully, as a combination of both. Such an approach would give us a deeper understanding of the nature and the life of these political ideas.[1]

In so doing, it is possible to come to a closer understanding of what a particular text is designed to do, and how it relates to the political culture in question. It is possible to argue about what particular context is most significant, but this approach serves historians much better than an eclectic search for political wisdom in the remains of the past. However, to focus on these texts at the moment of their creation does not necessarily provide insight into the subsequent life of these texts. It is, of course, possible to trace the life of those texts that are quoted, criticized and referred to in the

---

[1] See Richter (1990); Tully (1988); Mulligan et al. (1979).

work of others, and so follow the development of an idea or of a political language as it evolves through a number of different texts and contexts.

Another way that scholars have attempted to see the fate of ideas after an author has committed them to paper is by considering these texts as physical objects, and attempting to trace how they were distributed, who bought them and who read them. Robert Darnton has tried to reconstruct the lineaments of the book trade in early modern France.[2] Literary scholars have paid attention to what has been called 'reader-response' theory, and focused attention on the act of reading as well as the nature and distribution of the book as a physical object. A famous early example is the work of Jardine and Grafton on Gabriel Harvey's reading of the Roman historian Livy in sixteenth-century Cambridge.[3] In that instance, detailed information was available as to the particular circumstances of how this text was received and understood, but this is not always the case.

There have been attempts to examine marginalia, to reconstruct the contents of libraries and collections, and to examine commonplace books to see which passages especially interested readers. While such work has yielded some interesting results, it suffers from a familiar historical epistemological problem: the information we have is far outweighed by what we do not have. Of a print run of maybe 3,000, we may know five or six individual responses to a work; we may know the contents of one library in ten or twenty. While this may not be too much of a problem for a literary scholar who wishes to say certain things about certain texts, for the historian it raises tremendously important questions. To predicate a general idea of how a text was received from the chance remains that have come down to us would be irresponsible, however interesting individual responses may be.

This means that there is no simple way to bridge the gap between a history of political ideas, and a history of political culture. A notion of political culture that is derived from a *mentalité* tradition, or one coming from an idea of decoding the symbolic power of actions in the public sphere, remains in many ways incommensurate with a detailed examination of literary and political writing, yet it also seems perverse not to attempt in some way to combine the two.

Looking at translation can give us an opportunity to bridge this gap, and aid our understanding of the history of ideas in early modern Europe. When we are examining a text, one of the most important aspects of the context we should consider is the national tradition within which it was

---

[2] Darnton (1982).   [3] Grafton and Jardine (1990).

created: this is true of both an intellectual and a political context. When a text is translated, it is uprooted from the culture of its creation and placed somewhere new. This can show us what sort of texts and ideas appealed across cultural boundaries, and what it was that people in the early modern period felt to be of value in other cultures. We can learn something important about common concerns and problems and how they could be approached.

This can be especially interesting as it is the early modern period which saw an increase in the importance of the idea of nation and *patria*: national traditions were becoming more important in political culture. Such national traditions can be thought of as in some ways exclusive – defining a national tradition of literature or law was necessarily an exclusive act. At the same time, the sixteenth century was a time when many countries were discovering a national past, and a national constitution that grew out of that past.[4]

Europe, in the early modern period and especially after the Reformation, was a divided continent. Both international and civil war were common and there was extensive international involvement in civil conflicts. It was also a time of immense social, political and constitutional change across the entire continent. The consequence is that much of the political literature is extremely polemical, and even authors whom we would consider representatives of high culture often engaged in the most vicious invective. Even texts which did not contain arguments so specific to a particular situation might present arguments that would be acceptable in one culture and not in another. When censorship was commonplace, and authorship could be dangerous, translating a work which was in any way critical of those in power could also be extremely perilous. Being on the wrong side of a confessional divide could get one burnt at the stake.

It is therefore important to see what could be translated from one culture to another, and how that which was translated could be adapted and packaged in order to suit its new context, because this could change the nature and significance of the text. It could also be the case that there was little adaptation: something from one culture was often simply dumped into another with little explanation. Many early modern Europeans crossed cultural boundaries without the benefit of translators. They saw and reported what went on in other countries, and read the literature of those countries just as they did their own.

---

[4] Burgess (1992), 3–18.

Cultural boundaries, and even the strong religious boundaries that existed, were often crossed with impunity. For instance, it was commonplace for young English aristocrats in the sixteenth century to visit Italy, and learn Italian: the existence of the antichrist in Rome did not prevent them. Philip Sidney, the great Protestant hero, was one of those who did this, learning and absorbing and adapting the poetics of this Catholic culture.

It is the activities of these individuals, and the acts of translation that they performed, which allowed the culture of translation to exist in early modern Europe. However, this ability to translate means that we can be misled if we assume that an untranslated text had no influence: it was by no means necessary for something to be translated for it to be powerfully influential in another country, at another time, in another place. Queen Elizabeth I of England was by no means exceptional in being fluent in French, Italian and Latin: in the sixteenth century, to be educated would mean just that.

One aspect of this automatic crossing of cultural boundaries was the existence of a lingua franca in Europe – Latin – at least in written form (above, pp. 65–80). When Hobbes met Hugo Grotius in the Netherlands, it is reported they conversed in Latin – though Grotius declared that he could not comprehend a word! The existence of a text in Latin could preclude the necessity of its being translated, or demonstrate that it was intended for an educated audience. One aspect of the early modern period is the increasing importance of the vernacular languages of Europe: relatively few political treatises were written in a vulgar tongue before Machiavelli's *Il principe* of 1513, but by 1700 relatively few were written in Latin.

Translation in and out of Latin is therefore a vital part of this story, as Latin could be used as a European language in a debate that was meant to have an international audience. James I and Robert Bellarmine could exchange Latin tracts, and publication in Latin remained strong in Hungary and elsewhere throughout the sixteenth and seventeenth centuries. Milton defended the English people in Latin for a European audience, while defending the Republic at home in English.

The classical literary and political tradition was of course of huge importance. This is something that was drawn on as a commonplace, in terms of both texts and histories – Shakespeare in *Macbeth* could refer to Tarquin's creeping steps without necessarily having read Livy. It is beyond the scope of this essay to discuss the fate of classical political texts in the Renaissance, but it is important to remember their continued presence and significance alongside contemporary works. They existed both in their original Latin or Greek, and increasingly in translation as demand grew for ancient political wisdom. These texts and their various interpretations form a sort of background to the texts we are considering. Early modern political actors could and did take things straight from Greece or Rome without the assistance of their contemporaries.

In taking translation as historical evidence, a further caveat is necessary. One aspect of the past that is often inaccessible is the motives of the translators, some of whom were anonymous and often obscure. Texts could be translated as interesting or eye-catching, or because of their relevance to a particular political situation, or because of a more general significance. A text could be translated for profit – one of the major reasons for the increased importance of writing in the vulgar languages was the development of printing at the end of the fifteenth century. There was a new audience for texts of all descriptions – religious, literary or political – that was not necessarily literate in Latin. This audience grew with time, as did that section of the population that could be considered as part of the political nation, so that during the great crises of the seventeenth century, such as the English Civil War or the Fronde, huge numbers of people were reading and acting on political literature. Translators could even be mistaken in thinking there was a demand for a particular text, and so deceive us as well.

Despite this, it is permissible to assume that a translated text was felt to be appropriate or interesting for its new political culture – it is unlikely the effort of translation was very often undertaken in vain. We can also perhaps deduce something from that which was not translated, and what people did not seem to be interested in, to help us trace the lineaments of their political culture, though this is a riskier enterprise (above, p. 24). It should therefore be possible to see what was translated, from what into what, and when, and so delineate the lineaments and contours of these relationships. The transformations the text goes through in the act of translation can also be seen, including what sort of adaptations have to be made in presenting the text in another culture. This aspect of the problem is made more interesting in that, for a modern translator, the aim is to render as closely as possible the original, even if we realise the impossibility of such a task.

In the study of the early modern period, no such assumptions can be made. Fragments of texts were used, there was no sense of copyright, and texts were often bound and sold with other texts, even without translation. For instance in some Dutch Latin editions and some other languages, Machiavelli's *Il principe* was bound with the *Vindiciae contra tyrannos*. Does this tell us anything about how these two, seemingly opposite views on royal domination, were regarded in the early modern period? At other times, it is a translated or second-hand version of the text that a translator uses, and the new version is one more step away from the author.

A great deal can be said about the political concerns of early modern Europe, and the intellectual lineage of various ways of thinking about politics, from translation. There are, however, some difficulties: for instance, in the area of jurisprudence and natural jurisprudence. It is a commonplace that one of the most important developments in political theory of the early modern period was in the area of natural law and natural rights. This could mean two things: firstly, the elucidation of a set of moral orders or political rights, and secondly, the idea of basing political association upon a transfer of rights which were at some point inherent to individuals. This was first expressed by the writers of the Second Scholastic in Salamanca, and later by the Dutch jurist Hugo Grotius, and by Thomas Hobbes in England.[5]

The problem is that much of this literature was written in Latin for an audience of lawyers who dealt in Latin every day. Mostly it stayed in that language, at least until the eighteenth century when there was a greater demand for the wider dissemination of such ideas. For instance, the civil lawyer Alberico Gentili, an Italian fugitive from the Inquisition who ended up teaching law at Oxford, had great influence on the English civilian tradition and international law in general. However, neither his *De iure belli*, nor his absolutist text *Regales disputationes* of 1605, were translated, although there was a Latin edition of the latter at London in 1644 during the English Civil War, presumably from a royalist press.

The Spanish natural jurisprudential tradition of the later sixteenth century also tended to remain in Latin. Juan de Mariana's *De rege et regis institutione libri III*, Luis de Molina's *De justitia et jure*, Domingo de Soto's *Libri decem de justitia et jure* and Francisco Suarez's *Tractatus de legibus ac Deo legislatore* all remained untranslated into any vernacular tongue. This is perhaps because of their highly technical nature, and because their intended audience would be one trained in a similar legal tradition. It would perhaps take some intermediary stages for such ideas to make their way into the mainstream.

---

[5] Brett (1997); Tuck (1979).

Later in the seventeenth century and into the eighteenth century, theorists of natural law acquired a wider following. Hugo Grotius is probably one of the most famous. His *De iure belli ac pacis*, in contrast to similar works from Spain, was often translated, but mostly after his death in 1645. It was first published in Paris in 1625, and thereafter there were eight editions in the seventeenth century and three in the eighteenth. The first translation was, predictably enough, into Dutch in 1635, and then there followed an English translation by Clement Barksdale in 1654 and another more accurate one by W. Evats in 1682. There was a French translation in 1687 by de Courtin, and then a new translation in 1724 by Jean Barbeyrac, then Professor of History and Civil Law at Lausanne.

A similar pattern can be discerned with editions of the German jurist Samuel Pufendorf's *De jure naturae et gentium libri octo*. After going through a number of Latin editions, in 1703 it was translated into English by Basil Kennett, President of Corpus Christi College in Oxford and a writer on Greek poetry, on which subject he often disagreed with French critics. When the second edition of this translation appeared, not only did it incorporate the annotations from Barbeyrac's French translation of 1710, but it was advertised as 'corrected, and compared with Mr Barbeyrac's French translation'. An Italian translation by Giambattista Almici followed in Venice in 1757.[6]

Pufendorf's shorter text *De officio hominis et civis*, which functioned as a compendium of the somewhat cumbersome *De jure naturae*, was very popular especially in England where it was printed many times in Latin at London and Cambridge. It seems to have functioned as an academic primer for the study of natural law at Cambridge University, as well as a more general introduction. Gershom Carmichael, Regent and then Professor of Moral Philosophy at the University of Glasgow, supplied notes and observations on the text for a 1724 edition at Edinburgh that came from his lectures on the subject. A French translation of *De officio hominis et civis* appeared in 1696, but evidently Barbeyrac thought it of insufficient quality and produced his own, with notes, in 1707.

The final work translated by Barbeyrac was Richard Cumberland's *De legibus naturae*, again with notes by the translator in 1744. Cumberland's great opponent Hobbes did not receive such a great deal of attention. His friend Sorbière, whom he had met in Paris while associated with Mersenne and his circle, translated *De cive* into French in 1649, and the *Elements of Law* in 1652. His *Leviathan* achieved an international audience primarily

---

[6] Bazzoli (1979).

through the author's own Latin edition of 1668, although there was a Dutch translation in 1667: the radicalism of this text maybe made it unsuitable for the conservative politics of Louis XIV's France.

While writings on natural law clearly had great resonance across borders and cultures in early modern Europe, works which concerned themselves more with the specificities of law tended to remain untranslated. One notable exception is Jean Bodin's *Six livres de la république* of 1576, which went through a number of editions in its original French, and was also translated into Latin by the author ten years later in an edition clearly designed for an international audience. Bodin was a French jurist and humanist who aimed, through the analysis of law, history and philology, to be able both to describe the political and legal customs of a wide variety of cultures, and to draw conclusions about issues as diverse as sovereignty, taxation, revolutionary change and national character.

It was perhaps the catholicity of Bodin's aims which made this text so appealing in such a wide variety of contexts: while much of the material was made up of legal specifics, it aimed to provide more general political and legal definitions. There followed translations into Spanish and Italian, and in 1606 a composite English translation from both the Latin and French versions appeared. This was clearly a highly popular and important text, which became accepted as authoritative on the nature of law and sovereignty: the English judges in the Ship money trial of 1637 quoted Bodin in defining the nature of the monarchy of Charles I.

More specific works had less broad appeal however. At the end of the sixteenth century, legal antiquarianism promoted ideas of constitutional arrangements that could be thought of as having been in place throughout the history of a nation or a state. Such ideas were often used to defend rights of cities, corporations or even peoples against the encroachment of monarchs. Despite the centrality of these texts to political struggles across early modern Europe, they were very rarely translated into other languages.

Fortescue's *De laudibus legum Angliae* (On the Praises of the Laws of England) was translated from the Latin into English by Robert Mulcaster in 1567, and remained a key text with an English context, as it moved from being a purely legal text to having a wider political significance. There was a new translation in 1616, this time with additional notes by the jurist and antiquarian John Selden, and this went through six editions, the last in 1775. In 1714, the year that George Elector of Hanover was made King, an English edition was published under the title *The difference between an absolute and a limited monarchy, as it more particularly regards the English Constitution*. Thus a fifteenth-century text, written in exile in order to persuade Edward IV to rule in a particular fashion, became a key part of the Whig interpretation of English constitutional history as that of a limited monarchy ruling a free people. Fortescue, however, never appeared in any other language.

There was a continental Latin edition, by John Budden, in 1610, of Sir Thomas Smith's *De republica Anglorum: The maner of Gouernment or policie of the realme of England* of 1576, which went through a number of editions. This was not so much a legal text as an account of England and how it was governed, as might be given by an informed traveller.

Similar works from other countries had similar fates. Claude de Seyssel's *Grande monarchie de France* of 1519 had a number of Latin editions in the seventeenth century, and was sometimes bound with Plato's *Laws*. It was also translated into German by George Lauterbeke under the title *Vom Ampt der Könige und Regierung des gemeinen Nutzes in der löblichen Kron Frankreich*, maybe because of the relevance of French claims in the Holy Roman Empire contained in Seyssel's work.

The later *Francogallia*, by the French Protestant François Hotman, was translated from Latin into French almost immediately upon its first publication in 1574. This text was designed to demonstrate the independence of French from Roman law, and the existence and validity of institutions that could act as a check on royal power. The French and Latin editions were part of a concerted campaign to describe a limited French monarchy during the Wars of Religion, but the texts were not translated into any other languages. Despite the possible relevance of such a text to the debates over the English constitution, it did not make it into English until 1711, when it was published under a title which shows the Whig prejudices of the translator – *Franco-Gallia, or an Account of the ancient free state of France and most other parts of Europe before the loss of their liberties, written originally in Latin by the famous civilian Francis Hotman in the year 1574*. By and large, however, those texts that dealt with constitutional matters, be they English, French, Danish or German, did not find an audience outside their original context.

GENRE II – MONARCHS AND REPUBLICS

One debate within the politics of the early modern period is whether a monarchic or a republican constitution would be best. In fact, this question was rarely debated explicitly. Rather the advantages and value of one form of government were extolled at the expense of the other: the real debate tended to be about what form of republic would be best, or how a monarch should act.

Since the Second World War much attention has been paid in scholarship to the republican tradition in European and American political thought. The political ideas of the Italian city republics, especially Florence, have been extensively examined by historians such as Hans Baron, Quentin Skinner and latterly James Hankins.[7] They have emphasized the importance of the ideas of republican governance that emerged in that context, and their longevity within the English and American contexts.[8]

Given the importance of this intellectual tradition, fewer texts than one would imagine were translated and circulated in early modern Europe. Leonardo Bruni's panegyric on the city of Florence was not translated into any vernacular language, and Guicciardini's *Dialogo del reggimento del Firenze* (Dialogue on the Florentine Regime) remained in Italian. In terms of texts in translation, the republican tradition does not emerge as particularly deep. The text identified by Pocock as key in the transmission of this tradition, despite its relatively heterodox nature, was Machiavelli's *Discourses*. Jacques Gohorry, whose main interest was in medicine and drugs, translated it into French in 1571, superseding an earlier translation of 1544. The text was printed numerous times in France, and often bound with Gaspard d'Auvergne's translation of the *Prince*. There was a later translation in 1664, and yet another in 1694. In 1615 there was a Dutch translation, and in 1636 an English translation by Edward Dacres, who also translated the *Prince* four years later. The *Discourses* makes a good example of a text whose availability was not necessarily defined by its translation: it had been printed in London for an English audience in its original Italian.

Another important text is Gasparo Contarini's *De magistratibus et republica Venetorum libri quinque* (Five Books on the Magistrates and the Republic of Venice), which was completed in 1534 and published in Paris in 1543, and thereafter numerous times in Venice itself. Contarini described and praised the republican constitution of Venice, which in the sixteenth century remained a living example of republican politics, almost alone in Italy. The idea of Venice, and Venetian politics, was an important one throughout Europe. Charles I reacted to constitutional proposals by his Parliament by saying that they would reduce him to a 'Doge of Venice'. Domenichi's Italian translation of Contarini's text in 1544 was published numerous times in Venice, where its appeal was obvious. It did however find other audiences: there was a French translation by Jean Charrier,

---

[7] Hankins (2003–4); Skinner and van Gelderen (2002); Skinner (1978); Baron (1955).
[8] See Wootton (1994); Pocock (1975); Robbins (1959).

published by Galliot du Pré, and an English translation by Lewes Lewkenor in 1599. The example of Venetian republicanism was made available in two of the largest monarchies in Europe, and may well have had a greater impact on the development of republican thinking than more explicitly polemical texts, which remained untranslated. Later in the sixteenth century, in 1582, Paolo Paruta's panegyric of Venice, *Della perfettione della vita politica* (The Perfection of Political Life), was also translated into French. It was translated into English during the interregnum by Henry Cary, Earl of Monmouth, who translated Paruta's *Discorsi politici* (Political Discourses) around the same time.

Despite the importance of Venice, the number of texts that were circulated and translated which concerned monarchies rather than republics was huge. A good example is Antonio de Guevara's *Relox de principes* of 1529. Guevara (1480–1545) was a Spanish Franciscan who was employed in the household of Prince Juan, the son of Ferdinand and Isabella of Spain. Subsequently, he became a monk and an inquisitor, and finally Bishop of Guadix and Mondeñedo. He wrote a book in the mirror-for-princes tradition, which purported to be the advice of the celebrated Roman emperor and stoic Marcus Aurelius. After the *Libro aureo de Marco Aurelio* was published in 1528 at Seville, in what the author claimed was a pirate edition, he produced a second and expanded edition under the title *Relox de principes*, printed at Valladolid the following year. The second text was much expanded, better organized and less aphoristic, though in common with the first edition, much of what it contained was conventional Renaissance wisdom. It enumerated the virtues that a prince should display in order to rule well, combining the pagan virtues, as the title would suggest, with Christian virtues and exhortations to piety.[9]

Both versions of the text were instantly and consistently popular in Spain and beyond.[10] There was an almost instant French edition of the shorter version, by Berthault de La Grise in 1531, from the press of Galliot de Pré, which went through a large number of editions. The expanded text was translated by Herberay des Essars (who also translated the hugely popular romance *Amadis de Gaul* from the Spanish), as *L'orloge des princes*, in 1540, and again proceeded through a number of editions. The English translation of the first text, published in 1539 by John Bourchier, was taken not from the original Spanish, but from the French, along with the French preface. This was relatively common as a text moved between

---

[9] On Guevara see Grey (1973); Jones (1975).   [10] For Spanish editions see Foulché-Delbosc (1915).

different languages; French would have been better known than Spanish in England in the seventeenth century. By 1557 there was an English translation of the fuller text, by Thomas North, who was chiefly famous for his translation of Plutarch.

Mambrino Roseo da Fabriano translated the shorter version into Italian in 1543, where it was bound with his translation of Erasmus's *Institutio principis christiani* – making a sort of composite humanist advice book for princes. The fuller text was translated by Sebastiano Fausto da Longiano in 1553: both versions went through a great number of editions. Ægidius Albertinus translated Guevara into German in 1599, in an edition that went through numerous editions, and there was a Latin translation by Johannes Wanckel for the German market in 1601. At the end of the sixteenth century there was also a Dutch edition of the *Libro aureo*, and an edition of the full *Relox de principes* in 1617, taken in fact from the German, translated from high to low Deutsch. As we move into the seventeenth century, Guevara's text moved even farther afield. In 1610 there was a Hungarian translation by János Draskovich, made from Wanckel's Latin version. In 1616 there was a Swedish translation by Eric Schroder, and in 1738 there was even a translation by Gabriel Hamazaspean into Armenian.

What made this text so popular? Part of the reason must be that in Italy and elsewhere, Europe was dominated by monarchs, so texts concerning their proper conduct had obvious appeal. Despite the differences in political culture between the nations of Europe, they largely shared the institution of monarchy. The translation of this text and others shows that they not only shared the institution, but the understanding and views of that institution put forward by writers on political theory. What the history of Guevara's texts demonstrates is that a work about monarchy could have appeal across Europe, and across geographical and confessional boundaries. Perhaps the reason this text could also appeal to Protestants is that it is essentially a pre-Reformation text.

The universality of appeal of Guevara's text contrasts with that of some later texts that had a more definite confessional bias. The Spanish Jesuit Pedro de Rivadeneira's *Tratado de la religíon y virtudes que debe tener el príncipe cristiano* had in many ways a similarly conventional morality of princely action to that of Guevara. It was however clear in its targets – not only Protestants, but also those in Spanish affairs who advocated a *politique* strategy of temporizing with reform. After being published at Madrid in 1595, it was translated into Italian in 1599, Latin in 1603 and French in 1610. Within the context of its creation it was a popular text, but it was unsuitable for England, the Netherlands, Sweden or the Protestant princes of Transylvania.

Niccolò Machiavelli's altogether more controversial version of the mirror-for-princes genre, despite being put on the Papal Index, had a lively history in translation, perhaps as a subversive version of a genre that was very much in demand, and one that raised more complex moral issues than texts like Guevara's. *Il principe* went through a number of Italian editions in the first half of the sixteenth century, and was translated into Latin in 1560; there was a Dutch translation in 1615, and an English translation in 1640 from Edward Dacres. It received simultaneous translations into French by Guillaume Cappel and Gaspard d'Auvergne in 1553, and there was clearly great interest in this text in France. Richard Tuck has identified a Franco-Italian intellectual group active in France in the 1560s and 70s, who identified closely with the politics of Machiavelli and Guicciardini.[11] French interest in Machiavelli continued into the seventeenth century: there was a new translation of his entire works by Briencour in 1664, and in 1683 another translation of *Il principe* appeared, this time with notes, from the pen and press of Amelot de la Houssaye.[12] It was this edition that provided the stimulus to Frederick II of Prussia to compose his *Anti-Machiavel*, with which it was often bound in eighteenth-century editions. When this was translated into English in 1741, it came complete with a translation of Houssaye's preface to his edition of Machiavelli.

There were not only mirrors for princes in the early modern period, but also mirrors for those who served them as courtiers and counsellors. This literature grew in importance in the sixteenth century, as courts became more bureaucratic and centralized: there was a demand for an understanding of how to behave in such positions. The fate of Baldasar Castiglione's *Cortegiano* is well known: it became an instantly popular text across Europe, and from its beginnings in Urbino, defined and created the culture of courts in the early modern period.[13]

One good example is the Spaniard Federico Furio Ceriol's *El concejo y consejeros del principe* (The Council and the Councillors of the Prince) of 1559: this text was partly about the formal structure of the councils that formed royal government in Spain and partly about the character and qualifications of those counsellors who occupied places on them. Despite the specifics of Spanish politics, this text had wider appeal: the next year, an Italian edition appeared at Venice, translated by Ludovico Dolce, a man

[11] Tuck (1993), 40–5.   [12] On the importance of this edition, see Soll (2004).
[13] See Burke (1995), esp. 55–80.

best known today as an art theorist and friend of Titian, who supported himself with a variety of literary activities. In 1563, a Latin edition appeared, and in 1570, William Blundeville translated it into English under a title that implied that the hierarchy of Spanish councils was something to be emulated. A version of the Latin translation was published in Kraków, and two years later Ceriol's work was translated into Polish under the title *Rada pańska* (The Lord's Council). *El concejo* was one of the earliest works to consider the issue of counsel, and it proved popular from the west to the east of Europe.

The Polish kingdom, with an elective monarchy, obviously depended even more clearly on good counsel, and thus it is no surprise that this Spanish text should reach so far. One of the few texts to go in the other direction, from east to west, was Wawrzyniec Grzymała Góslicki's *De optimo senatore libri duo*, first published in Venice in 1568. Góslicki became a major political figure in Poland on his return from Italy, where the *De optimo senatore* had been written, and he became a counsellor with the qualities he attempts to describe. Latin editions were popular, and there was an English translation in 1598 – although the translator got the name wrong, having a copy of the text but being unfamiliar with its author. A second English translation appeared in 1660, the year of the Restoration, but with those sentiments which tended to the limiting of monarchy removed.

One other aspect of this literature that proved popular was that which was inspired by Louis XIII's first minister, Cardinal Richelieu. His opposition to Habsburg expansion, and thus to their project of Counter-Reformation, was hugely controversial, and so he encouraged writers to support his vision of government, and the role of a chief counsellor which he had made his own. Two of these works were translated into English, despite there being no equivalent person in England to whom such sentiments could be attached. Philippe de Béthune's *Le conseiller d'estat* of 1633 was translated into English the next year, and Jean de Silhon's *Ministre d'état* made the same journey in 1658.

Texts that concerned monarchs, and those which concerned courtiers, counsellors and those who served monarchs, were immensely popular across Europe in the sixteenth and seventeenth centuries. Political theory therefore focused on the necessary qualities required of the monarch or counsellor, and thus the differences between the political situations of monarchs in different European countries did not make such insights from one incommensurate with another, as had been the case with specifically constitutional arguments.

The dominance of the monarchic tradition also means that it is possible to say something of the republican tradition in early modern Europe whose transmission had to come not through a broad tradition but through a small number of key contemporary texts. This means that classical texts and examples, from both Greece and Rome, continued to have an important and direct influence on political ideas. Cicero, Sallust, Plutarch and Aristotle were the inspiration for much republican thinking into the seventeenth century, and were probably more significant than texts which came from centres of early modern republicanism like Florence or Venice. This might also be an indication that practice and experience of different forms of self-government, in the Netherlands and the cities of Europe, even those in monarchic states, was as important as any textual tradition.

GENRE III – REASON OF STATE

Reason of state is usually associated with monarchy but, of course, was not always necessarily so. Its practical and moral imperatives revolved around the state as an abstract entity, and the need to keep it in being, and this was an imperative that monarchs attempted to make their own. The moral consequences of the existence of the state apparatus were very important for early modern Europeans, especially in the seventeenth century. This becomes clear when the translation of texts is considered. One of the most famous texts from the reason of state tradition was Justus Lipsius's *Politicorum sive civilis doctrinae libri sex* (Six Books of Politics) of 1589. This text not only went through a large number of Latin editions, but also received very speedy attention from translators.

As a European hit, the *Politics* was translated by Charles Le Ber into French in 1590. In the same year William Jones translated it into English, and Marten Everart into Dutch. It appeared again in French, translated by Simon Goulart, in 1594; in Polish in 1595; in German in 1599, translated by Melchior Hagenaeus; in both Spanish and Italian in 1604, in Italian again in 1618 and finally in Hungarian in 1641.

Lipsius's text spoke of the moral imperatives of the state, but contained within the six books of his text was a more generalized political wisdom which clearly had a wide appeal. As a composite text of quotations collected into appropriate chapters, it was in some ways a generic innovation not unconnected with the birth of the essay, and this contributed to its popularity. Part of its appeal was also its confessional neutrality, which came from Lipsius's own: it had something to offer to both Catholic and

Protestant. By contrast, Giovanni Botero's *Ragione di stato* of the same year, which covered similar ground but from a more Counter-Reformation stance, was more Catholic and hence less catholic. Published in Latin in 1590, it was rapidly translated into Italian, Spanish and French, and it seems to have been very popular, but it was never translated into English, Dutch or Swedish.

Trajano Boccalini's satires on the statecraft genre, the *Ragguagli di Parnaso*, and the *Pietra del paragone*, were both hugely popular, possibly due to their lighthearted tone. Both texts were published over the course of the 1610s in Venice, where censorship was lighter and their scurrilousness not too inflammatory. They consisted of a number of short satires on contemporary political culture, 200 in the case of the *Ragguagli*. This meant that translators were free to pick and choose what they translated and what they did not, and so not choose that which would upset authorities or political sensibilities at home, while at the same time bringing in a truly cosmopolitan air.

The *Ragguagli* existed in a very malleable form – the Italian edition of 1624, after Boccalini's death, had some extra satires added by Girolamo Briani, and this was often the case when the text was translated. The French translation of 1615 was fairly faithful, but added a text supposedly by Lorenzo de' Medici. The Spanish translation of 1634 by Perez de Sousa selected only those satires which were not offensive to the Spanish Empire, and in later editions extra ones were added. A Latin edition appeared in 1640, followed by a German edition shortly afterwards, and a Dutch translation in the 1670s. In 1626, an English edition of selections appeared, a collaborative project by John Florio, William Vaughn and Thomas Scott – although it is not really possible to see much strategy in the selections, other than what took their fancy. An almost complete English translation was carried out in the 1650s by Henry Cary, Earl of Monmouth, who left out only two of the satires, which were particularly vicious about Queen Elizabeth I.

The appeal of these satires across different cultures and indeed different times is instructive; they had their own appeal as well as their adaptability, and this shows how important reason of state was. Girolamo Frachetta's discussion of reason of state was translated into French and included in the French translation of Ammirato's discourses on Tacitus. Even a text originally published in secret, Naudé's *Considérations politiques sur les coups d'état*, was translated into both English and German.

Texts which come under the heading 'reason of state' seem to have had wide appeal from the early seventeenth century onwards, and all but the most religiously radical seem to have been able to cross confessional boundaries. In the seventeenth century, any discussion of the state and the moral imperatives of its existence had appeal across Europe. The questions that reason of state addressed – how to preserve a state in danger, how would it be possible to create a viable body of knowledge referring to political and state affairs – were common questions, and this explains the popularity of translations of such texts.

GENRE IV – THE LITERATURE OF RESISTANCE

The theories of resistance to established authority that emerged in the second half of the sixteenth century have been seen as a very important part of the history of ideas, especially those that demanded action on behalf of a people who were constituted prior to the authority that ruled over them. Perhaps the most famous articulation of these ideas was the *Vindiciae contra tyrannos*, written by a Huguenot during the French Wars of Religion, but designed to appeal beyond a narrow confessional audience to moderate Catholics who also opposed the crown. This became a popular and important text. Probably written in Latin by Mornay or Languet, it was published in 1579. It was very quickly translated into French, probably at the instigation of its author, in 1581, and in substantially the same context. In 1588, the year of the Armada, an English translation of Book IV appeared, on the importance of defending religion – appropriate for Protestant England under threat. A full translation, by William Walker, appeared in 1648, on the eve of the regicide. Walker was a journalist and pamphleteer who was chaplain to Oliver Cromwell, and so close to him that he was called 'Oliver's priest'. It is highly significant that he should issue such a text at such a time: it could not have been done without Cromwell's approval. There was a Dutch translation in 1586 – a key point in the Dutch wars against the Spanish to establish an independent republic. Finally, there was a Swedish translation in 1639.

George Buchanan's *De iure regni apud Scotos* was first published in 1579, again in Latin; it was obviously rather more specific than the *Vindiciae*, being about Scotland. It went through quite a number of Latin editions, and there was a Dutch translation by Effert de Veer in 1598. For an English translation it had to wait until 1680 – the height of the Exclusion crisis, and a time of possible rebellion. There was another edition in 1689, after the Glorious Revolution had actually happened. These two events were important for stimulating thinking about resistance. The crisis of 1680 was the motivation for the publication of Sir Robert Filmer's highly conservative

Patriarcha, which elicited a number of responses that focused on ideas of resistance, and republicanism.[14] The radicalism of Algernon Sidney's *Discourses Concerning Government* led to his execution; it was translated into French in 1702.

More famous is Locke's *Two Treatises Concerning Government*. There was an almost immediate French translation in 1691 and a large number of French editions after that. Both Sidney and Locke were important for the development of French republicanism in the eighteenth century, and of course in their original versions for American ideas of independence. Resistance remained important for the whole of the early modern period, and a few key texts had a great deal of influence, especially on the political thought of France, Britain and the Netherlands.

TRANSLATION AND INTENTION I – JAMES I AND
THE *BASILIKON DORON*

One thing that complicates the history of translation is the different motives there could be for translating a text, and it is instructive to look at examples where such motivations can be deduced. One text where this is clear is the *Basilikon doron* of James VI and I, published by the King of Scotland on the eve of his accession to the English throne. It makes an interesting example because of the attempt made by James for his text to cross cultural boundaries and, especially significant at the end of the sixteenth century, confessional boundaries as well. The Greek title *Basilikon doron* means 'the kingly gift', and this text was an example of the princely literature so popular in Europe at the time. It was written in 1598, and addressed to his son Henry, by a king possibly worried about his death and the succession struggle for the English throne. The original manuscript was written in the Scots dialect, and the first printed edition contained some Anglicization: it was in a way the first translation. William Waldergrave printed seven copies in secret in Edinburgh in 1599, which were given to trusted servants of the crown, including Prince Henry's tutor.[15]

There ensued a battle with the Scottish Church when the book was censured, without mention being made of the identity of its author, for Erastian opinions on church government. When James became King of England in 1603, the book became part of a publicity campaign to show his capabilities as a monarch, and his right to rule the new kingdom, that of

---

[14] On Filmer and reactions too him, see Daly (1979).   [15] Craigie (1950), 4–8.

Great Britain. James faced a struggle to combine his two kingdoms into one, and to forge a political identity that would enable him to govern effectively in both kingdoms. Therefore there was a new and expanded edition published in 1603, with a greater degree of Anglicization, so that the inhabitants of his new kingdom could read the book. In a new preface to the reader, James asserted his religious orthodoxy and the probity of the advice in the book, enhancing the persona of the wise king that James wished to assume. He took his learning seriously, having been educated by George Buchanan, author of *De iure regni apud Scotos*, and took pride in his ability to dispute in Latin and other languages with his political and religious opponents, including, famously, with Cardinal Bellarmine on the Oath of Allegiance.

There was such demand for the text in England that the printing work had to be farmed out to several shops to keep up: James's subjects were keen to read of their new king. There was even a verse edition by William Willymat, consisting of the text rendered into parallel English and Latin verses. Contributing to the mirror-for-princes genre could not only show his ability to his new subjects, but to the wider world of European politics. In line with his irenicist ideas, there was initial interest from Catholic as well as Protestant Europe. The English Jesuit Robert Parsons read parts of it to Pope Clement VIII, and claimed that the pope was moved by the experience; 'and in very truth I do highlie admire many thinges in that booke, and could never have imagined that which I would see therein. Christ Jesus make him a Catholike for he would be a mirrour of all princes.'[16]

Parsons then made sure that a Latin translation was made for the pope's perusal, claiming in his letter accompanying it that it had been requested, and that it was a faithful translation: 'Con questa vanno l'ultimi folii della traduttione del libro del Re d'Inglaterra, commandatici da vostra Santità, il padre che l'ha tradotto è huomo dotto et confidente et s'ha sforzato d'esprimere la vera sentenza dell'autore, et reddere sensum sensui' (With this comes the final pages of the translation of the King of England's book ordered by Your Holiness, the priest who translated it is a learned and trustworthy man and he has tried to express the true meaning of the author, translating the sense rather than literally).[17]

The pope also received a copy of the Latin version printed in London in 1604 as the first part of a European campaign. Despite this interest, events

---

[16] Calendar of State Papers Domestic, 1603–10, 8. Quoted in Craigie (1950), 27.
[17] Fondo Borghese IV, 95, Vatican Library. Quoted in Craigie (1950), 28.

overtook the text. The aftermath of the Gunpowder Plot, the enforcement of an oath of allegiance on English Catholics and James's personal controversy with Bellarmine on the subject, led to the work being on the Index.

James still wanted to be a mirror for all the princes of Europe. Jean Hotman, son of the Huguenot jurist François Hotman, was commissioned by Thomas Parry, the English ambassador to Paris, to execute a translation, which James examined before he authorized it to be released. Although Hotman complained that he did not get paid, his work was a faithful rendering, with only those passages excised that were difficult for Catholics to swallow. It proved very popular in France after its publication in 1603, going through many editions in Paris and Lyon, including pirated ones. The next year the official Latin translation came out, of which there are copies in all the major libraries in Europe, the one in Uppsala having belonged to Sigismund III, King of Sweden and Poland.

Southern Europe was still problematic. James had made peace with Spain, and wanted his text to continue this rapprochement. Two Englishmen were commissioned to translate the text: John Florio (author of the first English–Italian dictionary and translator of Montaigne) into Italian and John Pemberton into Spanish. Both of these editions however failed to make it from manuscript into print – James's Protestantism was clearly making it difficult for him to have appeal across the confessional divide, despite the conventional nature of the text. *Basilikon doron* did better in northern Europe. There were two Dutch translations early on, and in 1604 a Welsh edition appeared, as well as a German translation by Emmanuel Thompson in 1604; Eric Schroder translated it into Swedish in 1606, and there was a Hungarian version by 1612.[18] Perhaps its very failure in southern Europe made it successful elsewhere, as this text was a Protestant version of a genre – the mirror for princes – which had been dominated by Catholics, and as such provided appropriate advice for a prince and head of a national Protestant Church. The princes of Germany, Sweden and Transylvania could learn how to be reformed, without taking reformation too far and becoming the pawn of a radical Church.

The rapid nature of the translations as they appeared across Europe after James became King must have been part of a concerted campaign to establish his kingly and intellectual credibility. Despite his Protestantism, there were aspects of this text that could appeal across boundaries; if Parsons is to be believed, even the Pope thought it had its good points.

---

[18] Craigie claims (2) that there was also a Danish version, but there is no evidence of this. On the Dutch translation, Stilma (2005), 159–237.

The impetus for translation was James's desire to be a *rex pacificus* in a divided Europe, and his identity no doubt helped to sell the work. Judging from the success of the text, his attempt may even have worked, at least in some parts of the Continent, and even for his own subjects.

TRANSLATION AND INTENTION II – JEAN BARBEYRAC AND NATURAL LAW

If, as an author, James VI and I could inspire translation then, conversely, sometimes it is a translator who determines a programme of translation and publication of texts which puts them in a new light. We have seen that many natural law texts were translated by Jean Barbeyrac in the first half of the eighteenth century, but it should be emphasized that this was a concerted attempt to bring something to French intellectual life that he felt was missing. In doing so, he presented a set of ideas that were hugely important for the progress of the French Enlightenment.

What made these translations so significant was the extent to which Barbeyrac introduced them, annotated them and attempted to shape the way they were perceived. They were for him part of a larger project – the presentation, in French, of a systematic moral philosophy that fitted with his religious and epistemological ideas. The first work he produced was a translation and annotation of Samuel Pufendorf's *De jure naturae et gentium*, a hugely popular work from its first publication in 1672, going through many editions in London and Amsterdam. He prefaced this with a history of morality which aimed to show why the work of Pufendorf in particular, and seventeenth-century natural law theorists in general, was so important.

It was the systematic nature of Pufendorf which appealed to Barbeyrac. This could successfully steer a course between a complete scepticism – he quotes Montaigne as an example of this position – and an ultramontane position, including a belief in innate ideas and a slavish following of the Catholic interpretation of Scripture: the piece contains a sustained attack on the Church Fathers. His impetus for this was partly because he was part of the Huguenot diaspora, the French Protestants who had been expelled from France in 1685, who were behind a number of different critiques of French Catholic moral and political doctrine.[19]

To justify this project, Barbeyrac appeals to Locke's *Essay Concerning Human Understanding* (he praises Coste's French translation): Locke

---

[19] Hochstrasser (1993) has put Barbeyrac into this religious context.

attacks innate ideas, yet also provides a basis for believing in human reason. He was sufficiently invested in this position to spend some time attacking Sherlock's religious critique of Locke and reassertion of the notion of innate ideas. A rational, empiricist, moral system was the ideal. Pufendorf is praised as the culmination of Grotius's project, after the interruption of the misguided Hobbes, which serves as an antidote to deceptive priestcraft:

They have not left us a methodical System, they do not exactly define all the Virtues, they enter not into Particulars, they only give, as occasion requir'd, general Precepts; from whence we must draw Consequences, to apply them to the State and Circumstances of particular Persons; as it would be easy to shew, by many Instances, if the Thing was not evident to all who read, with ever so little Care, the Holy Scriptures. And from thence it appears, to mention it only by the Bye, how far we ought to rely upon the Expedient of those, who after have made it their Business to ruin the Certainty of the Light of Reason, refer us to the Light of Faith, for the resolving of our Doubts: As if the light of Faith did not necessarily suppose that of Reason. (Pufendorf 1749, 72)

By contrast, for Barbeyrac, Pufendorf's systematic philosophy demonstrates the conformity of reason and Scripture: to prove this he quotes Richard Cumberland, whose *De legibus naturae* he was later to translate. Barbeyrac's presentation of the text included making alterations as he translated, to correct what was, in his eyes, the barbarism of Pufendorf's Latin. His translation left out some passages, especially those of extensive quotation from other authors as proof, and added others, many from Pufendorf's shorter work, *De officio hominis et civis*, which had become a popular university textbook. If he felt that the explanation was insufficient, then he would expand it, according, as he saw it, to Pufendorf's principles. It was an overall process of clarification and presentation, which he trenchantly justified (this passage of the introduction was not included in the English version as Kennet had not changed the text in the same way):

Pour les autres, s'ils veulent admirer jusqu'aux négligances, & aux bevûes d'un Auteur d'ailleurs très-estimable, ce n'est pas en leur faveur que j'ai soûtenu un si long & si pénible travail: ils peuvent le mépriser, & s'en tenir au Latin; il n'est point craindre que l'Original se perde. [As for the others, if they wish to admire even the carelessness and the mistakes of an author who is otherwise most worthy of esteem, it is not for them that I have carried out this long and painful work. They can despise it if they like and keep to the Latin, there is no danger that the original will be lost.] (Pufendorf 1706, sig m, lv)

His notes completed this project, creating a composite text that was part Pufendorf and part Barbeyrac. There he defended Pufendorf's ideas, and occasionally criticized them, adding passages from other authors and those of Pufendorf himself. This was an eclectic process, and one that Barbeyrac understood blurred the boundaries between author and editor. He includes the thought of others:

I have often given only their general Sense, in my own Way; so that, unless where I cite their own Words in *Italic*, or mark'd with inverted Comma's, he must not impute all I say to the Author, from whom I borrow any Thought. I have used the same Method, with regard to the lost Reflections of the Author, which I have remov'd to the Notes; for I have not always exactly distinguish'd the Things I have interspers'd, or added. (Pufendorf 1749, 74)

Barbeyrac's presentation of a rationalist systematic morality was immediately popular and famous across Europe. He tamed Pufendorf's German Latinity for a French audience for whom literary style was as important as logical exactitude, and in doing so gave it a new lease of life.

His project did not stop there: he went on to translate Grotius's *De iure belli et pacis*, and finally Cumberland's natural law treatise. The importance of his work was clear when the second edition of Basil Kennet's English translation of 1703 appeared, which Barbeyrac regretted not having seen prior to his own work. Not only were Barbeyrac's notes, and later his preface, included, now translated into English, but the text itself was advertised as compared with and corrected according to Barbeyrac's text. The same was done with the English translation of Grotius.

The progressive import of Barbeyrac's work was clear during the conflict between Low and High Church Anglicans in England in the 1720s. The Whig Thomas Gordon, who along with John Trenchard wrote *Cato's Letters*, which became a classic expression of Whig ideology and hugely influential in both Britain and America, used Barbeyrac for his own purposes. Gordon took the attack on the Church Fathers from the recently translated introduction to Pufendorf, and printed it with an introduction of his own. At a time of great crisis in the English Church and state, it was an attempt to rebut the accusation of fanaticism the Dissenters were often subject to, by pointing out the dubious philosophical basis of High Church, as opposed to Low Church morality, and was thus a commensurate project with Barbeyrac's own.

The example of Barbeyrac illustrates both the importance of translation in the transmission of ideas, and the variety of roles involved in such transmission. His translations were immensely important for eighteenth-century moral and political ideas. In his choice of texts, and his reworkings of sometimes obscure pieces, he attained a level of agency at least equivalent to that of the authors themselves. Thus, the influence of a dedicated translator could extend far and wide in both time and geographical extent.

CONCLUSION – BOUNDARIES OF DIFFERENCE

Translation reveals much about intellectual and moral boundaries in early modern Europe, and how porous they were. There was relatively little political thought translated between Eastern and Western Europe, although this may not reflect incommensurability between the two, but rather the continued importance of Latin in the East, where there was a greater density of vernacular languages within the same states and empires. There was also a greater degree of censorship within the Habsburg Empire in the East, which affected such centres as Prague and Graz. Confessional boundaries also loomed large, and became increasingly important after the Council of Trent and the hardening of religious differences between Protestant and Catholic. While some texts, such as Guevara, made it through, others, like James I's *Basilikon doron*, did not. This continued to affect writing of many types into the eighteenth century: the French works of the Protestant diaspora, which did so much to stimulate the French Enlightenment, were published at Amsterdam rather than at Paris: books could evade boundaries through physical movement as well as translation.

What was translated reveals the importance of the monarch in early modern Europe, and the fact that political ideas often centred on that figure or those who served him. Monarchy and the state were great themes that attained a universality, which enabled texts that dealt with them to move between West and East, Catholic and Protestant. This dominance does not tell the whole story however, because of the persistence of classical republican texts, and their adaptation and importance within these monarchies. The example of Rome and the practice of self-government in the cities could make alternatives to monarchy readily available to the early modern mind.

Translation also means adaptation, and the eclectic and at times mercenary attitude of early modern translators meant that there was always a flow and flux of political ideas across early modern Europe. Texts could be censored or altered for a particular audience, sometimes at the behest of the author, and sometimes by a translator keen to make a market or to present new ideas. Adaptation could be a positive process, allowing a set of ideas to flourish in a new context, and providing inspiration to a new and different generation. The political ideas of the eighteenth and nineteenth centuries owed a great deal to the efforts of early modern translators.

CHAPTER 7

Translating histories

Peter Burke

Following the anthropological model suggested in the introduction, this chapter will examine translations of historical works as evidence of what readers in different countries found particularly interesting or alien in other cultures in the early modern period. A survey of general trends will be followed by case studies of the translations of Francesco Guicciardini's *History of Italy* and Paolo Sarpi's *History of the Council of Trent*.

I

What exactly counts as a work of history is not as easy to decide as one might think. The term 'history' itself in different languages, from the ancient Greek *historia* onwards, presents a challenge to translators.[1] The frontier between history and fiction was a porous one, and some scholars may object to the inclusion here of translations of Eustache Le Noble's quasi-historical works. The frontier between history and biography was also open. In what follows, biographies are generally omitted, but they are included in the cases of Alexander the Great, Charles II of England, the emperor Charles V, Charles IX of Sweden, Columbus, Cromwell, Gustavus Adolphus, Henry IV of France, Henry VII of England, the emperor Leopold, Louis XI, Olivares, Philip of Spain, Richelieu, Sebastian of Portugal, Pope Sixtus V and Wallenstein.

What counts as a translation is equally difficult to say with any precision. For example, a book by the Tuscan humanist Leonardo Bruni about the Goths is sometimes described as a free translation of Procopius and sometimes as an original (though derivative) work ('stolen' according to Gibbon), which was itself translated into Italian, French, German and English. Here the text will be treated as original, following the author's description of the work as 'not a translation but a book written by me' (*non*

---

[1] Lianeri (2006). My thanks to the author for showing me this chapter in advance of publication.

translatio sed opus a me compositum). A similar problem occurs in the case of Bruni's history of the Punic War, in this case based on – or freely translating – Polybius.[2] Again, the French humanist Blaise de Vigenère produced an edition of the medieval chronicler Villehardouin to which he added a version of the text that he described as 'more modern and intelligible'. Although it was made from French into French, this version will be counted as a translation.

Unlike some other chapters in the volume, this one is concerned only with published translations. Some translations did circulate in manuscript in the period, including a medieval Russian translation of Josephus, German and Spanish translations of the Jesuit Maffei's history of the Indies, a Spanish translation of Cambini's history of the Turks, German and English translations of the work of the Italian humanists Sabellico and Polydore Vergil, and an Italian and a Russian translation of the Romanian Dimitrie Cantemir's study of the Ottoman Empire. All the same, the volume of published translations relative to the few that remained in manuscript is so overwhelming that little will be lost by omitting the latter from this overview.

The importance of early modern translations from the ancient historians is only to be expected. In the first place, translations from Greek into Latin. At the Renaissance, some were undertaken by well-known humanists such as Lorenzo Valla (who translated Herodotus and Thucydides), Poggio Bracciolini (Diodorus and Xenophon) and Angelo Poliziano (Herodian). In the vernaculars, at least 274 translations of 25 ancient historians were published in the 350 years between the invention of printing and the end of the eighteenth century, more exactly between 1476 and 1792. The translation of the classics reached its peak in the sixteenth century. The slow decline thereafter may signify a loss of interest in the classics but it may simply mean recognition that the task had already been completed. Some of these texts were successful commercially over a long period. Baldelli's Italian version of Caesar, for instance, Lauterbach's German Josephus and Hooft's Dutch Tacitus all passed through many editions. The French translator Nicolas Perrot d'Ablancourt, notorious for his freedom (above, p. 29), translated Arrian, Caesar, Tacitus, Thucydides and Xenophon.

The 'top ten' ancient authors were as follows: Tacitus (28 translations of either the *Annals*, the *Histories*, or both); Josephus (26 translations of either

---

[2] Bruni quoted in Botley (2004), 36–7. On the relation to Polybius, Botley hesitates between 'translation' (26) and 'reworking' (33).

the *Antiquities* or the *Jewish War* or both); Sallust (21 translations of *Catiline, Jugurtha*, or both); Caesar (18); Curtius (15); Xenophon (14 translations of the *Anabasis*, the *Cyropaedia*, or both); Justinus (12); Thucydides (11); Polybius (11); Diodorus Siculus (11).

These are not exactly the authors we might expect. Take the first thirty years of printed translations, 1476–1505. The seventeen translations published in this period do not include anything by Herodotus, Thucydides or Tacitus. Instead we find four translations of Curtius, four of Valerius Maximus, two apiece of Caesar, Josephus, Livy and Plutarch, and one of Justinus.

Eighty translations of twenty-seven 'medieval' texts were published, ranging from the history of the Church by Eusebius (translated eight times) and other early Christian writers to Froissart (translated twice). They included Bede's *History of the English Church* (twice translated into English) and the Danish chronicle of Saxo Grammaticus (twice translated into Danish), signs of interest in national history. The inclusion of four chroniclers of the Crusades (Benedetto Accolti, Robert the Monk, Geoffroi de Villehardouin and William of Tyre) is a reminder that medieval historians were not necessarily despised in the age of the Renaissance.

Thirteen translations of seven historians from the Muslim world, writing in Arabic, Turkish or Persian, appeared in print at this time. They included an anonymous Ottoman chronicle and the annals written by Sa'duddin bin Hasan Can (otherwise known as Khojah Efendi), tutor to Sultan Murad III, published in Latin, German, Czech, Italian and English versions. On the other hand, they did not include Ibn Khaldun, whose fame in the West came only later. Again, there was only one translation from the Chinese, a French version of the work of Sima Guang by the Jesuit J. A. M. de Moyriac de Mailla (1777–85). The interest in the history of Islam was a sign of Western anxiety about the expansion of the Ottoman Empire.

II

In what follows the emphasis will fall on what has been least studied so far, the work of 'modern' Western historians from Leonardo Bruni to William Roscoe, the historian of Lorenzo de' Medici. It is difficult to think of any way of compiling a complete list of these historians, but as in the case of translation into Latin (above, p. 65) I think I can claim to have looked at a large sample. So far 553 published translations of 340 texts written by 263 modern historians have been discovered.

As the introduction to this volume suggested, something can be learned from both the 'export' and the 'import' of texts, in other words the languages from which and the languages into which texts were translated.

Italian (with 93 texts) led the list of languages from which historians were translated, followed by French (90), Latin (70), English (36, mainly into Dutch until the eighteenth century), Spanish (25), German (10), Portuguese (5), Dutch (3), Greek (2), Czech (2) and Catalan, Hebrew, Polish and Swedish with 1 translation apiece.

English led the languages into which texts were translated, with 140 items, followed by Latin (121), French (102), Dutch (88), German (80), Italian (59) and Spanish (30). The remaining languages had low scores: Swedish (8), Polish and Russian (7 each), Portuguese (4), Danish and Greek (2 apiece), and Arabic, Hungarian and Romansh (1 each). The unexpected importance of English and the low performance of Spain should be noted. As in the case of translation in general (above, p. 18) Sweden came on-stream in the seventeenth century and Russia in the eighteenth.

Most of the translations were concerned with the history of Europe or of particular countries within it in the medieval and modern periods. About sixty-four texts were concerned with antiquities. Around fifty dealt with the world outside Europe, whether they took the form of world histories or focused on regions such as the Ottoman Empire, China or Spanish America. Around forty texts focused on religion, whether on church history, heresy or the missions.

It is worth noting, as usual (above, p. 24), what was not translated and for what reasons. Machiavelli's presence on the Index, for example, explains how his *History of Florence* failed to be translated into Spanish. It is no surprise to learn that Protestant historians were rarely translated in the Catholic world – it is the exceptions to the rule that are interesting. The Lutheran Johann Sleidan's history of the Reformation appeared in Italian in 1557, just before the Index of Prohibited Books was made binding on the whole Church, while the German humanist Johann Carion's *Chronicle*, despite being edited by Philip Melanchthon, appeared in Spanish in 1553, before being placed on the Index in 1559. In the Protestant world, on the other hand, a number of books by Catholic priests such as Paolo Sarpi, Famiano Strada and Louis Maimbourg were published in translation – but sometimes disguised as Protestants, as we shall see.

The most interesting, or at any rate the best-documented, example of a non-translation, or more exactly of the non-publication of a translation, concerns a Spanish version of William Robertson's *History of America*. Proposed by the Academy of History, supported by the Count of Campomanes and translated by Guevara y Vasconcelos this text was forbidden publication by royal decree.[3]

As for language problems, British historians suffered from the fact that English was not well known on the Continent before the end of the seventeenth century. Costantino Belli, who translated Paul Rycaut's account of the Ottoman Empire from the French, excused himself in the preface with the remark that 'this history was written in English, perhaps the most difficult language of Europe'. That Francis Bacon's history of Henry VII appeared in two translations, French and Latin, in 1627 and 1640 was quite unusual for the time. However, the situation was gradually changing. Gilbert Burnet's history of the Reformation was translated into Dutch in 1686, French in 1687 and Latin in 1689, while Lord Clarendon's history of the 'great rebellion' appeared in French in 1704–9, and Burnet's history of his own time in German, Dutch and French between 1724 and 1735.

III

The most successful historians may be worth examining more carefully: the sixteen authors whose eighteen texts were translated five or more times apiece, making 120 translations in all (see Appendix 1).

One text was translated eleven times, Philippe de Commynes's memoirs of Charles the Bold and Louis XI. As we have seen (above, p. 73), the Latin translations alone went through at least fifteen editions. Another first-hand account, the Italian Jesuit Martino Martini's history of the fall of the Ming dynasty in China, was translated nine times. Thanks to its Dutch and English translations, Martini's work was used as a source for plays by Joost van Vondel (*Zungchin*, 1667) and Elkanah Settle (*The Conquest of China*, 1676).[4] Francesco Guicciardini's *History of Italy* was also translated nine times.

Two texts were translated eight times each: Sleidan's *Commentaries*, which might be described as a political history of the Reformation, and Sarpi's *History of the Council of Trent*. Two were translated seven times: the *History of Inventors* by the Italian humanist Polydore Vergil and the political theorist Samuel Pufendorf's *Introduction* to international history, which was probably used as a textbook in colleges.

---

[3] Cañizares-Esguerra (2001), 171–82.   [4] Hsia (2000).

Five texts were translated six times apiece: the Italian bishop Paolo Giovio's *History of His Own Time*, Machiavelli's *History of Florence*, Sleidan's *Four World Empires*, the Jesuit Strada's *Netherlands War* (a history of the revolt against Spain) and the ex-Jesuit Maimbourg's *History of the Crusades*. Like the translations of the chronicles by Villehardouin and others mentioned above, the success of this particular work by the prolific Maimbourg testifies to continuing European interest in the Crusades, a movement that in a sense did not come to an end until the end of the seventeenth century, when peace was made between the Ottoman and Habsburg empires.

Six texts were translated five times apiece: the Jesuit José de Acosta's *Natural and Moral History of the Indies*, Luis de Avila's account of the wars of Charles V, Fernão Lopes de Castanheda's *History of the Discovery of the New World*, Enrico Caterina Davila's *Civil Wars of France*, Paolo Sarpi's *History of Benefices* and the *History of the Conquest of Mexico* by the Spaniard Antonio de Solís, who was better known as a playwright and is almost forgotten today.

The eighteen texts include a number of classics, notably the works by Commynes and Guicciardini, but there are also surprises for modern readers, notably the presence of Solís, Martini and Avila. The place of Avila in the list is probably due to a deliberate attempt at propaganda (above, p. 17). As for Martini, he had the advantage, like Strada, Acosta and (for a time) Maimbourg, of being a Jesuit, since as we have seen (above, p. 15) the order was deeply involved in translating. Leading Enlightenment historians such as Gibbon and Robertson would also have appeared in the list if the dates of this study had been extended a few more years (two works by Robertson appeared in four languages apiece before 1800 and in other languages in the nineteenth century).

Political history takes the first place in this list, with eleven texts. It may be significant that three of them deal with civil wars, in China, the Netherlands and France. Religious history is represented by Sleidan's history of the Reformation, Sarpi's account of the Council of Trent and his history of benefices, but the histories of the Crusades, the Indies, the revolt of the Netherlands and the civil wars in France all had a good deal to say about religion. Of the sixteen authors, six were clerics.

The eighteen texts were translated from six languages: Latin (6), Italian (5), Spanish (3), French (2), Portuguese (1) and German (1), and into eleven languages: English (22), French (21), Dutch (15), German (14), Italian (11), Latin (10), Spanish (7), Swedish (5), Polish (3), Danish (2) and Portuguese (1). In other words they more or less follow the pattern for translations of modern history in general.

IV

Who read all these translations? The figures for different languages, listed above, tell us something important, even though it is necessary to remember that a translation into a given language may circulate outside the area in which it is the mother tongue. In the eighteenth century, for instance, some Brazilians read Robertson's history of America in French.[5]

Patronage offers further clues to the readership of translations, suggesting the importance of history for the ruling class. Antoine Macault translated Diodorus into French for King Francis I (a painting of him survives showing him presenting his book to the king), while the translator of Guicciardini into Latin dedicated the book to King Charles IX. In Saxony, Georg Forberger dedicated his translation of Guicciardini to the elector, who gave him a pension in order for him to translate more works of history.

In England, the Duke of Norfolk asked Barclay to translate Sallust. Queen Elizabeth's minister William Cecil asked Arthur Golding to finish the translation of Curtius begun by Brend. Christopher Hatton, a leading figure at the court of Elizabeth, was the dedicatee of Bedingfield's version of Machiavelli's history of Florence. Three translators were close to King Charles I. The king himself encouraged William Aylesbury to translate Davila. Aylesbury was helped in his task by Charles Cotterell, master of ceremonies at the court. Sir Robert Stapleton or Stapylton, who translated Strada, was another courtier as well as a former Benedictine monk who had been converted to Protestantism. The last French translator of Sarpi, Pierre-François Le Courayer, dedicated his work to Queen Caroline of England, who had asked him to undertake the task and granted him a pension. In the case of Le Courayer, the translation was published by subscription so that we know that the book was bought – if not read – by the great and the good such as bishops, peers and heads of Oxford and Cambridge colleges.

Libraries and their inventories also have much to tell us about the readership of historical works in translation as well as in the original language. For example, William Cecil owned a copy of Guicciardini in its Latin translation, as did Philip Marnix, counsellor to William the Silent, King James VI and I, and Andrew Perne, Master of Peterhouse. Seven Cambridge colleges still own copies of Guicciardini in Latin which were probably acquired at this time. Again, William Camden and Andrew Perne

---

[5] On Canon Luis Vieira, Maxwell (2003), 114.

owned Commynes in Latin translation, like six Cambridge college libraries, while Lancelot Andrewes owned Sarpi in Latin.

Turning to English versions, Andrewes owned Commynes and Machiavelli's *History of Florence*, Thomas Baker owned Bentivoglio, Lady Anne Clifford Commynes, Sir Christopher Hatton Machiavelli and Sir Edward Coke both Machiavelli and Guicciardini. Sarpi's *History of the Council of Trent* in English could be found in the libraries of Sir Edward Dering, a leading Member of Parliament; of the diarist Samuel Pepys; and of William Byrd, plantation owner in Virginia, who also owned Guicciardini and Davila in English.

A few case studies of the 500 early modern translators of historical works may be illuminating at this point, since translators may be regarded as particularly well-documented readers.

Fourteen individuals published five or more translations each, or eighty-nine texts altogether. Some of these men may be described as 'humanists', and specialized in translating ancient history: the German Hieronymus Boner, for instance, the English schoolmaster Philemon Holland, and Claude de Seyssel, a bishop who was also counsellor to Louis XII of France.

Others were professional writers, like the Venetian *poligrafi*.[6] Four of the fourteen individuals just mentioned worked for a single publisher, Gabriel Giolito, who had the idea of launching a series or 'necklace' (*collana*) of classical texts in translation together with more recent 'historical jewels' (*gioie historiche*). Tommaso Porcacchi edited the series for Giolito from 1550 onwards, translating five texts himself. Ludovico Domenichi also translated five, while the poet Francesco Baldelli translated eight texts, so Giolito must have thought that translating history was good business.[7] The Spanish exile Alfonso Ulloa also worked for Giolito, translating among other works the history of the Portuguese in Asia by João Barros, Zárate on the conquest of Peru, Lopes de Castanheda on the Indies and a history of the voyages of Columbus.[8] Giolito was not alone in his conviction that history would sell, for at least eight historical works were translated by another *poligrafo*, Pietro Lauro, who worked for various Venetian publishers.

Most of the texts translated by the *poligrafi* were the work of ancient historians, but the moderns included Carion's chronicle, Paolo Giovio's history of his own time, Olaus Magnus on the history of the north of Europe and Polydore Vergil's history of inventors.[9] In other countries a

---

[6] Bareggi (1988).   [7] On the *collana*, Grendler (1969), 158; cf. Cochrane (1981), 383, 388, 420, 487.
[8] Cochrane (1981), 317–19; Binotti (1996).   [9] Bareggi (1988).

few professional writers, such as the Dutchman Lambert van den Bos and the retired English soldier Captain John Stevens, specialized in translating works on modern history. So did the noble amateur the Earl of Monmouth, who concentrated on recent Italian texts such as Guido Bentivoglio on the revolt of the Netherlands and Paolo Paruta on Venice.

V

Some translations were advertised on their title-pages as particularly faithful. Paolo Sarpi's *History of the Council of Trent* was described on the title-page of the German edition of 1621 as 'carefully and faithfully translated' (*fleissig und trewlich versetzt*), while the version of Sarpi's *History of Benefices* published by Carlo Caffa in 1681 was described as 'translated from Italian into Latin, following the letter and the style of the author' (*Ex Italico in Latinum versus, iuxta Literam Stylumque Authoris*).

Despite these claims, the interlingual translation of historians was at the same time a form of cultural translation, in other words an adaptation to the needs, interests, prejudices and ways of reading of the target culture, or at least of some groups within it. Take the case of the English translation of Pedro Mexia by William Traheron, who continued the history of the emperors up to his own time and also, 'for some reason', as John Pocock recently observed, omitted 'an eloquent account of the valour and antiquity of the nobles and kings of Spain'.[10]

Works of history, ancient and modern, were generally read in the early modern period as examples of behaviour either to imitate or to avoid. As a Latin translator of Guicciardini pointed out in 1597 (ironically enough, in the dedication to a collection of the author's maxims, *Hypomneses politicae*), history teaches 'not by means of naked and cold precepts, but by famous and living examples' (*non nudis ac frigidis praeceptis, sed illustribus et vivis exemplis*). The importance of exemplarity may be illustrated by the attention given to speeches and aphorisms.

Today, readers may well be tempted to skip the speeches that they find in ancient or early modern histories, speeches which they know to have been invented by historians, not delivered by the historical agents. In the early modern period, by contrast, the speeches were treated like the arias of an opera, in other words the best part. Anthologies of speeches were produced and translated. For example, Livy's speeches appeared in French in 1554. General anthologies of speeches from historians ancient and

[10] Pocock (2003), 251.

modern appeared in Italian (in two volumes edited by Remigio Nannini, 1557 and 1561), French (edited by François de Belleforest, 1572, an amplified version of Nannini) and Latin (edited by Justus Gesenius, 1674, and Christoph Keller or Cellarius, 1699).

The organization of these anthologies gives some idea of how they were used. Nannini and Belleforest each produced a volume of military speeches, while Nannini also edited a volume of 'civil and criminal' orations. Prefaces suggest that the target audience was that of counsellors, ambassadors and captains.

As for aphorisms, the dismissive reference to 'naked and cold precepts' should not be taken too seriously as evidence of a general attitude, since some editions of Guicciardini (the Venice 1574 edition for instance) furnished the text with a *gnomologia* or index of aphorisms, allowing readers to find them without reading the book through (the aphorisms were also signalled in the margins). Guicciardini makes a paradoxical example in this context because, unlike his friend Machiavelli, he was suspicious of general rules which did not pay enough attention to what we call 'context' and he called 'circumstances'.

All the same, the general remarks about particular events that Guicciardini offered in his history were given particular emphasis and sometimes taken out of context by his editors, translators, printers and readers. Anthologies of these aphorisms were published separately and also translated into Latin. In similar fashion a *gnomologia* was added to the Geneva 1594 edition of Procopius, while the volumes edited by Nannini and Belleforest mentioned above were also furnished with indexes of 'aphorisms worthy of note'.

The cultural translation of histories will now be pursued a little further via case studies or micro-histories of the European reception of Guicciardini and Sarpi, and in particular the accommodation of their work to the Protestant world.

VI

No really thoroughgoing comparison of the early modern translations of Guicciardini's *Storia d'Italia* (nine translations of a long text into six languages) has ever been made.[11] It would probably be revealing, given the freedom normally exercised by translators in this period to amplify as well as to abbreviate the original text (above, p. 31). For a tiny example of

---

[11] Some editions and translations are discussed in Luciani (1936).

the process of amplification at work, one might take Georg Forberger's German version of the famous pen-portrait of Alexander VI, where the author's 'more than barbarous cruelty' (*crudeltà più che barbara*) becomes 'more than Turkish tyranny and cruelty' (*mehr denn Türckische tyranny und grausamkeit*).

For a slightly more extended example of cultural translation, one might turn to the relatively little-known Dutch version of Guicciardini's book, published at Dordrecht in 1599 under the title *De oorlogen van Italien* (The Wars of Italy), a title that was presumably chosen because an emphasis on wars in which Spain took part would appeal to readers in the Netherlands at this time. The translator's name is not known but there are clues to his religious allegiance. The long introductory letter to the reader describes Guicciardini as a good Catholic but one who was aware of the misdeeds of the papacy, and interprets the Italian wars as examples of 'God's just judgements' (*Godes rechtveerdige oordeelen*). Printed marginalia reinforce the religious message, introducing references to God where the text does not. The notorious character-sketch of Alexander VI appears with a marginal gloss noting that the pope's behaviour was far from the perfection St Paul wanted to see in a bishop, while in book four, in which Guicciardini discusses the Papal States, the marginalia turn into miniature essays on the early Church, something that would interest Dutch Calvinist readers of the time.

The fate of the censored passages of Guicciardini's history makes another vivid illustration of cultural translation. The original – posthumous – edition of the *Storia d'Italia*, published in Florence (1561–4), was not a complete text. Certain cuts were made by Bartolomeo Concini, secretary to the Duke of Tuscany. As a result the book made its first appearance minus an important 'digression' on the origins of the temporal power of the popes, as well as certain critical remarks on papal conclaves and an unflattering portrait of Leo X. By contrast, the still more pungent portrait of Alexander VI was retained in the first edition, although it disappeared from the Spanish translation by Florez de Benavides (1581), whether for religious or for 'national' reasons (since Alexander, originally Rodrigo Borja, was a Spaniard).

The first translators, including some Protestants, were apparently unaware that the text from which they were working had been cut. Hence the first editions of the Latin version by Celio Secundo Curio, a Piedmontese Protestant refugee to Switzerland (1566), the French version by Jérôme de Chomedey, a *conseiller* in the Parlement of Paris (1568), and the English version made – from the French – by Sir Geoffrey Fenton (1579) all lacked the censored passages.

Fenton was a little behind the times, since by 1579 it had become public knowledge that the text of the first Italian edition was incomplete, and at least one copy of the original manuscript was in circulation (the Latin version published at Frankfurt in 1609 claims to be taken 'ex autographo florentino'). The offending passage about the temporal power was published separately (in Latin and French as well as the original Italian) in Basel in 1569 by Pietro Perna, the Italian Protestant refugee who had published Curio's translation, and again in London (this time with the addition of an English version) in 1595. It was restored in later editions of the French and English translations (in English, beginning with the third edition of 1595), in the Dutch translation of 1599 (with a note saying that the passage was omitted from the Italian edition) and also in an Italian edition published in Geneva in 1621. Between 1602 and 1739 the text was reprinted separately at least eleven times in one or more of the four languages mentioned. Rarely has a censored text achieved such a wide circulation, especially in translation.

Although Guicciardini did write these passages, we may still say that their appearance in print reveals a Protestant reading of his work. He wrote in the 1530s and died in 1540, at a time when it still seemed as if the split between Catholics and Protestants might be repaired. Appearing a generation later, with the special emphasis given by separate publication, the critique of papal power was perceived as much more radical. One might say that Protestant readers began to view Guicciardini as an ally.

VII

This is also what happened in the case of Paolo Sarpi, notoriously described by Bossuet in his *Histoire des variations des Eglises protestantes* (1688) as 'Protestant habillé en moine' with 'un coeur calviniste'. Even the first Italian edition of Sarpi's *Historia del Concilio Tridentino* (1619) was 'translated' in the sense of published abroad, in London, after the manuscript had been smuggled out of Venice via the British embassy (an unusually dramatic book history).[12] In the paratexts of the first edition the *Historia* was reframed as a Protestant work, or at least as one more violently and openly anti-papal than the text itself.

For example, the title-page drew attention to 'the artifices of the court of Rome to prevent the spread of true doctrines and the reform of the Church' (*l'artifici della corte di Roma per impedire che né la verità de dogmi se*

---

[12] Yates (1944); Burke (1967).

palesasse, né la riforma del Papato e della Chiesa si trattasse). There was also a dedication to James I by yet another Italian refugee, Marco Antonio De Dominis, formerly Archbishop of Split but by this time Dean of Windsor. The dedication referred to 'free spirits' who were aware of 'the deceits and tricks' (*le frodi et inganni*) of the court of Rome, its 'diabolical inventions and stratagems' (*inventioni e stratagemi diabolici*).

Some index entries supported this message. Winston Churchill was not the first person to use the index of a book – in his case the history of the Second World War – as a polemical weapon ('Baldwin, Stanley, confesses to putting party above country'). The Dutch translation of Guicciardini, discussed above, includes an index entry under P, 'Pope squeezes a lot of money out of the Jubilee' (*Paus vischt groot ghelt uit de Jubelee*), and another under G, pointing to Guicciardini's critical discussion of the rise of the Papal States.

In Sarpi's case this idea was taken still further. For example, the index to the first French translation includes entries on 'Reformation frivole de Pie IV', 'Servitude du concile par les commandements de Rome' and 'Usurpation et artifice notable de Rome'. The Latin translation includes entries such as 'Paulus III se Concilii cupientissimum simulate' (Paul III pretended enthusiasm for the Council), 'Translationi Concilii color queritus' (the search for an excuse to move the Council) and 'Valdenses per multa secula soli pontificiae tyrannidi contrarii' (the Waldensians, for many centuries the only opponents of papal tyranny). The English translation is cool by contrast, although we do find an entry under 'Paul III', 'His chiefest virtue was dissimulation.' The index to the mid-eighteenth-century German translation is also a mild one, except where Cardinal Sforza Pallavicino, who wrote against Sarpi, is concerned.

Sarpi himself preferred the language of irony and insinuation to direct statement, and the debate over his religious attitudes still continues, but it is particularly interesting in this context to note that the author was embarrassed by the way in which his book was reframed in the first edition in order to appeal to Protestant readers. Sarpi's secretary Micanzio wrote to De Dominis complaining of 'that inappropriate title-page and that terrible, scandalous dedication' (*quel titolo impropriissimo e quella dedica terrible e scandalosa*).[13]

Sarpi himself, hearing that Jean Diodati, a Calvinist of Italian origin who lived and taught in Geneva, was planning to publish a second edition of the history, wrote to ask him to omit the dedication, which is also absent

[13] Bianchi-Giovini (1836), vol. II, 308.

from the English translation of the history, published in 1620.[14] It is worth
noting that the subtitle of the English translation is milder than that of the
first Italian edition, referring simply to 'the practices of the court of Rome,
to hinder the reformation of their errors, and to maintain their greatness'.[15]

The German translation of 1620, on the other hand, included the
'scandalous' dedication and, if anything, sharpened the language of the
title-page: 'Darinn alle Räncke un(d) Practicken entdecht warden/mit wel-
chen der Bapst und der Römische Hoff den Keyser und die Stände des
Reichs wegen dess begerten Concilii eine lange Zeit geäffet' (the reference to
'making apes of' the Estates of the Holy Roman Empire is interesting as an
attempt to demonstrate the book's relevance for the German public).

Some other early readers reacted in a similar way. The French scholar
Pierre Dupuy, for instance, wrote to his friend William Camden that the
book would have been better without the dedication and the subtitle
(*Utinam abesset praefatio et etiam pars ultima tituli*). Another French
scholar, Nicolas Claude Peiresc, also writing to Camden, agreed, calling
it a pity that the editor was not as moderate as the author but unable
's'abstenir non seulement de l'arraisonnement qu'il a ajouté au titre, et des
mots piquants et partiaux qu'il a entrelacé en l'indice des matières, mais
aussi de son épître liminaire'.[16]

The intentions of De Dominis (as of Sarpi himself) may have been
ecumenical rather than Protestant, but they were understood to be
Protestant by the Englishmen most involved with the publication of the
history, Archbishop George Abbot, the diplomat Sir Dudley Carleton and
the lawyer Sir Nathaniel Brent (a client of Abbot).

The paratextual message was driven home in the translations of the
Historia that appeared in the Protestant world in the seventeenth century,
including the English translation (1620) by Brent, the anonymous German
translation of 1620, the anonymous Latin translation (also 1620), actually
made by Sir Adam Newton, Dean of Durham, the French translation by
Diodati (1621) and the Dutch translation of 1621 by a certain Marcus de
Rogeau.

The Dutch translation, which is limited to the first five books of the
history, includes a long prefatory letter to the States-General commenting
on the persecution of Protestants in the Netherlands in the time of Charles
V and criticizing the pope, or more exactly what the writer calls the two
popes (the second one being the general of the Jesuits). There is no index

---

[14] Malcolm (1984), 57, 126.   [15] Viallon and Dompnier (2002), xliv–li.
[16] 13 July 1619; quoted in Vivanti (1974), xci.

but the strong language of the English title-page is retained and the English dedication by De Dominis is translated. Generally speaking the translation itself is faithful: it is by contrast the marginalia that gave Sarpi a Protestant flavour. They emphasize papal deceits and do not so much summarize as moralize, with a regular use of exclamation marks, especially when commenting on papal hypocrisy.

One Catholic translation requires to be mentioned here, because it is an anti-papal one (though the author added to the text a declaration of his Catholicism). The version of Sarpi by Amelot de la Houssaye was published in France in 1683, just after the famous assertion of independence by the French ('Gallican') Church in the Four Articles of 1682. The book contains anti-papal and anticlerical index entries as well as marginalia that are sometimes so long that they wind around the page. Under the entry 'Moines', for example, we find 'Envieux les uns les autres' and 'comment ils s'enrichissent', while a marginal note compares one pope with Tiberius (Houssaye was a great admirer of Tacitus) on account of his skill in dissimulation: 'Plus ce pape tenoit le concile en brassière, plus il affectoit de paroitre populaire dans son discours.'

The tradition of publishing the *History* in Protestant countries continued into the eighteenth century. The French translation of Sarpi published in 1736 appeared in London, the work of Pierre-François Le Courayer, a priest who left France following his defence of the validity of Anglican orders and was given a pension by the British government. This edition is also noteworthy for its visual paratexts, an allegorical frontispiece including an old man with a lantern and a vignette of the attempt by the court of Rome to assassinate Sarpi in Venice. Other works by Sarpi on the Venetian interdict, on the history of benefices and on the Inquisition were presented in a similar way in their various translations.

As in the case of Guicciardini, these many versions of Sarpi have never been examined in as much detail as they deserve, although the controversies about them (in particular about the three French translations) suggest the potential interest of such a study.[17] In his preface, Houssaye, for instance, accused Diodati of failing to understand both Italian and French, and declared that 'ceux qui confronteront nos deux traductions croiront quasi que nous avons traduit deux different auteurs'. Le Courayer repeats this criticism of Diodati and adds his own of Houssaye. These controversies make very clear how small details may make a great contribution to a book's effect. Details that, as we have seen, were not always provided by the author.

---

[17] A beginning has been made by Viallon and Dompnier (2002).

APPENDIX I: THE MOST TRANSLATED HISTORIANS

1. José de Acosta, *Historia natural y moral*, Italian (Galucci) 1591; Dutch (Linschoten) 1598; German 1598; French (Regnault) 1598; English (E. Grimestone) 1604.

2. Luis de Avila, *Commentario*, Italian, French, Flemish, Latin, English (Wilkinson) all 1555.

3. Philippe de Commynes, *Memoires*, Italian (Raince) 1544, (Conti) 1612; Latin (Sleidan) 1545–8, (Barthius) 1629; English (Danett) 1596, (Uvedale) 1712; Dutch (Kiel) 1612, (Haes) 1757; German (Klosemann) 1643; Spanish (Rizo) 1625; Swedish (Schroder) 1624.

4. Enrico Caterina Davila, *Guerre*, French (Baudoin) 1644; English (Cotterell and Aylesbury) 1647; Spanish (Varen de Soto) 1651; Latin (Cornazanus) 1735; English (Farnesworth) 1758.

5. Paolo Giovio, *Historia sui temporis*, French (Sauvage) 1550, (Parq-Champenois) 1555; Italian (Domenichi) 1555; Spanish (Villafranca) 1562; German (Forberger and Haluerius) 1570; Dutch (Heyns) 1604.

6. Francesco Guicciardini, *Storia d'Italia*, Latin (Curio) 1566; French (J. Chomedey) 1568; German (Forberger) 1574; English (G. Fenton) 1579; Spanish (Florez de Benavides) 1581; Dutch 1599; Spanish (epitome, Nato) 1683; English (Goddard) 1735; French (Favre) 1738.

7. Fernão Lopes de Castanheda, *Descobrimento*, French (Grouchy) 1553; Spanish 1554; Italian (Ulloa) 1577; English (N. Lichefield) 1582; Dutch (Hoogstraten) 1670.

8. Niccolò Machiavelli, *Historia Fiorentina*, French (Brinon) 1577; English (Bedingfield) 1595; Latin (Turler) 1610; English (M. K.) 1674; French 1694; Dutch (Ghys) 1703.

9. Louis Maimbourg, *Croisades*, Dutch (Broeckhuizen) 1683; Italian (Emiliano) 1684; English (Nalson) 1685; Polish (Andrzej) 1707; Latin (Więtrowski) 1723; German 1776.

10. Martino Martini, *De bello tartarico*, German (Paullinus) 1654; French (Girault) 1654; Dutch (GLS) 1655; English 1654; Italian (Latini) 1654; Spanish (Aguilar y Zuñiga) 1665; Portuguese (Goméz Carneiro) 1657; Danish, Swedish (Nidelberg) 1674.

11. Samuel Pufendorf, *Einleitung*, Swedish (P. Brask) 1680; German 1682; Dutch (Vries) 1684; French (Rouxel) 1685; Latin 1687; English (Bohun) 1695; Russian.

12. Paolo Sarpi, *Historia del Concilio di Trento*, English (Brent) 1620; Latin (Newton) 1620; Dutch (Rogeau) 1621; French (Diodati) 1621; French (Houssaie) 1683; French (Le Courayer) 1736; German 1620? (Rambach) 1761.

13. Paolo Sarpi, *Beneficii*, English (Denton) 1681; Latin (Caffa) 1681; French (Houssaie) 1685; German 1688; English (Jenkyns) 1727.

14. Johann Sleidan, *Quatuor imperia*, German (Koch) 1557; English (Wythers) 1563, (Darcie) 1627; French (Le Prévost) 1557; Dutch 1583; Swedish 1610.

15. Johann Sleidan, *Commentaria*, Dutch (Deleen) 1558; English (Daus) 1560, (Bohun) 1689; French (Le Prévost) 1557, (Le Courayer) 1767; German (Pantaleon) 1557; Italian 1557; Swedish (E. Schroder) 1675.

16. Antonio de Solís, *Conquista*, French (S. de Broë) 1691; Italian 1699; English (Townsend) 1724; Danish (Lang) 1747; German 1750.

17. Famiano Strada, *De bello belgico*, Italian (Papini and Segneri) 1638–; Flemish (van Aelst) 1645; French (Du Ryer) 1644; English (Stapylton) 1650–, (Lancaster) 1656; Spanish (Novar) 1681; Polish (Poszakowski).

18. Polydore Vergil, *Inventores*, French (Michel) 1521, (Belleforest) 1582; Italian (Lauro) 1543, (Baldelli) 1587; German (Tatius) 1544; English (Langley) 1546; Polish 1608?

APPENDIX 2: EDITIONS OF GUICCIARDINI ON THE
ORIGINS OF THE PAPAL STATES

1569 *Loci duo ... quae ex ipsius historiarum libris iii et iv non leguntur*, Basel (Latin, Italian, French)

1595 *Two discourses of Master Frances Guicciardin, which are wanting in the thirde and fourth bookes of his Historie*, London (English, Latin, Italian, French)

1602 *Francisci Guicciardini loci duo*, s. l. (perhaps Geneva) (Latin, Italian, French)

1609 'Discursus de ortu pontifici imperii', in *Monita politica*, Frankfurt (Latin, Italian, French)

1609 *Paralipomena quae ex ipsius Historiarum libris iii, iv et x in exemplaribus hactenus impressis non leguntur*, Frankfurt (Latin)

1618 Guicciardini, *History of Italy*, London, 'with restitution of a digression towad the end of the 4th booke, effaced out of all the Italian and Latine copies in all the late editions'

1629 'A part of the Historie of Francis Guicciardine, stolen out of his third Booke concerning Pope Alexander the sixt', 'A second place conteining a large discourse by what meanes the Popes of Rome attained to that greatnesse which they now enjoy' and 'A part of the histoire of Francis Guicciardine stolen out of his tenth Booke' (English)

c. 1650 'De origine secularis potestatis in romana ecclesia', in H. Conring, *De imperio romano*, Lyon (Latin)

1663 'Paralipomena', repr. A. Wicquefort (ed.), *Thuanus restitutus*, Amsterdam (Latin, Italian, French)

1684 'F. G. Historia Papatus', in J. H. Heidegger, *Historia Papatus*, Amsterdam (Latin)

1705 'Guicciardini's account by what means the popes usurped their temporal power', in *The Present State of Europe*, London (English)

1712 *The History of the Papacy wrote by Francesco Guicciardini ... which was fraudulently left out of the 4th book of his history*, London (English)

1739 *Deux passages très importants dans l'histoire de François Guicciardini*, The Hague (Italian)

CHAPTER 8

The Spectator, *or the metamorphoses of the periodical: a study in cultural translation*

Maria Lúcia Pallares-Burke

The fortunes of the English *Spectator* (1711–14) and its followers, in Europe and elsewhere, may be said to represent one of the most successful enterprises of both literal and cultural translation in the history of printed communication. Its study provides a vivid illustration of the problems and dilemmas of what was known in the eighteenth century as good and bad imitation, while we now describe it as cultural translation – in other words, the adaptation of a text to new contexts. A daily paper published intermittently between 1711 and 1714, *The Spectator* was not the first periodical to be edited by the English men of letters Joseph Addison and Richard Steele. They had already collaborated on *The Tatler*, which appeared three times a week between 1709 and 1711. Its name means 'someone who gossips', and indicates the conversational tone as well as the topicality of the paper.

However, it was in *The Spectator* that they found the formula for both national and international success. Even the beginning of this trend gives testimony that *The Spectator*, the so-called original model of the *Spectator* genre of journalism, did not involve a complete break with older trends, as is usually presented; it involved, in fact, a work of cultural translation and is best described as the culmination of tendencies in the history of the seventeenth-century press. So, this essay will start by going back to the periodical traditions which the spectator model followed, and then will show how the journal was itself a creative adaptation of earlier periodical traditions, political, learned and fashionable – the *Gazette*, the *Mercure galant* and the *Journal des savants*.

The second part, which deals with the *Spectator*'s imitations, will focus on a case study of the *Spectator* genre of journalism, the work of Jacques-Vincent Delacroix. Since Delacroix was one of the most, if not the most tireless, convinced and persistent of the followers of the English model of journalism, his work not only illuminates the history of the *Spectator* genre, but also gives some insights into the debate on cultural translation that it provoked.

THE RISE OF THE PERIODICAL, 1450–1700

A brief survey of the development of the European periodical press testifies to the important role it played in the process of cultural exchange and to the cultural and literal translations that it involved. Between c. 1450 and c. 1600 the news entered print in 'occasional' rather than periodical form, via proclamations and pamphlets of various kinds, whether they were concerned with battles, natural disasters, or religious changes such as the Protestant Reformation.[1]

Then, in the first decade of the seventeenth century, in Germany, we see what may be called the invention of the news-sheet, news-book or periodical, in the sense of a series of texts published at regular intervals, whether annually, quarterly, monthly, weekly, bi-weekly or even daily, in order to offer new information to readers (hence the term 'news'). Issues were generally numbered so that readers would know whether or not they had missed one. The print run of seventeenth-century news-sheets was generally around 1,500 copies and one press could produce 600 in a day.[2]

The wars of the period – the Dutch war for independence from Spain (1568–1648), the Thirty Years' War in Central Europe (1618–48), the English Civil Wars (1642–51) and so on – doubtless boosted the sales of this new form of literature. It normally took the form of a number of reports from different cities – Venice, Rome, Paris, Vienna, London and so on, situated on the major postal routes. By the 1660s there were about fifty European newspapers, published in Latin, Italian, French, English, German, Dutch and Danish. Most were monolingual but in the 1660s Georg Greflingen of Hamburg published news in German, French, Italian and English. One of the most famous periodicals of the eighteenth century, best known as the *Gazette de Leyde*, published in French in the Dutch Republic from 1677 to 1811, was originally entitled 'Traduction libre des gazettes flamandes et autres' (Free translation of Flemish and other gazettes), making available to French readers news that would not normally be published in France itself.

One newspaper often appropriated material from another. For example, a study of the transmission of the news of the events of 1669 shows that one paper, published in Copenhagen, regularly borrowed from others published in Hamburg a few days earlier.[3] However, the editor selected information that would appeal to his Danish target audience as well as

---

[1] Seguin (1964).   [2] Schröder (1995), 5: cf. Raymond (1996).   [3] Ries (1977).

translating from German into Danish. In that sense we might speak of the cultural and well as the literal translation of the news.

The rise of the periodical and of the market for periodicals led to increasing specialization by function. Three different kinds of periodical developed, specializing in different kinds of information: political, social and scholarly.[4]

Take the case of France. Political information was to be found in the *Gazette*, founded in 1631 by Théophraste Renaudot. Published with the assistance and according to the requirements of the government, this journal appeared twice a week and presented brief and impersonal accounts of major political events, national and international. It was edited in Paris but also published in the provinces. There were rival papers, such as the weekly *Nouvelles ordinaires*, but the support of the government ensured the success of the *Gazette*.[5]

In the second place, social information could be found in the *Mercure galant*, founded in 1672, which appeared every month and offered news of the court and the world of fashion (in interior decoration as well as in clothes), as well as stories and competitions (to solve enigmas, for example, or to write verses on a particular theme), for a wider and especially a female readership. This journal too was financed by the French government, but unlike the *Gazette* it did not give the impression of being official, thus making its regular praises of King Louis XIV more persuasive.[6]

In the third place, scholarly information was provided by the *Journal des savants*. The first issue, published on Monday 5 January 1665, contained a note from the printer about the policy of the journal: 'Le dessein de ce journal estant de faire savoir ce qui se passe de nouveau dans la République des Lettres' (The aim of this journal being to make known what is new in the Republic of Letters), and it would contain four kinds of items: summaries of new books, obituaries of scholars, accounts of experiments and decisions of legal tribunals. The last feature may seem odd today but reflects the fact that many French scholars of the time were lawyers or had been trained to be lawyers. The plan was for the journal to appear weekly before the news went out of date ('parce que les choses vieilliroient trop'). In practice, however, the *Journal des savants* appeared once a fortnight. The subjects discussed included literature, church history, coins and medals, and natural philosophy.[7]

All three models were imitated outside France, thus illustrating the process of cultural exchange. For example, the *Gazette* model was adopted

---

[4] Sgard (1991).   [5] Feyel (2000).   [6] Dotoli (1983); Vincent (1979).   [7] Morgan (1929).

in the England of Charles II and the Russia of Peter the Great as well as in Spain. In London, it appeared twice a week and was edited by an under-secretary of state. A French translation of the *London Gazette* was published from 1666 to 1705, while in the mid-eighteenth century the *Gazette of St Petersburg* appeared in French and German as well as in Russian.

The *Mercure galant* might be described as the first women's magazine, even if it was also read by men. The first volume appeared in English translation, as 'The Mercury-Gallant', in 1673. This enterprise was not continued but a number of the main features of the French journal were imitated by English competitors such as the *Athenian Mercury*, produced by the English bookseller John Dunton and targeting women as well as men, with special 'Ladies issues' and a short-lived sister journal, *The Ladies' Mercury*. Some of the special features have survived in women's magazines to this day, notably the love stories, news about the latest fashions, competitions and letters from readers, sometimes taking their problems to the 'agony column'.[8] Journals specializing in fashion appeared somewhat later, among them the *Courrier de la mode* (1768–) and the *Cabinet des modes* (1785–).[9]

As for the *Journal des savants* model, it was followed in a long series of European learned journals. Among the most important of these was the *Philosophical Transactions of the Royal Society of London*, which began publication in 1665 and paid more attention than the French journal to natural philosophy. Another major periodical was the *Acta eruditorum* (1682–), produced in Leipzig in Latin for an international learned public, and including more material on the humanities than its London competitor and less material on *belles-lettres* than its rival in Paris.[10]

Most famous of all, there was the *Nouvelles de la république des lettres* (1684–) edited by the French critic Pierre Bayle from his place of exile in Rotterdam and aimed at general readers as well as scholars.[11] Its rival was the *Bibliothèque universelle et historique*, edited in Amsterdam from 1686 onwards by the Swiss Protestant exile Jean Leclerc, which justified its existence on the grounds that rival editors did not know enough foreign languages and promised accounts of 'discoveries' in humanities as well as in mathematics and medicine. In 1687 and 1688, some of the book reviews that appeared in the *Bibliothèque* were written by John Locke.

In all these scholarly journals one of the most important features was a new literary genre, the book review, an invaluable aid to selection and

[8] McEwen (1972); Berry (2003).   [9] Roche (1989).   [10] Laeven (1986).
[11] On Bayle, Labrousse (1963–4).

discrimination at a time when readers risked drowning in the 'deluge' of new publications (this vivid image comes from the pen of a seventeenth-century librarian). While the early seventeenth century was the crucial moment for the development of the news-sheet, the late seventeenth century was the formative period for the more substantial monthly or quarterly journal.

These periodicals both drew on and contributed to the process of international collaboration. The editors depended on scholarly informants from different countries. Books published in one language were often summarized at length in another, offering a temporary substitute for translation. There were plans to translate some of the journals themselves, and for a few years the *Transactions of the Royal Society of London* was made available in Latin to the many scholarly readers of the time who did not know English.

Bayle's career is a good example of the importance of the great Huguenot diaspora for the rise of both journalism and translation in the late seventeenth century. After the Revocation of the Edict of Nantes in 1685, 2 million French Protestants faced the alternatives of conversion to Catholicism or expulsion from France. Of the 200,000 who chose expulsion, there were many Calvinist ministers. They tended to migrate to Protestant cities such as Amsterdam, London or Berlin. The supply of ministers in these places far exceeded the demand, and it was necessary for most of the new arrivals to find an alternative occupation. Highly articulate as many of them were, a literary career was an obvious choice, whether as authors, editors or translators, or in the new profession of 'journalist' (a word that was just coming into use at this time in French and English).[12]

Translation was another of their main activities, and French culture was spread in the Dutch Republic, Britain and Prussia, and English culture in France, thanks to the efforts of Huguenots such as Abel Boyer, translator of Racine into English; Pierre Coste, most famous for his translation of Locke into French; Pierre Des Maizeaux, who translated Bayle into English; and David Mazel, who translated Gilbert Burnet and John Tillotson into French.

THE FORTUNES OF *THE SPECTATOR*, OR A CASE STUDY
IN CULTURAL TRANSLATION

Many of the features of the periodicals mentioned above could be found in the short-lived but extremely influential journal *The Spectator*, which

[12] Yardeni (1985), 201–7.

stands out as a creative adaptation of earlier periodical traditions, political, learned and fashionable. One may say that this early eighteenth-century periodical effectively founded a new genre of journalism by drawing on the three models already in existence, thus combining elements that used to be separated, as well as adding something of its own.

To start with, Joseph Addison and Richard Steele, the main authors, were both involved in the politics of their day, and their journal made comments on politics, claiming, as the name 'spectator' implied, to stand above party and present an 'impartial' view in the age of the great conflict between the Whigs and the Tories. Like the *Mercure galant* and other social journals, *The Spectator* also offered information about the latest fashions and trends, though it wrote from a more detached and critical viewpoint than its predecessors, as in the famous example of the article on the use of the fan (no. 102), which appealed to so many writers outside Britain, including faraway Brazil.[13] Like the *Athenian Mercury*, it continued the traditions of encouraging and discussing letters from its readers. Finally, like some of the learned periodicals, *The Spectator* frequently discussed literature, science and philosophy, although – as the statement of intent published in the first issue made very clear – the aim of the editors was to bring down philosophy 'from heaven to earth' and to appeal to a non-academic public, female as well as male. Here too it offered both information and critical comment.

This creative synthesis might be viewed, therefore, as a cultural translation of earlier traditions and genres into a form appropriate for certain kinds of English reader at the beginning of the eighteenth century. It was an instant success, selling about 4,000 copies a day, while its transformation into book form occurred at a time when the daily issues were still coming out.

However, what is truly remarkable about this journal is that although it was written day by day and was addressed to the concerns of people living in a certain place at a certain time, its appeal turned out to be much wider, crossing frontiers and even centuries, as the great number of translations and imitations testifies. Addison and Steele's journalism was also translated, so to speak, into other genres, since *The Spectator* is widely recognized as having made an important contribution to what literary critics describe in retrospect as the tradition of the English essay. These two journalists have turned, therefore, into 'classics'. One might even say that

---

[13] *The Spectator*, 1711, no. 102; on the adaptations made by the Brazilian follower *O carapuceiro* (1837), Pallares-Burke (1994a).

posterity has 'translated' them into classics. Whether he would have been pleased by this fate or not, Addison's literary reputation has long rested on his articles for *The Spectator* rather than on more ambitious works such as his tragedy, *Cato*.

The success story of *The Spectator* on the Continent starts with the literal translations – never complete, but only partial.[14] They were pioneered by the French in 1714, followed by the Germans, the Dutch, the Swedes, the Italians, the Portuguese and the Russians.[15] The journal went through no less than eighteen editions in the Netherlands, fourteen in France and four in Germany, and it became the object of what contemporaries themselves described as a 'cult'.

The reason for this huge appeal is clearly stated by the first translator, who raised the issue: why translate? Spelling it out in the preface to *Le spectateur ou le Socrate moderne, où l'on voit un portrait naïf des moeurs de ce siècle* (1714), he proudly placed himself in the position of mediator between Great Britain and 'foreign countries' and argued that it was a work worth translating because it could be meaningful for other readers other than for the ones originally intended. He was moved, he confessed, by the ambition that the translation would be followed elsewhere with the same 'good effects' as in Britain, and was supported by 'the hope of bringing men back from their deviation and inspiring them with the principles of Honour and Virtue'.

As the introduction to this volume suggests, translation between languages is a form of translation between cultures, and the modifications that a text undergoes in translation are not the result of linguistic factors alone. So we see, for example, St Paul's Cathedral becoming the Kremlin Palace in the Russian translation, slaves and tropical fruit juices being added to the Brazilian version of the English essays, and so on.

As a model for more or less free or creative imitation, for what came to be known as the 'moral weeklies', *The Spectator* was once again an instant success. But contrary to what might be expected, the local imitations did not take the place of the translations of the English original in the

---

[14] Partial translations range from volumes of selections, under the title of *Zuschauer, Le spectateur ou le Socrate moderne* etc. – as in the case of the French, Dutch, German and Italian translations – clearly acknowledging the source, to the publication of individual articles from *The Spectator* in various journals without explicit acknowledgement, as in the cases of Swedish, Portuguese, Spanish and Russian.

[15] On the German followers and translations, Martens (1968); on the Dutch, Van Boheemen-Saaf (1984) and Schoneveld (1984); on the French, Gilot (1975) and Gilot and Sgard (1981); on the Swedish, Gustafson (1933); on the Portuguese, Picwnik (1979); on the Italian, Anon. (1753), *Scelta delle più belle et utili speculazioni dello* Spettatore (Livorno); on the Russian, McKenna (1977).

preference of the public. Indeed, the translated original *Spectator* continued to compete with the numerous imitations throughout the century, despite the effort of some of its local descendants to rise to its level.

The letters of Goethe to his beloved sister Cornelia offer a rather telling testimony of the long-lasting appeal of *The Spectator*. Dissatisfied with the German imitations, which were bad because they copied the outward appearance, but not the 'actual essence of the original', Goethe urged the fifteen-year-old Cornelia to start the 'improvement' of her 'understanding and will' by carefully reading the English *Zuschauer*. His advice was categorical: 'Take one number after the other, in order, read them attentively, and when it does not please you, read it again . . . They are better and more useful than if you would read 20 novels.'[16]

More impressive testimonies to the *Spectator*'s reputation throughout the century come from the findings of Daniel Mornet, whose analysis of 500 catalogues of French private libraries from 1750 to 1780 revealed that *The Spectator* occupied a leading position, appearing more often than works by Voltaire, Locke or Rousseau.[17]

The list of the followers of the journal begins as early as 1711 with a Dutch journal published in French, Justus Van Effen's *Le misanthrope*.[18] In the Netherlands, there were about seventy such followers, published in either Dutch or French. In England, imitations have been described as 'countless'.[19] In France, at least 100 imitations of *The Spectator* were published before the Revolution, and as an eighteenth-century French reviewer testified in the *Journal étranger* in June 1757, the excellence of this work stimulated imitation: 'The fate of the good originals is . . . to produce an infinity of copyists and the English *Spectator* is the Father of a numerous posterity.' In the German-speaking world, the number of descendants was so great that as early as 1739 Louise Gottsched, the second translator of *The Spectator*, declared in her preface that there was such a 'multitude of imitations that it was difficult to list them'.

Famous followers of the journal include *Der Patriot* (Hamburg, 1724), *Der Freymaurer* (Leipzig, 1738), the *Patriotiske Tillskuer* (Copenhagen, 1761), *El pensador* (Madrid, 1762). And jumping into the nineteenth century, the successful Brazilian *O carapuceiro* gives, as late as the 1830s and 1840s, further evidence of the long-lasting and wide appeal of the *Spectator* genre.[20]

---

[16] J. W. von Goethe (1951), *Briefe der Jahre 1764–86* (Zürich), 26–8.   [17] Mornet (1910).
[18] On the international history of the *Spectator* genre, Rau (1980) and Pallares-Burke (1996).
[19] Stephen (1910).   [20] Pallares-Burke (1994a).

One important form of adaptation was the translation from one gender to the other, as in the case of *The Female Spectator* (Eliza Heywood, London, 1744), *La spectatrice* (1728), *La spectatrice danoise* (1748), *Die vernünftigen Tadlerinnen* (Halle, 1725) and *La pensadora gaditana* (Cadiz, 1763–4).[21] Some of these adaptations were themselves translated. *La spectatrice danoise*, for instance, which was actually written by a man, Laurent de La Beaumelle, was translated into German in 1756 under the title *Des Herrn de La Beaumelle Gedanken*.

The great number of its followers that spread in Europe like a 'torrent', or grew like 'mushrooms' (to use common contemporary descriptions of this literary phenomenon), provides a most vivid illustration of the problems and dilemmas of cultural translation. One of these problems, as Peter Burke has suggested, is that the translator of a text and the cultural translator face the same dilemma between intelligibility and fidelity.[22]

This was, in fact, the problem that Borges tried to solve with the concept of 'creative infidelity' that he began using in the 1930s. According to the Argentinian writer, what should be praised in a translation is not so much its fidelity to the original text, but the audacity with which the translator lies, or, in other words, its 'creative infidelity'. Mardrus's translation of the *Arabian Nights*, according to Borges, shows that the more a translator dares to lie the more valuable he is, since his additions, innovations and twists allow an enriching dialogue between cultures to take place.[23] It is, in fact, extremely interesting to note that there were actual controversies in the eighteenth century over what was or was not a true and faithful imitation of *The Spectator*, revealing that there was contemporary awareness of the process that we now call 'cultural translation'.

It is at this point that the work of Jacques-Vincent Delacroix (1743–1831) becomes extremely relevant. In the international history of the *Spectator* genre, this man of many parts – journalist, lawyer, historian, teacher and translator – stands out as the most convinced and persistent of the French followers of the English model, and his long-lasting career provides a wonderful standpoint from which to observe the development of the genre and the debate on cultural translation that it provoked.[24]

---

[21] Pallares-Burke (1994b); for a comparison between the French, English and Spanish female *Spectators*, Pallares-Burke (1993).

[22] Interview with Peter Burke in Pallares-Burke (2002), 141.   [23] Borges (1936).

[24] For his biography, see the entry by M. Gilot on Delacroix in Sgard (1976), 109–12; on his *Le spectateur français*, see the entry by Sgard in Sgard (1991), 1218–21; on Delacroix as a follower of *The Spectator*, see Pallares-Burke (2004), which gives exact references for the quotations from him in the following paragraphs.

Starting in 1767 with his *Spectateur en Prusse* and ending in 1830 with the *Nouvelles étrennes du spectateur français*, no fewer than fifteen of Delacroix's works carry the title of *Spectateur*. Of these, three at the very least, and probably more, are periodicals – *Le spectateur en Prusse* (1768), *Le spectateur françois, pour servir de suite a celui de Marivaux* (1771–3), *Le spectateur français, ou le nouveau Socrate moderne* (1791) – while the others employ the persona of the philosopher-journalist *Spectateur* as an authority-figure, as, for instance, in *Opinion du spectateur français sur la proposition de supprimer la peine de mort* (Opinion of the French *Spectator* on the Proposition to Abolish the Death Penalty), or *Le captif littéraire, ou le danger de la censure, par l'auteur du spectateur français* (The Literary Prisoner or the Danger of Censorship, by the Author of the French *Spectator*).

In most of these works Delacroix makes references to *The Spectator* of Addison and Steele, a model or tradition from which he seems unwilling or unable to distance himself. In 1823, for instance, he bids farewell to the genre, writing *Les adieux du spectateur du monde politique et littéraire*. Nevertheless, one year later he returns with his last farewells, *Les derniers adieux du spectateur français*, which were again to be followed, three years later, by a letter that *Le spectateur français* addresses to the Parisians. Finally, in 1829, Delacroix announces his awakening, publishing *Le réveil du spectateur français*, to be followed, one year before his death, by some 'gifts' to the public, with his *Nouvelles étrennes du spectateur français* (1830).

Delacroix shared some important common features with other followers of *The Spectator*. In the first place, like the majority of the imitators, he often refers to the English *Spectator* as an immortal work whose perfection could not be equalled. The words of the first of them, the Dutchman Justus Van Effen, who wrote *Le misanthrope*, had set the tone of this admiration with great eloquence: 'What is good in the good *Spectators* is so excellent that I cannot see how the human mind can achieve anything beyond it' (*La bagatelle*, 21 November 1718).

As if they were not putting themselves in the position of competitors, the great majority of the followers seem not to have experienced any 'anxiety of influence'. On the contrary, they sound extremely proud to be following in the footsteps of the English model, even competing with each other over the faithfulness of their imitation.[25] Following the common pattern, Delacroix admits that 'there are original books which are inimitable. Such was the case of the *Spectateur anglois* which appeared at the beginning of this century' (*Le spectateur français*, 1791).

[25] Pallares-Burke (1996).

In the second place, the followers seem to have been united in the criticism they made of other products of the press. Too many periodicals, they claimed, were concerned with fame for themselves and to achieve this they cared only to flatter and entertain the readers, rather than teaching them anything of value; alternatively, they offered nothing but news and partisan opinions. Unlike all these journals, the *Spectator's* disciples claimed to follow the original model, by inaugurating in their local environment a new type of journalism which concentrated on the education of its readers and was devoted to uniting men rather than encouraging their division into parties.

The imitators generally agreed that their interest in the common good was the main reason which made them walk the same path as the original *Spectator*. The reading of the English periodical and its followers was presented many times as an activity as good for the health of the mind as the swallowing of a good medicine. Van Effen, for example, even defined the ideal *Spectator* as a 'physician of manners' (*médecin des moeurs*), while there were correspondents who referred to the different issues of the original *Spectator* as regular 'doses' of an 'effectual remedy', or as 'excellent cleansers of the brain'.

A third point that united the whole family of *Spectators* was their need to adopt the persona of an Olympian observer of the human condition on the model of the original Mr Spectator, a silent and attentive observer of men who had developed 'a more than ordinary penetration in seeing' (5 March 1711). Following this tradition, *Le misanthrope* of Amsterdam, *Der Patriot* of Hamburg, *La spectatrice* of Paris, *The Female Spectator* of London and *La pensadora gaditana* of Cadiz, among numerous others, presented themselves as privileged observers who assume the role of moral guides in the name of public interest. The world is for them a theatre that they claim to observe with the impartiality and detachment of a spectator. 'Nothing that interests men and relates to their happiness is indifferent to me,' says Delacroix following the same tradition (*Le spectateur français*, no. 4 (1791) discourse 4). The stage of his silent observation is Paris, and he wanders around the Luxembourg Gardens, the Opéra etc. – as Marivaux and Madame Spectatrice had done before him – claiming to be able to see through social appearances to the underlying reality.[26]

One last point that united the whole family of *Spectators* is the need for collaborators. In spite of their claim to a wide and privileged vision, the editorial personae also tend to present themselves as incapable of

---

[26] On Marivaux's *Spectateur français*, Gilot (1975); on *La spectatrice*, Pallares-Burke (1994b).

embracing the whole spectrum of human experience alone. The constant refrain of the followers of Mr Spectator is the need for sharing their public mission with other people who would also play the role of spectators. This collaboration could be either the work of specific friends who provided the journal with a great variety of information and points of view, or of any reader who had information to offer, questions to raise, criticisms to make, favours to ask etc.

The Female Spectator (1744–6), for instance, relied on the help of an educated married lady with 'sparkling ideas', a beautiful girl and a 'widow of Quality', not counting the 'friendly spies' who sent information from places as distant as 'France, Rome, Germany' etc. The more daring Danish *Patriotiske Tilskuer* (1761–3) even introduces a peasant into the 'congregation' that helped in the organization of the periodical (see the German translation, *Der patriotische Zuschauer*, 1769, no. 3).

As for the participation of readers through correspondence, the followers of the English *Spectator* seemed to be aware of the importance of readers' letters, real or fictitious, as a strategy to involve the public and to make it an accomplice in the Enlightenment project of the periodical. Following the same trend, Delacroix claims to be happy to have, like Socrates, stimulated men to give birth to their own ideas and to have published the letters of readers who, as he says, 'supplement the knowledge which I lack' (*Le spectateur français avant la Révolution*, discourse 25).

The Swiss Bodmer, another member of the *Spectator* family and author of *Die Discourse der Mahlern* (1721–3), made a quite revealing comment when he said that the role of the letters from the public in *The Spectator* was so great that the authorship of the journal should be attributed to the 'whole city of London' rather than to 'Mr Richard Steele and his club' (vol. III, no. 24).

THE '*SPECTATOR* QUESTION' AND THE DEBATE ON CULTURAL TRANSLATION

The phenomenon of the 'countless' imitations of *The Spectator* even gave rise to a debate in the Republic of Letters on what one might call the '*Spectator* Question', raising many of the issues discussed today under the heading 'cultural translation'.[27]

The Paris periodical *Le journal étranger* (1754–62), a journal devoted to discussing the Republic of Letters and its vices, testifies to a general context

[27] Pallares-Burke (1996).

in which these concerns grew in the eighteenth century. With the aim of emphasizing both the value of different cultures and their interdependence, one of the journal's central themes was literary imitation; as they made it clear, looking for the 'us' in the 'others' and for the 'others' in 'us' was a way to demonstrate that borrowing was relatively inevitable and constructive. Thus the February 1755 issue claims that Goldoni's comedy *Pamela* has surpassed the original novel by Richardson. Pope's imitation of Horace and Dr Johnson's imitation of Juvenal are also described as 'preferable to the originals'. In September 1755, there was a long discussion of an English imitation of a French imitation of a Chinese tragedy, Arthur Murphy's *Orphan of China*, which derived from Voltaire's *Orphelin de la Chine*, which in turn followed a French translation of a Chinese play, the title of which was transliterated as *Tchao Chi Cou Ell*.[28]

But what counts as a good or faithful imitation? This question became the theme of an international polemic, revolving around the true meaning of being a *Spectator*, of writing as a *Spectator*, of persuading as a *Spectator*. As if the English text had become sacred or canonical, the value of its followers was measured in direct relation to their faithfulness to what was believed to be its original form of teaching and even to the original title.

Three centres can be said to have been the scenes of the main debates about good and bad imitations, or, as we might say, successful or unsuccessful cultural translations, legitimate or illegitimate uses of the *Spectator* model: Zürich, Copenhagen and Paris.[29]

In Zürich, Bodmer and Breitinger, authors of the first German-language imitation of *The Spectator*, led something of a campaign against the unfaithfulness of *Der Patriot* from Hamburg and *Die vernünftigen Tadlerinnen* from Halle, on the grounds that they were not loyal to the 'nature of a spectatorial text', and did not obey the rules of verisimilitude, impartiality and the personification of the characters under which they wrote. It was for instance quite implausible that the Halle periodical was the work of three female friends. Gottsched's personae, remarked Bodmer, should have first been legitimized before they were given 'male arguments'.[30]

In Denmark, the writers Holberg and Schlegel referred to an actual internal war among the *Spectators* which, in the middle of the century, competed with one another for the legitimate role of teachers of morals. Their testimonies reveal some of the main issues at stake in the debate. The occasion for the polemic was the publication in Copenhagen of some

---

[28] Pallares-Burke (1994–5), esp. 192–3.   [29] Cf. Pallares-Burke (1996), 7–8.
[30] J. Bodmer (1728), *Anklagung des verderbten Geschmackes* (Frankfurt and Leipzig), 41.

rather incisive and bold periodicals which, naming themselves *Spectators*, declared war on public and private vices. Their authors were criticized for their harshness, their teaching as 'men of truth' and for assuming that the 'conversion' of people to morals could be the 'work of a week'. Instead, the critics claimed that a journalist should be more like a 'gentle teacher', who with 'softness and gracefulness' worked for the eradication of vices and faults. All the same, the critics did not approve of the tender and gay manner of the French writers whom they considered not truly 'spectatorial' either, since they failed to go deep into human vices and remained at the level of trivial faults of etiquette.[31]

In Paris, the French debate seemed to corroborate such points and there is plenty of evidence about the terms of the debate in the reviews and comments from the *Bibliothèque française* (1724) and the *Journal encyclopédique* (1759) to the *Année littéraire* (1777, 1784), which over the years made comparisons between the new *Spectators* and the model they were expected to follow. To entitle itself *Spectateur* (or *Censeur, Observateur, Menteur* etc., all titles which alluded to the *Spectator* tradition), implied a commitment to a certain way of writing which, if not complied with, was a fault to be denounced in the Republic of Letters.

The importance of Delacroix in this debate is due in particular to his work being the object of discussion among the critics, who viewed him through the lens of that debate. It is interesting to note that the reception of his work in the Republic of Letters was, if not always warm, at least encouraging by the reaction it provoked in people as different as Fréron, Voltaire, Grimm and the journalists of the *Journal encyclopédique*. Voltaire was impressed by his *Spectateur* of 1771 and welcomed him in a letter of that year as a legitimate heir of Addison and Steele, a praise which Baron Grimm considered absolutely inappropriate and damaging to the *Spectator* tradition, especially considering that this praise encouraged undeserved subscriptions to Delacroix's work.

It is a 'sacrilegious compliment' to call this Delacroix a true descendant of Addison and Steele and only the 'divine mercy' can pardon this 'blasphemy', says Grimm in his bombastic manner. He linked Delacroix to 'a troop of irritable prophets' and declared that it was not possible to have a *Spectateur* in France with this kind of pretentious journalist. It seems that what made Delacroix unspectatorial, according to Grimm, was his lack of modesty.[32]

---

[31] L. Holberg (1754), *Geschichte verschiedenes Heldinnen* (Copenhagen and Leipzig), preface; Holberg (1748–9), *Pensées morales* (Copenhagen), preface; J. E. Schlegel (1745–6), *Der Fremde* (Copenhagen), no. 1.

[32] Baron Grimm (1830), *Correspondance littéraire* (Paris), 406–7.

Amazingly similar to Grimm's opinion was Fréron's in the *Année littéraire* a few years later when reviewing a new edition of *Le spectateur* of 1770–2, where Voltaire's praise is again attacked. Delacroix's style is too 'pretentious', 'pompous', with too many images, everything 'strangely out of place' in a *Spectator* which aims at 'painting the manners of its century'. Along the same lines is his criticism of the immodest way *Le spectateur* praises the *philosophes* as 'celestial men' by whom humankind can be released from the darkness they linger in; equally anti-spectatorial is the way *Le spectateur* performs his educational role. The first aim of a *Spectator*, he says, is surely to instruct, but he should never do this as a 'new Prometheus' who delivers 'light' to humankind; on the contrary (and just as the Danish commentators had said earlier), he should do it gently and unobtrusively as Socrates, 'this ancient *Spectator*', had done (*L'année littéraire*, 1777).

Enthusiastic about a periodical which had the merit of both pleasing and instructing the public at the same time, the *Journal encyclopédique* (1777) regrets, though, that in spite of his talent Delacroix had not worked as a true *Spectator*, and this for one of the reasons also pointed out by *L'année littéraire*: his unwillingness to leave his 'cabinet' where he studies mainly books and himself, instead of real men. It is impossible to be a faithful 'painter' of 'our ridicules, of our defects, of our vices, of human nature', without exercising the talent for observation.

Steele and Addison, Fréron had also remarked in his review of Delacroix's new edition of *Le spectateur français*, did not announce themselves as solitary men, but, on the contrary, as 'voyeurs' who observed men in the public squares, in the assemblies, at the theatres, boudoirs, ateliers, in the 'noisy liberty of the bourgeois orgies', from which they would gather material for the 'moral magistracy' they had undertaken – and which those who followed them were, as a matter of fact, expected to undertake as well.

In short, some rather interesting points stand out from the comparisons made by the French Republic of Letters between the new members of the *Spectator* 'family' and their model. A *Spectator* must not be sad, solitary or contemplative, but a joyful and active spy who, in various places, gathers material for his 'moral magistracy', that is, for correcting morals and manners and attacking vices. Its spirit should be similar to that which prevails in a 'comic theatre', where the scene is marked by 'delight' and 'cheerfulness', while social criticism is being made.

This type of work was even described by a reviewer as the 'supplement to comedy', which would do all the time what the theatre does only on the day of the performance, that is 'to apply prompt remedy' to the foolish acts which 'succeed one another on the stage of the world'. But above all, this 'remedy' should be prescribed with grace, with tact, so as to be swallowed by the 'patient', almost without noticing (*L'année littéraire* (1771), VII, 124–7).

In this debate on *The Spectator*, a second important thing to note is Delacroix's reflexivity, that is, his role as a spectator of the *Spectators*, his repeated reflection on the spectatorial part he had performed in France during so many decades, from the late 1760s till 1830, surviving the regimes of Louis XV, Louis XVI, the Revolution, the first Republic, Napoleon, Louis XVIII, Charles X and Louis Philippe. As we listen to his repeated reflections on his role as a spectator and to his reply to the critics, we can glimpse some of the ways this appealing eighteenth-century genre was appropriated and translated, that is, adapted to the different circumstances it encountered throughout his long-lasting career.

Delacroix himself makes comparisons between the circumstances in which the original daily *Spectator* was published and his own enterprise. The English one, Delacroix reminds his readers in 1770, was addressing its pages to a society which had already gone through a major revolution and the editors were simply trying to consolidate it by converting the whole nation to the new way of thinking and behaving associated with the new regime. And because Addison and Steele had to fight only against the taste of their public and not against the fury of the *censeurs*, they needed only to have enough talent to disguise their teaching with amusement so as to appeal to the public. They could, though, dare to enlighten their public with 'great truths', and could talk about everything: 'politics, legislation, government, ministries'; while he, Delacroix, had to keep distant from such 'great subjects' and, contenting himself with a 'much narrower range of things', simply observe men as they are 'without daring to say what they should be'.

So, the criticism of his observations as being frivolous and thin was unjust, he argued, and did not give him credit for the courage required to play the part of a spectator at a time when there was prejudice against this 'mere title'. Years later, after the Revolution, he thought that the acclaimed freedom of expression had granted him the right not to talk about trivialities and to be able to repeat what his English model had done, that is, to speak clearly and without many innuendos about what he had been forced earlier to disguise entirely. In 1791 he was so misled as to think that the new political regime allowed him to imitate Addison and Steele, by delivering in the periodical pages the most useful course of 'practical morality'. 'The vices and the faults of the great which were formerly hidden behind their titles, their rank and their distinctions, appeared in broad daylight', in the English *Spectator*, said Delacroix in 1791. 'Those who had believed themselves above criticism, thanks to their wealth or status, were unmasked.'

No real change had happened though, and when in 1793–4 he – gently and with care – dared to criticize the revolutionaries in power and suggest what they should do, he almost lost his head. He was arrested and prosecuted as a royalist and a 'public enemy' of the Revolution for daring to advise the Convention to consult the people and not to judge the king.

As time went by and Delacroix continued to act as a spectator and reflect on the role with which he identified himself so completely, it becomes clear what he understands as its true meaning: to be a spectator is to be first of all not a royalist or a republican, but a moralist who believes that the happiness of the state depends on respect for morals (*moeurs*); and who, out of his love of humanity, tries to intervene, as far he can, in human affairs in order to minimize the sufferings and pain he sees and foresees.

What Delacroix took, then, from the original English text was, so to say, the inspiration for a kind of writing that complied with his humanitarian beliefs and offered him an essential strategy for success in the role of a moralist whose aim is, as he insisted, to produce 'le bien général'.

This was fundamentally the strategy of disguising oneself as an impartial and apolitical observer, of pretending not to belong to any sect, party or class, and thus having no personal interest to blind his eyes. The original *Spectator* (16 October 1711) had defended what he called 'the Socratical way of reasoning', that is, the strategy of not allowing one's antagonist to notice that you had a 'firmly fixed' opinion and that you were 'endeavouring to bring over another to your opinion' – a strategy completely the opposite of the political writings and actions of the French censors and government, who think they can bring others to their opinions by 'insults', 'threats' and 'denunciations'. Only those who have not reflected on human history can think that it is possible to produce 'a revolution' in people's minds and affections by means of 'terror', argued Delacroix in a truly spectatorial way.

Following this strategy, Delacroix's work would follow, he said, the 'form' of the English *Spectator*, including 'several discourses without real link, many letters real or fictitious, confidences that might never have been really genuine, projects which might have come from my own imagination, etc'. If the aim is to improve manners and morals, Delacroix argued, 'it does not matter under what veil reason and truth are hidden, as long as one can recognize their language'.

If he varies so much in tone – going from grave and serious to frivolous and mundane – and introduces 'different characters' into his 'conversations', it is to captivate the public more successfully, he explains in 1824. In short, as seen through the gaze of this 'spectator of the spectators', for a cultural translation of the *Spectator* model to be effective, the model should be considered a 'canvas'; as Delacroix put it, *The Spectator* was a 'pretty canvas' that Addison and Steele had left for posterity to fill in, taking into account the generational differences as well as national and historical ones.

As if corroborating Borges's idea of 'creative infidelity' being the rule for a successful translation, Delacroix says that 'it would be against the artistic rules to employ the same colour to paint two different nations', suggesting that he clearly realized that to continue to be faithful to the *Spectator* tradition, and keep on correcting morals and manners, he had to be different – in other words, that he had to keep changing in order to remain the same, that is a true joyful and active *Spectator*.

Delacroix did not have the talent of Addison and Steele (as indeed nobody else seems to have had), but he did have an individual contribution to make as the most systematic spectator of the *Spectator* genre itself, and perhaps as one of the most insistent followers of Addison and Steele, who made a number of successive attempts to translate a set of ideas and practices (originally designed for early eighteenth-century England) to the new and ever-changing contexts of French culture.

PART III

Translation and science

CHAPTER 9

The role of translations in European scientific exchanges in the sixteenth and seventeenth centuries

Isabelle Pantin

DEFINITION OF THE CORPUS: A PROCESS OF REDUCTION

The aim of this chapter is to study the role of translations in the spread of scientific texts from the sixteenth to the end of the seventeenth century.[1] My personal interests, my training and the lack of primary research in the field have all influenced the method followed here. The necessary means to study translations as a general process which could be quantified, or even mapped, are lacking for this period, unlike for the twentieth century.[2] In any case, scientific books represent but a small part of the mass of translations made during the period considered, and I am not convinced that a quantifying approach would be particularly illuminating. This study examines the extent to which translations reveal not so much the transformations of the scientists' work, than the transformations of its cultural context. Being mainly concerned with the motives and aims of the translations, I have resorted, for the most part, to case studies.

This general orientation also justifies the decision to leave aside the most obvious corpus, and the largest one, in other words the translations of the works of the past (essentially from antiquity, but also from the Middle Ages), and to concentrate on modern works. This choice may seem debatable in a research programme of which almost half concerns the Renaissance, given that at the time the scientists themselves accorded the greatest importance to the legacy of the past, all of which is fully evident in the intellectual movement of humanism: quotations, editions and commentaries of ancient texts were often a means to convey new ideas.

All the same, the corpus of 'modern' translations can be justifiably set apart because it poses special problems. Considered in itself, it throws useful light on the ways in which recent scientific information was

---

[1] Waquet (1998); Grant (1954); Chartier and Corsi (1996); Burke (2004).
[2] Milo (1984) has applied quantitative methods to a twentieth-century corpus.

exchanged. Besides, it requires an analysis that is quite complex, while translations of ancient works are more straightforward. As far as science is concerned, the purpose of the latter, all things considered, is always the mastery of a branch of knowledge. The translation of modern works, of course, aims at that too, but also answers other needs. This study is essentially a survey of these needs, based on the analysis of diverse examples, which should ideally represent the rest. However, there is no pretence to have covered the whole field of scientific translation.

As mentioned before, there is no comprehensive inventory of this field. Hence instead of trying to picture the world of scientific translations in all its extension, richness and variety, I have resigned myself to focusing on its most prominent features. I have considered only printed translations, although the circulation of manuscripts was far from negligible in the early modern period. This is obvious, for example, in the case of Paracelsus, whose influence slowly spread over Germany and Switzerland before his main works were printed. Even after his disciples had edited and translated them (below, pp. 172–3, 175), Paracelsian texts and fragments continued to circulate in manuscript, notably in England, as Charles Webster has convincingly shown.[3] The printing of a text simply suggests that its editors and publishers thought that it could attract a reasonable number of customers (the usual print run was of 600 copies). In the case of translations (especially Latin translations), a portion of these expected customers were foreigners; I have therefore attached particular importance to the international book trade, which was concentrated in a definite area.

According to Henri-Jean Martin,[4] the principal towns involved in this trade, before the Thirty Years' War, were Frankfurt (the venue of the greatest book-fair and the most international), Leipzig, Cologne, Basel, Geneva, Venice, Paris, Lyon, Strasbourg, Amsterdam, Antwerp and Leiden. From the beginning of the seventeenth century London became more and more active, while Spanish librarians were virtually absent. During and after the war against Spain, towns in the Netherlands (especially Amsterdam) grew in importance. For instance, according to a catalogue published in 1634, the Elsevier had in stock more than 3,000 books in Latin (433 from Paris, 231 from Lyon, 932 from Frankfurt, 201 from Leipzig, 286 from Cologne, 169 from Basel, 456 from Geneva, 164 from Venice, 34 from London etc.); more than 500 in French (322 from Paris, 103 from Geneva, 27 from Lyon etc.); 307 in Italian; 32 in Spanish and only 7 in English.[5]

---

[3] Webster (1979).   [4] Martin (1969), 303–11.   [5] Martin (1969), 311.

For these reasons, the Hispanic world, the New World and Eastern Europe are generally omitted from this study. To compensate for this obvious gap, more attention has been paid to countries having for different reasons a complex experience of the problems of language and the transmission of knowledge, England, because of its insularity, and the Netherlands, which had to deal with multilingualism.

A purely descriptive survey would have been unsatisfactory, since the description would not have been faithful or reliable, for the reasons already mentioned. So what follows will focus mainly (though not exclusively) on works that underwent what might be called 'massive' (or, at any rate, significant) processes of translation. The heroes of this chapter are Paracelsus, Ambroise Paré, Simon Stevin, Galileo and William Boyle rather than the modest schoolmasters and surgeons whose manuals may have been published in more than one language. This choice is certainly debatable; it is even, perhaps elitist. All the same, it is not arbitrary.

FROM ONE VERNACULAR TO OTHERS

During the period considered, it was not common – but not exceptional either – for recent works to be translated shortly after their first publication. For the most part, these translations were made from Latin into the vernacular and from the vernacular into Latin, thus revealing the basically bilingual character of European culture up to the end of the eighteenth century. By contrast, translations from one vernacular into another were much rarer, especially in the field of science (in the case of novels or propaganda, it is obvious that the situation was quite different).

The translations that avoided passing through Latin can mainly be found in marginal subjects, especially utilitarian books: practical manuals, astrological pamphlets or prognostics about the effects of comets, popular pharmacopoeias and books of secrets. For example, Leonardo Fioravanti's Italian books (*Secreti medicinali*, 1561; *Compendio di tutta la cirugia*, 1561; *Capricci medicinali*, 1564; *Specchio di scientia uniuersale*, 1564; *Regimento della peste*, 1565) were translated into French and English.

In the Netherlands, printers or booksellers often managed to publish the same text in different languages: Jan van Waesberge of Rotterdam, for example, printed the Dutch and the French versions of Simon Stevin's books on fortifications. This was particularly easy when printers specialized in cartography and in books on instruments and navigation, of which the main part consisted of engravings. Willem and Jan Blaeu adopted this practice for their collections of maps and guides for navigation (which sometimes involved little more than changing the title). Willem's *Licht der zeewaert* (1608) thus became *The Light of Navigation* (1612) and *Le flambeau de la navigation* alias *Le Phalot de la mer* (1619).[6]

However, works other than popular manuals and illustrated technical books were involved. Alessandro Piccolomini's innovative cosmological textbook *De la sphera del mondo* (Venice, 1540) was translated into French by Jacques Goupyl. In these two versions the choice of the vernacular was made not only on account of the target audience, but also to 'illustrate' or raise the status of the Italian and the French languages respectively (this topic will be discussed below). *Mutatis mutandis* the French translations of Galileo's books – completed or only planned – by Mersenne and Carcavy (*Les mécaniques*, in 1634, *Les nouvelles pensées*, an adaptation of the *Discorsi*, in 1639, and the projected *Dialogue*) are exceptions of a similar kind: they were prestigious specimens showing that modern languages were appropriate for conveying a new philosophy.

However, the increasing number of scientific publications in English after the foundation of the Royal Society (when the English language was still little known outside Britain) occasioned some translations in French, though noticeably few: such translations lacked sufficient justification, either commercial or scientific. Whereas the whole of Boyle's work was translated into Latin (below, pp. 171, 173, 177–8), only a few dispersed tracts circulated in French.[7]

Paracelsus deserves a special mention.[8] His most widespread medical treatises, originally written in German, were soon translated into Dutch or into French (the English printed translations were more extensive, but did not appear before the second half of the seventeenth century, and the Italian *paracelsica* were few and late). All were published in Antwerp, where Philip Hermann made compilations in Dutch: *Dat secreet der philosophizen, Die peerle der chirurgijen* (from *Die grosse Wundartzney*, first printed in 1536) and *Een excellent tracktaet* (from the tracts on syphilis and its cure, *Vom Holtz Guaiaco . . .* and *Von der französischen Kranckheit*, first printed in 1529 and 1530). Pieter Volck Holst, a surgeon, translated *Die grosse Wundartzney* (*Die groote chirurgie*, 1555), and Martin Everart the *Labyrinthus* (1563). Everart later translated the other surgical books: *De Cleyne Chirurgie ende Tgasthuys Boeck vanden seer Vermaerden* (1568). Then appeared *La grande, vraye, et parfaicte chirurgie* (1567), based on the improved edition of *Die grosse Wundartzney* by Adam von Bodenstein

[6] For other examples, Keuning (1973). [7] Jones (1953).
[8] For bibliographical details, Sudhoff (1894).

(1564). Pierre Hassard also produced *De la peste, et de ses causes et accidents* (1570), gathering several tracts on the plague from two different German collections.

The purpose of these translations was clear: they were made by practitioners for practitioners, with the idea that they could spread new and useful information on the most frequent or dangerous infirmities and diseases, paying increasing attention to exhaustiveness and clarity. The next French translation of the *Chirurgie* to appear, in 1589, was made by Claude Dariot, based on the Latin version by Josquin Dalhem (1573). The dedication of the latter text to Pierre de Grantrye, signed by Pietro Perna, the publisher, mentions that Dalhem has replaced Paracelsian invented words with normal medical vocabulary, and quotes a letter where the translator affirms that he had paraphrased the obscure passages.

In this case, we encounter once more the common process where Latin intervenes, as in the case of Simon Stevin's Dutch *Mathematical Memoirs* (*Wisconstighe ghedachtenissen*), translated into Latin by Willebrord Snellius and into French by Jan Tuning. Willem Blaeu's instruction manual for the users of his terrestrial and celestial globes 'the one according to the opinion of Ptolemy ... the other after Copernicus's natural position', underwent a similar process. Written in Dutch, it was soon translated into Latin by Martinus Hortensius and then into French and English. The technical character of the book justified this series of translations. What was more significant was its ostensible Copernican sympathies. Even the apparently simplest cases reveal the possible complexity of the factors involved.

LATIN VERSUS VERNACULAR: RESHAPING THROUGH TRANSLATION

The translation of a modern work could serve different purposes. Its original language – either Latin or vernacular – was chosen according to the requirements of the context. As a rule, the decision to translate it did not mean that this context had changed, but that the role assigned to the work and the way in which its reception was envisaged, were altered. Two principal factors came into play: the new public and the prestige associated with a change in the status of the work.

One of the signs of these factors is that changing the language often provided an opportunity for altering the text. An example is Ambroise Paré's *Opera*, published in 1582, under the supervision of Jacques Guillemeau, one of Paré's disciples. This Latin book is not a pure and simple translation of the *Œuvres*, but almost a new version, in which details that might be unimportant or unintelligible for foreign readers have been cut out, and in which 'aids for the reader' (a system of titles, marginal notes etc.) have been improved.[9]

There are other examples, sometimes in the other direction: Laurent Joubert first wrote his *Paradoxa* in Latin and afterwards his *Erreurs populaires* in French, which were expanded and more vivid and picturesque than the original version. In extreme cases, the adaptation resulted in the composition of a completely different book. Thus Francis Bacon's *Advancement of Learning* (1605) was considerably enlarged and transformed when it became the *De augmentis scientiarum* in 1623. These two books addressed different audiences: in the first case the king and his entourage, in the second, professional philosophers.

As a rule (though there were exceptions), Latin translations tended to lengthen the texts, and vernacular ones to shorten them. In 1542 Leonard Fuchs published in Basel, with Isengrin, his *De historia stirpium commentarii*, which already possessed elements of multilingualism: plants were examined in alphabetical order under their Greek names, but they were listed in a four-part index which presented their names in Greek, in classical Latin, in medieval Latin and in German. The work was abridged, adapted and translated into German in order to be accessible to apothecaries and gardeners. In the *New Kreuterbuch*, once again published by Isingrin, the alphabetical order is under the German names that also provide the first entry in the multilingual index (where Greek names have been transliterated). This abridged version was translated into Dutch (*Nieuwe herbarius*, 1549), yet again published by Isengrin.

However, this simple scheme is slightly complicated by the career of the book in France. A French translation was made by Eloi Maignan directly from the Latin version (*Commentaires tres excellens de l'hystoire des plantes*) and published in Paris and Lyon, and a new epitome was prepared, with a Latin and French title, and the names of the plants in Latin, Greek, French, Italian and German. These few diverse examples suggest that vernacular translations were not all at the same level. Nor were the Latin ones.

THE CULTURAL STATUS OF LANGUAGES

As the Renaissance came to its close, Latin was still the principal language for scholarly activity throughout the whole of Europe, but decisive changes had occurred foreshadowing its slow decline. These changes involved the

---

[9] Pantin (2003).

vernacular languages, which, one after the other, set themselves up as languages of culture, transforming scientific life as well as the habits and requirements of scientists, without forgetting certain political features. Dante had introduced the notion of *vulgare illustre* (illustrious vernacular) and from the sixteenth century on, the close ties between national pride and the defence of a country's language were recognized everywhere.[10]

The two fields considered essential for appreciating the value of a language were, on the one hand, poetry, and on the other, 'philosophy', which, in traditional acceptance, covered what we now call 'science', since from the beginning of the sixteenth century the Aristotelian separation between natural philosophy and mathematics was contested. Theology, which the theoreticians defending languages often preferred to leave out of the discussion, will be omitted here as well.

Sperone Speroni, in his *Dialogo delle lingue* (Venice, 1542), and Joachim Du Bellay in *La défense et illustration de la langue française* (Paris, 1549) affirmed that vernacular languages were capable of expressing the highest philosophical conceptions. Jacques Peletier du Mans, a poet and mathematician, justified the use of French in both domains. Simon Stevin was deeply influenced by the ideas of the humanist circle of Hugo Grotius and repeatedly defended the thesis that Dutch was probably the oldest language in the world, particularly apt for expressing scientific ideas.[11] The position defended by the Royal Society concerning language is well known. John Wallis, professor of geometry at Oxford, wrote the first 'philosophical grammar' of English.[12]

Thus putting a work into a vernacular language did not only (or even always) imply a desire to popularize it. The most complete version of Oronce Finé's *Sphæra mundi* was the French one of 1551. Finé was the first holder of a royal chair in mathematics at the Collège Royal (where the lectures were delivered in Latin), and raising the prestige of the French language through the publication of scientific works of quality was at that moment one of the royal lecturers' duties. Besides, for both thinking and communicating between scholars, the essential advantages of a maternal language were recognized. Within different countries, more and more people worked, corresponded and published in the vernacular.[13]

On the other hand, when it was a question of communicating at the level of the whole of Europe, Latin had no serious rival. The big international centres of the book trade were mostly situated in the Germanic parts of

---

[10] Scaglione (1984); Chiappelli (1985); Burke (2004), 61–88.   [11] Wal (2004), 171–7.
[12] Jones (1953), 252.   [13] Pantin (1998).

Europe (with the book-fairs of Leipzig and Frankfurt), where Latin had maintained its role. Galileo himself failed to make Italian a European scientific language (it is not even probable that he really attempted it: the readers whom he wanted to convince were essentially Italians), and the spread of French, during its glorious heyday (towards the end of the classical period), produced a great number of original scientific publications in that language, but no significant series of translations. We could make similar remarks concerning the scientific English fostered by the Royal Society. The volume of translations – and this is a passing thought – could thus provide a criterion allowing one to differentiate a language of the elite from a language capable of imposing itself on all sectors of scientific activity.

However, at the end of the age of humanism, Latin was still much more than an easy medium for international communication, and putting a work into this language did not always imply wanting to spread it across national borders. When Jacques Peletier du Mans transformed his *Algèbre* (1554) into *De occulta parte numerorum* (1560), his reasons were complex. The desire to raise the prestige of French by using it to spread the sciences was no longer as important as it had been a few years earlier.[14] On the contrary, the use of Latin seemed appropriate to give algebra a dignity equal to that of the traditional mathematical disciplines. The fact that Peletier had recently become a mathematician of international renown, through the publication of his Latin commentary on Euclid (1557), constitutes only one reason among others.

In mathematics, it was difficult to be fully acknowledged and consecrated without Latin; but such was also the case with disciplines that had conceded much more place to the use of the vernacular, like medicine. Ambroise Paré, who had suffered the persistent hostility of the Parisian *doctores* because of his insufficient humanist training, enjoyed a kind of revenge when his *Œuvres* appeared as *Opera* (above, pp. 167–8).

LATIN, REFERENCE EDITIONS AND COLLECTED WORKS

In any case, when a book circulated in two versions, the Latin one was often the more 'living', the one that received commentaries or new materials. This is illustrated by Descartes's *Geométrie*; the editions of the original French text remained quite unchanged from 1637 to the beginning of the eighteenth century, while the Latin version received additions by Franz van

[14] On the 'return to Latin' in France at that period, Faisant (1979).

Schooten, Johann de Witt and others, thus proving the fecundity of the text. The same point could be made about Wallis's *Algebra*. The Latin edition included the first complete series of appendices, and thus constituted the 'classical' standard version of the book. More generally, the notion of 'reference edition' (the edition which receives successive improvements, thus becoming the definitive one), like the notion of 'corpus' – in the sense of 'collected works' – was often closely associated with the use of Latin. Of course there were exceptions: the definitive collective edition of Stevin's work was *Les œuvres mathématiques*, prepared and partly translated by Albert Girard (1634).

Latin played its expected role in the diffusion of Boyle's books. They were widely spread in English, but their first collected edition was published in 1677 by Samuel de Tournes, who circulated them in Latin (using the translations supervised by Boyle himself and first printed in England when they were available, or else getting 'continental' ones). This fact remains significant, even if commercial motives were prevalent. The Genevan bookseller was an international dealer, a regular attender of the Frankfurt book-fair, and he had already published collected scientific works, notably those of Paracelsus (1658).[15]

In any case, the collection was unauthorized: Boyle was averse to any form of systematization and on the first news of the publication, he had a quite negative review published in the *Philosophical Transactions* (14 December 1676), making clear that the edition had 'been put out without the consent and knowledge of the Author'. It also criticized the misleading arrangement of the treatises (which ignored their chronology), and complained that there was 'no mention made in the General Title, nor in any Advertisement, that these Books were all of them Translations out of English'. Besides, *Form and Qualities*, an essential philosophical treatise, had been omitted (it was added to the collection in 1687).[16]

Samuel de Tournes, for his part, was probably convinced that he was making a valuable contribution to the Republic of Letters. He took pains to gather all the available material, commissioned some new translations and arranged the innumerable tracts according to thematic order. His prefatory letter to the reader about the scientific value of the edition was more than commercial propaganda.

---

[15] Bonnant (1978), esp. 98, 147–8.
[16] Johns (1998), 508–10. Johns views De Tournes as a pirate pure and simple, whereas Hunter's judgement is more balanced (Hunter and Davis, 1999, lxxx–lxxxi).

The long process of the publication, Latin translation and collection of the works of Paracelsus gives a somewhat different impression. The border between the vernacular and the Latin versions is not so clearly marked in this case. The editors of the German texts had more or less the same background as the Latin translators, and on some occasions they exchanged their domains. Gerard Dorn remained constantly 'Latin', but Georg Forberger both edited German texts and translated others into Latin.[17] Adam von Bodenstein and Michael Toxites, who were clearly situated on the 'German side', sometimes edited and annotated treatises that were available only in early Latin versions.[18] Moreover, their productions seem often to have been bought and read by the same people. Even if the Latin editions were mainly aimed at the non-German market and played an essential role in spreading Paracelsianism through France, Belgium, England and, perhaps, Italy, they also had a wide circulation in Switzerland, Germany and Scandinavia, as is suggested by the number of copies now in libraries in those countries.

On the other hand, the German editions were not exclusively destined for German customers. The catalogue which John Dee prepared in 1583 attests that he then possessed forty-one German books by Paracelsus (plus nineteen in Latin and two in Flemish).[19] Paracelsus's work was perfectly 'in keeping with the new spirit of cultural assertiveness of the nations of northern Europe' (in Webster's words), and it was acknowledged as the first scientific masterpiece in the German language (just as Luther's was the first theological one).[20] Thus a Latin translation could add no prestige; the fact that some works were known only through early Latin translations was generally deplored as an irretrievable loss. Huser's German collection (published in Basel, by Waldkirch, in 1589–91) was considered to be the definitive one. No true adept could completely forget that Paracelsus had strongly expressed his dislike of Latin.

From the beginning, the Paracelsians were inspired by a kind of philological zeal (of course, they were more or less successful depending on training, talent and luck). They searched for manuscripts in their quest for authentic original texts, and, as they had to deal with dispersed and often fragmentary texts, they tried to gather different tracts together in order to publish sufficiently substantial books. However, the 'collecting spirit' was more present on the Latin side. Pietro Perna, who dealt with three translators, Gerard Dorn, Josquin Dalheim and Georg Forberger, had

---

[17] Sudhoff (1894); Zaunick (1977), 37–9.   [18] Sudhoff (1894), nos. 98, 126, 144, 160, 162.
[19] Webster (1979), 331–2.   [20] Webster (1979), 316.

conceived the project of a complete Latin collection.[21] The two volumes *Operum latine redditorum*, prepared by Georg Forberger in 1575, was only a partial achievement.[22] It could not be compared with Huser's ten massive volumes (eleven with the *Chirurgischer Bücher*).[23] As soon as the monumental German edition had appeared, however, Zacharias Palthen, an important bookseller in Frankfurt, gave it to a team of translators who produced eleven volumes (1603–5).

In 1658, Jean Antoine and Samuel de Tournes published a new edition in folio, *Opera omnia medico-chemico-chirurgica, tribus voluminibus comprehensa*. It had been prepared by Fridericus Bitiskius who boasted that his translation was more complete and truer to the originals, although he was heavily indebted to the Palthen team. However, the important thing is that a new complete Latin collection could still be planned, after so many editions, and at a time when the essential elements of the Paracelsian doctrine had been integrated into the works of prestigious disciples and followers, from Petrus Severinus to Jan Van Helmont.

COMMERCIAL INTERESTS VERSUS IDEOLOGICAL MOTIVES

These different examples show that two main factors were involved (and often mingled) in the process of translation: to put it crudely, ideological motives and commercial interests. If the latter were relatively constant, the former were more varied: prestige, desire to spread knowledge, to affirm an identity (requiring the marks of linguistic distinction), to defend the ideas of a group of individuals, or even to assert and protect intellectual property, as in the case of Boyle, who wished to guard against plagiarism. In a letter of 6 August 1665 he confessed his 'discouragement to the publication' of *Forms and Qualities*,

that in case it come abroad in English any considerable time before it is ready to bee published in Latine, Divers of the Experiments which possibly will appear new & somewhat Curious, may be with or without little variation, adopted & divulged by others.[24]

'Ideological factors' were often prevalent when the translations were made by the authors themselves, or by people close to them, on their own initiative or on the initiative of those around them. Translations sometimes provoked international polemics. Philip Lansbergen, for

---

[21] Hieronymus (1995).   [22] Sudhoff (1894), nos. 165–6; Zaunick (1977), 39–43.
[23] Sudhoff (1894), nos. 216–25.   [24] Quoted in Hunter and Davis (1999), lxi.

instance, a Calvinist pastor relieved of his ministry in 1613 because of his impossible strictness, devoted himself to his second passion, astronomy.[25] He considered that his special vocation was to recover the perfect knowledge of celestial motions once possessed by the Hebrews, and after laborious observations, calculations and comparisons between systems, decided in favour of heliocentrism. Martinus Hortensius, a former student of Isaac Beeckman and Willebrord Snellius, was for him what Rheticus had been for Copernicus. Encouraged by this young enthusiast, he published in 1629 a singular treatise: the first defence of the Copernican cosmology, written in Dutch and aimed at a large unlearned audience, *Bedenckingen op den dagelyckschen, ende iaerlijckschen loop van den aerdt-kloot* (Reflections upon the daily and annual course of the earth. The same on the true image of the visible heaven; wherein the wonderful works of God are discovered).

Within a year of its publication, Hortensius produced a Latin translation which was read all over Europe and incurred attacks by Alexander Ross, Jean Baptiste Morin and Libert Froidmont, who were in their turn answered by Hortensius and Lansbergen's son, Jacob (Philip had died in 1632). This quarrel played a role in Galileo's troubles: Froidmont, a theologian of Louvain, published in his second response (*Vesta*, 1634) the letter addressed to Jansenius by the nuncio in Brussels that announced the condemnation and abjuration of the philosopher.

This condemnation (and the shameful publicity given to it) was precisely the stain that Galileo and his disciples wished to wash out by permitting his work to survive and be read by unprejudiced readers.[26] At this point it was felt more than before that the circulation of his books in foreign countries was of the utmost importance and various editing projects were fostered. In 1633, Galileo's Parisian friend Elie Diodati sent a copy of the *Dialogo* to Matthias Bernegger (in Strasbourg) so that he could translate it into Latin and, some years later, he set himself the same task for the *Letter to the Grand-Duchess Christina*. As we have seen, some translations into French were also undertaken. Galileo himself, who had been reluctant at first, decided to have his work completely translated into Latin under his own supervision.

Several projects for the complete publication of Galileo's works in Latin were conceived simultaneously in France, in the German Empire and in Holland, under the supervision of Carcavy, Giovanni Pieroni and the Elseviers respectively. At this time the Elseviers had branches in Leiden, The Hague and Copenhagen, and offices or contacts in Venice, Frankfurt,

[25] Vermij (2002), 73–90.   [26] Garcia (2004); Pantin (1999); Pantin (2000b).

London, Paris and Florence. Their plans resulted in only three Elsevier editions, the *Systema cosmicum* (the Latin translation of the *Dialogo*) in 1635, a bilingual edition of the *Letter to Christina* in 1636 and the *Discorsi* (in the original version) at the beginning of 1638.[27]

The 'Latinization' of Paracelsus by Gerard Dorn and others did not possess such dramatic urgency and it depended more on motives of interest. From the mid-sixteenth century, Paracelsus's fame had extended over a wide area, so his books had sales potential. However, Pietro Perna, who published a series of new Latin translations in Basel, was also influenced by philosophical and religious motives. He supported alchemy and chemical medicine, and he was a Protestant with some unorthodox tendencies, a feature often associated with Paracelsianism.[28] Besides, his translators, Josquin Dalhem excepted, were adepts of the new doctrine.

There were two principal reasons for editing and translating Paracelsus: to answer the professional needs of practitioners eager to learn new remedies and treatments, and to promote a new philosophy radically opposed to the Aristotelian conceptions of science, of man and of nature. The limited Latin collection published by Perna from 1568 to 1575 suggests that he cared for both. Moreover, his translations prepared or accompanied the progressive appearance of a new kind of Paracelsianism, less idiosyncratic and better adapted to a learned audience.[29]

Another sort of 'ideology' was involved in the translations designed to accommodate the needs and requirements of a professional group or, possibly, institution. For example, physicians put much effort into translation, defending Latin on the one hand, a sign of professional competence, and vernacular languages, on the other hand, to enable the distribution of useful and wholesome knowledge. Medicine was one of the fields in which the simultaneous circulation of the same text in two languages (Latin and the vernacular) was not exceptional, notably in the case of treatises on the plague.

Turning to institutions, the Universities of Oxford and Cambridge supported Latin. Hence, for example, the translation of John Wallis's *A Treatise of Algebra Both Historical and Practical*, which became *De algebra tractatus historicus et practicus* (1693). The Royal Society, on the other hand, used its influence to favour English. In this context, some English booksellers, often associated with the Society,[30] worked to build up for

---

[27] Willems (1880); Westman (1984).   [28] Perini (2002), 61–111, 149–60.
[29] Schott and Zinguer (1998); Grell (1998); Kahn (1998); Webster (1975); Shackelford (2004).
[30] Barnard and McKenzie (2002), 302.

themselves a rich stock of scientific works in English, the complete list of which was often printed in each book, by way of advertising.

In fact, this sort of linguistic competition took place in harmony and mutual understanding: the same author could be a professor at Oxford or Cambridge and a fellow of the Royal Society (this was the case for Wallis and for many others). It did not preclude joint interests: the university printers at Cambridge and Oxford were often associated – or at least linked – with booksellers in London who could offer the Latin and vernacular versions of the same texts for inland and foreign trade.[31]

Newton's *Opticks* and its translation by Samuel Clarke, rector of St James's (1675–1729), were both published by Samuel Smith and Benjamin Walford (and afterwards by William and John Innys). Walford had formed a partnership with Samuel Smith who was the publisher to the Royal Society; he succeeded to this office on Smith's death, and William Innys succeeded him (from 1711 onwards).[32]

In the translation business, the desire to facilitate communication between scientists was not the only – and not even the main – factor. Booksellers would rather include both the Latin and vernacular version of the same work in their catalogues. English booksellers largely imported learned books in Latin: so the export of the Royal Society scientific publications in translation was some compensation. Quite a modest beginning, and without real prospects: the great obstacle to the penetration of foreign markets by English books was their prohibitive cost of production.[33]

The most 'ideological' translation undertakings had to satisfy commercial requirements, as is obvious even in the case of the Galilean translations. When he wished to publish his works abroad, Galileo was informed that the use of Italian would put off many readers. His disciple Pieroni in Vienna argued in 1635 that he had numerous supporters throughout Europe who were eager to read his books, without being able to do so: 'If the *Dialogues* were in Latin, I think that they would be already reprinted in France, in Belgium and Germany, and in more places, because the curious are very numerous.' Other correspondents wrote that the booksellers strongly objected to publishing books in foreign languages, fearing that they could not find customers.

---

[31] McKitterick (2002).   [32] Plomer (1922), 167–8, 298–9.
[33] See the letter of Jan Van Waesberghe, a Dutch bookseller, to Samuel Smith (January 1685), quoted in Johns (1998), 507.

However, the project of a complete translation failed, as we have seen, for obvious reasons: it was hardly possible to print condemned books in Catholic countries, even in France, which prided itself on not following every injunction and edict issued in Rome, and the booksellers obviously thought that the books would not be sold easily. Elsevier only published works that had a certain – if not large – potential readership: the still unpublished book on the 'new sciences' of movement, which constituted the Galilean legacy to physics, and the highly controversial texts where the philosopher had tackled two crucial problems head-on: the cosmological reform (in the *Dialogo*) and the exegetical reform which was necessary to harmonize Scripture with heliocentrism (in the *Letter to Christina*).

The remarks of Galileo's disciples are interesting: they took commercial factors into consideration, but not to derive profit from them. Contrary to such authors as Boyle, they did not fear plagiarism and piracy: Pieroni dreamed of reprints 'in France, in the Spanish Netherlands and Germany, and in more places', although, if they had happened, he would scarcely have had control over them (either economic or scientific). This idealist confidence in the ability of good philosophy to spread itself *ad majorem veri gloriam* is typical of a certain milieu.[34] Nevertheless, this attitude was not representative.

Another sign of the importance of commercial factors was that in the case of translations, a greater proportion of privileges was granted to the booksellers. It would be more exact to say that the booksellers involved in the 'translation trade' were of the kind that obtained general privileges. For example, Ambroise Paré, from 1549 onwards, always took pains to obtain personal privileges; but the two privileges for his *Opera* (that of Rudolph II, for six years, and that of Henri III, for ten years) were granted to the bookseller, and the Imperial privilege also concerned a translation, the Latin version of Bodin's *Republic*.[35] Maximilian II bestowed a general privilege on Pietro Perna in 1567, one year before the publication of *Pyrophilia*, the first of Dorn's translations. It was valid for 'all medical, philosophical, historical, mathematical and poetical books, and those that helped the study of Hebrew, Greek or Latin'.[36]

The translations of Boyle's books do appear to be a case of real commercial dynamics: Boyle's treatises were almost always written and published in English, but 'the English Philosopher' commissioned Latin translations which were often printed in Oxford or London – although mainly for the foreign market. These first Latin versions, as well as some

---

[34] Garcia (2004).   [35] Charon (1991), 231.   [36] Perini (2002), 380.

new ones, were afterwards printed in Amsterdam and Rotterdam, in spite of Boyle's opposition; and finally, as we have seen, Samuel de Tournes, in Geneva, gathered together all the existing translations, had the works still available only in English translated and published a complete Latin collection. However, in his notice 'Lectori benevolo', the bookseller stressed his ideological motivation.

In any event, the publishing career of the Latin Boyle remains an exception. In the sixteenth and seventeenth centuries, the translation of modern scientific books was only a marginal phenomenon without significant economical importance, even in the case of England – I should rather say of London – where there was a truly dynamic confrontation between Latin and the vernacular. It is significant that the chapter entitled 'Science and the book' in the *Cambridge History of the Book in Britain* does not discuss the problem of translations, and that, on the other hand, the part concerning 'vernacular traditions' does not deal with scientific literature, except via the 'periodical press'.[37]

CONCLUSION: TOWARDS THE CONSTITUTION OF A
UNIVERSAL *BIBLIOTHECA PHILOSOPHORUM*?

Thus there was no large flow of scientific translations; and the corollary was that works were rarely translated only to supply the market. The great majority of translations were from the vernacular into Latin, and had special motives. Above all, they were a sign of value. In the prefaces, they were often presented as proof of the international importance of the work, with the topos of the eagerly awaiting foreign audience. Jacques Guillemeau in the dedication to Marc Miron of Paré's *Opera* (1582) affirmed that all the surgeons he had met on his travels, Italian, German or Spanish, crave for the translation and so the book will have a great international career. We find the same topos in the Latin editions of Paracelsus.

Franz van Schooten expresses a similar idea with more sobriety when he presents Descartes's *Geometria*: the work, published in French twelve years before, has won the admiration of the *literati et ingeniosi*; therefore a translation, with explanatory notes, seems necessary to enlarge its readership, and Jean Maire, the bookseller, has managed to have it made. Again, the editor of the authorized Latin version of Boyle's *Spring of the Air* alludes to pressing requests from prestigious people.

[37] Johns (2002); Nelson and Seccombe (2002).

Latin translations were, for the writers, a means to establish themselves in the dignified Republic of Letters, and they were all the more significant when they concerned books which had first been written in the vernacular for important special reasons, like Galileo's *Dialogo*, or Lansbergen's treatise on the motion of the earth. On the other hand, they often reduced the authors' control over their own work. Several factors contributed to this effect, from the initiatives taken by disciples or distant followers (and the liberties taken by the translators), to the strategies of the booksellers. Robert Boyle had only too keen a perception of the unpleasant aspects of the process, whereas Galileo eventually submitted to enduring them, seeing that he thus secured the survival of his work. However, the most important thing was probably that the audience of the books changed: it became larger, more foreign, often ignorant of the circumstances of the first publication, and freer in its interpretations. Henceforth the work was a kind of common property (*bonum publicum*), it belonged to the whole community of philosophers and lettered persons.

CHAPTER 10

Scientific exchanges between Hellenism and Europe: translations into Greek, 1400–1700

Efthymios Nicolaïdis

THE LAST BYZANTINE DECADES

The fifteenth century is the century of the shift of power in the Balkans and Asia Minor, from the declining Byzantine to the rising Ottoman Empire. As Byzantium lost lands and power, its emperors looked forward more and more to help from Western Europe against Ottoman military conquest. In order to motivate Catholic Europe to assist the Orthodox 'heretics', a plan for the union of the two main European Christian Churches was put forward, and discussions organized between them. A side effect of these contacts was an intensive cultural exchange between the two sides, and as far as concerns science, the exchange of manuscripts and in some cases their translation as well.

During the last Byzantine dynasty of the Palaiologues, state officials and scholars belonged to the same milieu. To rise in the state hierarchy, studies were virtually obligatory. Officials usually followed high-level courses, studying the *trivium* (grammar, logic and rhetoric) and the *quadrivium* (music, arithmetic, geometry and astronomy). The training of these officials and the important position that what we call 'science' gained during this last Byzantine dynasty, led them to discuss natural philosophy rather than politics.

Indeed, political and religious debates between rivals trying to obtain the same high state office sometimes turned into scientific discussions. Moreover, appointments to some important political offices were made following scientific debates, as in the case of Metochites and Choumnos who disputed the office of first minister (*logothetis tou genikou*) debating on astronomy and not on politics or religion.[1] Metochites obtained this office after having demonstrated that he was a more able astronomer and natural philosopher than Choumnos.

---

[1] Sevcenco (1962).

This environment, together with a real enthusiasm for astronomy and especially for the computing of solar eclipses, is the reason why so many Byzantine officials of the state and the Church who came into contact with Western Europe were involved in science. It should be noted that the special interest in astronomy was closely related to computing horoscopes, since astrology was more and more in vogue in a civilization which was being defeated in the military field.

During the Byzantine period, three kinds of scientific text were translated into Greek, one from the East and two from the West: the texts of the astronomical school of Tabriz and Maragha in Persia, the texts from the astronomical school of the Karaite Jews in Provence and the texts of the Iberian astronomical school. The translations of the Persian texts into Greek would be of interest in Europe a century later, as astronomers from Western and Central Europe (Copernicus, for example), would study these texts from the Byzantine manuscripts.

The first group of translations, those from Persian into Greek, were in fact made during the fourteenth century, but became very popular during the fifteenth century, when they were copied again and again. During the fifteenth century these texts reached Italy, brought by Greek scholars who fled the Ottoman conquest. In the context of the revival of the Greek language among European scholars, these texts became important as they brought new knowledge to Italy. They include the astronomical corpus of Gregory Chioniades, who travelled to Tabriz at the beginning of the fourteenth century.

The most important text from this corpus – and the most copied – was edited in 1347 by George Chrysokokkes, and is entitled *The Persian Syntaxis in Astronomy*. This *Syntaxis* is based on the *Zîj-i lkhânî* of Nasîr al-Dîn al-Tûsî (1201–71), the founder and the most important astronomer of the observatory of Maragha. The book of Chrysokokkes is mentioned by the French scholar Ismale Boulliau (*Astronomia philolaica*, 1645); more than fifty manuscripts are preserved.

The history of the Greek translations of the Persian astronomical corpus goes back to the very beginning of the fourteenth century, when George Chioniades (whose monastic name was Gregory), following medical studies in Constantinople, went to Trebizond to obtain aid from the emperor Alexis II Comnenus (reigned 1297–1330) for travel to Tabriz. At that period, Tabriz was a renowned scientific centre where astronomy was taught by Shams al-Din al-Bukhari among others. Following this first visit, Chioniades returned to Tabriz as bishop of the Orthodox people of the town, sent by the Byzantine emperor Andronicus II (reigned 1282–1328).

From Tabriz, Chioniades brought back to Byzantium an astronomical corpus comprising the following Arab or Persian texts:

a) The *Zîj al'Alâ'î* by al-Fahhâd (c. 1176) as it was taught by Shams Bukhari.[2]
b) The *Zîj al-Sanjarî* by al-Khâzinî (c. 1135).[3]
c) Not yet identified tables beginning at the year 1093.
d) The tables of the *Zîj-i lkhânî* of al-Tûsî which inspired the *Persian Syntaxis* of Chrysokokkes.
e) Various short texts and figures, such as the famous *Figures of Heavenly Bodies* appearing in the Vatican manuscript Vat. gr. 211, fols. 115–21, inspired by the *Tadhkira* of Nasîr al-Dîn al-Tûsî.[4]
f) A treatise on the astrolabe, probably by Shams al-Bukhari.

As mentioned above, these texts circulated in Italy after 1400. Among them, the most discussed by historians is the text written by Chioniades, titled *Figures of Heavenly Bodies*. Based on the book *Tadhkira* of Nasîr al-Dîn al-Tûsî, it may have played an important role in the development of Copernican astronomy, as it presents the 'al-Tûsî mathematical couple', a geometrical tool which transforms circular movements into linear ones. This theorem can be considered as complementary to a theorem of Proclus that transforms linear movements into circular ones.

In *De revolutionibus*, Copernicus uses al-Tûsî's theorem in the theory of Mercury's motion.[5] The Polish astronomer, who could read Greek, probably found this information during his stay in Italy, in the manuscript Vaticanus graecus 211.[6] More generally, Persian astronomy of the school of Maragha became known in Europe after the fifteenth century through the above-mentioned Greek translations, as the Greek language became accessible to scholars during the Renaissance, and many Byzantine manuscripts were exported to Italy at the time of the fall of Byzantium.[7]

---

[2] Pingree (1985–6). See also Mercier (1988).

[3] Unpublished, Vatican Library, Vat. gr. 1058 and Vat. gr. 211, Laur. gr. 28/17.

[4] Paschos and Sotiroudis (1998). The authors argue that Chioniades has not only transmitted *Tadkhira* knowledge but has also modified and improved that knowledge (Mercury theory without the equant but with an elliptical trajectory for the epicycle centre).

[5] Remarked by Hartner (1971), 616.

[6] The first to note this was Neugebauer (1975), 1035. Cf. Swerdlow and Neugebauer (1984), vol. I, 47–8 and vol. II, 567–8. Nevertheless, Copernicus never mentions al-Tûsî, while he does mention Proclus. Some historians have concluded that he was inspired by Proclus' complementary theorem and rediscovered the same theorem as al-Tûsî.

[7] Note that as far as that period is concerned, a bibliography exists studying the sources of the Greek translations. Some of the Greek texts have been edited with extensive commentaries, mainly in the series of the 'Corpus des astronomes byzantins' (Université de Louvain-la-Neuve), directed by Anne Tihon. But there is still a lot to do in that field, as the main text, that of Chrysokokkes, remains unedited.

The second group of scientific translations into Greek during the last Byzantine period is the work of Karaites – Jewish fundamentalists who rejected the rabbinical tradition – in the south of France. During the thirteenth and fourteenth centuries, in Provence and Languedoc, the Karaites, these 'Protestant Jews', were known as the scientists of the diaspora. The Karaite astronomers and mathematicians were influenced by the Arabs and they made an important contribution to the spread of science in Europe. The Karaite community of Provence was in permanent contact with the Karaite communities all around the Mediterranean, among them those of Salonika and Constantinople. The Karaites were translators from and to various languages, such as Hebrew, Latin, Arabic and Greek. At the end of the fifteenth century, one of the most important Karaite scholars, Kaleb Afentopoulo (Elijah), who wrote mathematical and astronomical books, was living in Constantinople.

The mathematician Immanuel ben Jacob Bonfils de Tarascon wrote many books and one of them was the *Kanfe nesharim* (Eagle Wings), known as *Sepher shesh kenafayim* (Book of Six Wings) because of the division of the astronomical tables in six groups, in reference to Isaiah. These tables were a European success, due to which Bonfils was nicknamed 'master of the wings' (*Ba'al kenafayim*). His book comprises an introduction commenting on the tables and was written in Hebrew about 1365 (some manuscripts extended the tables until 1490). The book was translated into Latin in 1406 by Johannes Lucae e Camerino and was used by Pico della Mirandola. It was later translated into Greek and also, under the title *Shestokryl* (Six Wings) into Russian. The Greek translation was made by Michael Chrysokokkes in 1435. This translated text spread widely in the Greek world, and more than a century later, in 1574, Damaskinos Stoudites, Bishop of Lepanto and Arta, updated the translated tables.[8]

The translation of this text into Greek was probably due to the network of the Karaite communities, and the contacts between the Balkans and the south of France via these communities. We know many commentaries on Bonfils's *Kanfe nesharim*, written by Karaites and explaining how to adapt the tables (originally calculated for the latitude of Tarascon, 33.30°) to the latitude of Constantinople and the Crimea.

How did Michael Chrysokokkes find and translate that text? It has been suggested that he collaborated with Ioannes Kavoutzes at Phocea.[9] In any case, information on Michael Chrysokokkes is scarce. We know that he

---

[8] Παρέκτασις των ιθ΄ετηρίδων Μιχαήλ του Χρυσοκόκκου, Library of the Annex of the Patriarchate of Jerusalem in Constantinople, MS 317.

[9] Diller (1972).

was *notarios* of 'the Great Church', in other words the Patriarchate of Constantinople, during the second quarter of the fifteenth century. It has been suggested that he is the same person as Manuel Chrysokokkes, deacon and *Megas sakelarios* of the Patriarchate who was present at the Council of Ferrara and signed the Union of the Churches.[10] In that case, he became deacon after 1435 and then changed his name to Manuel.

The *Wings* had an important diffusion during the Byzantine and post-Byzantine period. At least fifteen manuscripts have survived, together with commentaries and additions such as those of Damaskinos Stoudites. It has been demonstrated that the main object of the *Wings* was the computing of the solar and lunar eclipses; this computing had been a real fashion among Byzantine scholars of the fourteenth and fifteenth centuries, which could explain the success of Bonfils's tables.[11]

Jacob ben David Yom-tob, or Bong'oron or Bonjorn or Yom Tov Poel (there are still other versions of his name), was astronomer to King Pedro IV of Aragon, 'the Ceremonious' (reigned 1336–87). His father was a maker of instruments in Perpignan; his son, an astronomer too, converted to Christianity at the end of the fourteenth century. Jacob ben David's astronomical tables for use at the latitude of Perpignan and beginning at the year 1361, aim in particular, like those of Bonfils, at the computing of solar and lunar eclipses. Written in Hebrew, they were translated into Latin and Catalan, became popular and were used or commented on by later astronomers such as Abraham Zacuto of Salamanca.

The Greek translation of Yom-tob's tables was due to the contacts made at the time of the Union of the Churches. Marcos Eugenikos (c. 1394–1445), Bishop of Ephesus, was sent to Italy to participate in the discussions. He was the Orthodox representative who refused to sign the decree of the Union in 1439. In Italy, he found the Latin version of the Jewish text of Yom-tob and translated and adapted it into Greek.

The third group of translations comes from the regions ruled by the descendants of the Crusaders and they date from the fourteenth century. These translations came from the Iberian astronomical tradition, where Arabs and Europeans met. They did not have any significant influence and do not appear in many manuscripts afterwards.

To mention them in brief: there were the *Toledan Tables*, of Arabian provenance, adapted from Latin; some Latin treatises on the astrolabe based on Arab sources (the treatises of Messahalla and Maslama); and finally the famous *Alphonsine Tables*, ordered by Alfonso X, 'the Wise', the future King

---

[10] Lampsides (1937), 313.   [11] Solon (1968). See also Solon (1970), with bibliography.

of Castile and Leon (calculated for 30 May 1252), which were a great European success for more than two centuries. All these texts were translated and adapted into Greek c. 1340 by the Cypriot nobleman George Lapithe and his circle. The *Alphonsine Tables* circulated in Constantinople at the beginning of the fifteenth century, adapted for this city by Demetrius Chrysoloras (c. 1360–1416), a high official who was a partisan of the anti-Unionists.

THE GREEK COMMUNITIES OF THE OTTOMAN EMPIRE

The influence on European science of the Byzantine scientific manuscripts brought to Western Europe a few years before, during and after the fall of Byzantium, has already been pointed out by historians. Many European editions of ancient Greek scientific texts published in the fifteenth, sixteenth and seventeenth centuries were based on the corpus of scientific manuscripts belonging to Cardinal Bessarion and other Greek scholars who fled to the West. It is the complementary opposite trend that will be discussed here: the translations into Greek of contemporary scientific texts, mainly written in Latin languages.

During the sixteenth and seventeenth centuries, an important Greek community flourished in Venice and at the end of the sixteenth century it established a Greek College in order to prepare Greek students to enter the University of Padua. In 1623 a similar college was established in Padua itself. As for Rome, a College for Greek Catholics had been founded in the sixteenth century.

The fact that the Ottoman Empire did not have a higher education system – apart from the *medrese*s or mosque schools (discussed below, p. 193) – encouraged Greeks in the Ottoman Empire to study abroad during the sixteenth and seventeenth centuries. Padua was the favourite university for these visiting students, some of whom would go on to teach science in the colleges of the Greek communities of the Ottoman Empire. The manuals they wrote for use in their teaching were mainly compilations based on books they read during their studies in Padua.

The sources of translations and compilations in Greek in the sixteenth and seventeenth centuries have not yet been determined. The situation is very different from both the Byzantine period and the eighteenth century, when many Greek books on science, including translations, were printed: for that period too, the majority of the sources are well known.[12]

---

[12] A bibliography of history of science of the post-Byzantine period (about 2,000 titles) of Greek authors is available on-line at the web address: http://www.eie.gr/institutes/kne/ife/index.htm

During the sixteenth and seventeenth centuries, there are few translations of entire books, and these translations date mainly from the end of the seventeenth century. Anastasios Papavasilopoulos, a priest-teacher from Janenna, wrote two manuscript treatises at the end of the seventeenth century: an 'Introduction to Mathematics'[13] and a 'Physical Philosophy',[14] both of them translated from Latin. The sources of these two translations have not yet been discovered.

The books are school manuals of arithmetic, geometry and physics (from 'modern and ancient sources') to be taught to his pupils at the town of Tyrnavo, in Thessaly. The 'Introduction to Mathematics' was translated in 1695; it is a second level (for that period) educational book presenting definitions of geometrical figures, basic arithmetic and calculation of surfaces and volumes. The 'Physical Philosophy' was translated in 1701 and presents a knowledge of natural philosophy at the same level as it would have been taught at the colleges preparing for entrance to the University of Padua.

The first printed book which can be considered as a translation is a book on practical mathematics, in other words arithmetic for merchants and also pupils at what might be called a primary level of education. This book was printed in Venice in 1568, and republished nineteen times until as late as 1818! The author, Emanuel Glyzounis (1530–96), came from the island of Chios, went to Italy to study and settled in Venice, where he became a printer. His *Practical Arithmetic* is a translation from one or many Italian books called *Abacci*, very common at those times. These were books presenting basic arithmetic (addition, subtraction, multiplication and division) and also methods for solving problems with one unknown number. Glyzounis added a method to calculate the date of Easter, as the book was addressed to Orthodox Greeks. This book was the most popular book for practical arithmetic in the Balkans until the nineteenth century; it was even translated into Romanian in 1793.[15]

---

[13] Εισαγωγη μαθηματικης εκ της των Λατινων φωνης μεταχετεσθεῖσα ... (Introduction to Mathematics Translated from Latin ...), National Library of Greece, MS 2139, eighteenth century, fols. 38a–66a. Karas (1992) has found six manuscripts of this text, all from the eighteenth century.

[14] Εγχειρίδιον της αναζησασης φυσικης φιλοσοφιας ... (Manual of Physical Philosophy Revived ...), National Library of Greece, MS 1331, fols. 1a–98a. Karas (1992) has found two manuscripts of this text, both dated 1701 (the year of composition).

[15] Βιβλιον προχειρον τοις πασι περιεχον την τε πρακτικην αριθμητικην ... (Book Easy for Everyone, Comprising Practical Arithmetic ...), Venice, 1569. All editions until 1818 were published in Venice. On the history and the contents of this book, Kastanis (1998), 31–58; Kastanis (2004), chapter 2.

We know at least two other Italian *Abacci* which were anonymously translated by the eighteenth century. These translations have never been printed and were overshadowed by the success of Glyzounis's book.[16] Between Glyzounis, who translated a practical arithmetical book for everyday life from Italian in the middle of the sixteenth century, and Papavasilopoulos, who translated secondary-level books for teaching from Latin at the end of the seventeenth century, education was reorganized in the Greek communities of the Ottoman Empire. Indeed, after the fall of Byzantium, where there was a three-level system of education, some Greek communities in the Ottoman Empire gradually organized a local two-level system: *hiera grammata* (mainly reading, using ecclesiastical texts) and in some communities a 'college' where secondary education was provided, often by Greeks who had studied in Padua. Until the beginning of the seventeenth century, it was rare for science to be taught in these schools.

In 1620, however, Cyril Lukaris became Patriarch of Constantinople. He was the first patriarch to have studied in Italy. Lukaris asked his friend Theophylos Corydaleus, who had also been a student in Italy, to head the Patriarchal School of Constantinople. Corydaleus, who had studied theology, philosophy and medicine in Padua, introduced science teaching in the Patriarchal School and continued that teaching after he settled in Athens in 1640. His teaching of Aristotelian physics (following the course at the University of Padua) had a great influence all over the Balkans until the introduction of the new natural philosophy in the middle of the eighteenth century. Corydaleus had studied physics with Cesare Cremonini, the well-known Aristotelian scholar (he copied some of Cremonini's books while he was a student in Padua). The two main manuscripts written by Corydaleus, 'Geography' (1626) and 'Aristotle's Physics' (1634), are not literal translations from Italian books, but they are strongly influenced by the books Corydaleus had seen, possessed or copied in Padua. 'Aristotle's Physics' became one of the most widely used books of physics in the Balkans: more than 143 manuscripts still exist and a printed version was published in Venice in 1779.

Along with Corydaleus, a number of scholars constituted a seventeenth-century Greek 'School of Padua', teaching philosophy and Aristotelian science to Greek communities: Georgios Korressios (1570–1660), Nikolaos (Nicephorus) Klarontzanos (d. 1645), Meletios Syrigos (1586–1664),

---

[16] See Karas (1992), vol. I, 157 and *infra*: 1) National Library of Greece MS 1107, sixteenth century, fols. 42a–76b; 2) Vaticanus graecus, MS 1699, seventeenth century.

Nikolaos Koursoulas (1602–52), Nikolaos Kerameus (d. 1663), Gerasimos Vlahos (1605/7–85), Mathaios (Meletios) Typaldos (1648–1713) and Georgios Sougdouris (1645/7–1725).[17] Gerasimos Vlahos wrote a book in 1661 for his teaching at the Greek College in Venice, entitled 'Harmonia definitive entium'[18] and based on various Italian and Greek sources. This consists of a sort of lexicon written in two languages, Latin and ancient Greek, with definitions for material and non-material beings by ancient and sometimes by Byzantine authors.

In 1680, Ioannis Skylitzes wrote an 'Introduction to the Cosmographical Sciences'.[19] In this manuscript the Copernican system was for the first time presented at length in the Greek language. As yet we know neither the sources Skylitzes used nor those of the 'Epitome of Astronomy' of Meletios Mitros, Bishop of Athens, written in 1700 (or a few years before that date).[20] In the first part of his book, Skylitzes discusses the constellations of both hemispheres, and presents elements of geometrical cosmology (divisions of the cosmological sphere), of the diurnal motion of the earth and of the equinoxes and the methods for determining latitude at sea. In the second part he presents the planets and the three theories of the system of the universe: the geocentric ('that of Pythagoreans'), the Copernican and the Tychonian. He gives some information about the size and motion of the sun, about the size of the solar sphere (the 'solar heaven') and about the calendar based on the sun's movements. Most probably this book was based on a number of sources; many such 'cosmography' books existed in Europe in those days.

The book of Meletios Mitros is much more important (320 manuscript pages). It may be considered as a simplified manual of astronomy in which the reader finds an extensive introduction to geometrical cosmology, a method for computing tables for the movements of the planets, the size,

---

[17] Petsios (2004).

[18] The Greek title is Αρμονια οριστικη των οντων, MS, collection of the Institute of Byzantine and post-Byzantine Studies in Venice. A small description is given in Tatakis (1973).

[19] Εισαγωγη εις τας κοσμογραφικας επιστημας και τεχνας (Introduction to the Cosmological Sciences and Arts . . .), Patriarchal Library of Jerusalem, MS 267, fols. 9b–47a. Karas (1992) has found ten manuscripts of that text: two of the seventeenth century (one dated 1680) and the others of the eighteenth.

[20] Βιβλιον αστρονομικον, και περιεκτικον, αμα τε και αποδεικτικον, των τε παλαιων και νεων (ων εφευρων) απο Αδαμ μεχρι πτολεμαιου και κοπερνικου . . . (Astronomical Book Comprising and Sometimes Demonstrating from Ancients and Moderns (Those Having Made Discoveries) from Adam to Ptolemy and Copernicus; making clear from when and from whom we have been taught science and wisdom of that astronomical art). Library of the Annex of the Patriarchate of Jerusalem in Constantinople, MS 420 (20 folios + 320 pages). Karas (1992) has found nine manuscripts of that text, all of the eighteenth century.

distance and movements of the sun, the moon and the five 'minor planets', and an extensive presentation of the constellations including those 'unknown to the Ancients'. Meletios Mitros presents in nine pages the three main theories of the cosmological system (Ptolemaic, Copernican and Tychonic). The remark about the sources of Skylitzes is valid for Mitros as well.

One of the rare translations is that of some Ottoman astronomical texts by Chrysanthos Notaras (d. 1731), who had his secondary education in Constantinople before leaving to study in Padua in 1697 and in Paris in 1700. In 1680, before his travels, he translated three astronomical texts from Arabic. In fact they were texts of Ottoman astronomy, descriptions of problems solved by the astrolabe quadrant, a popular astrolabe among the Turks.[21] The first text, titled 'Explanation and Description of the Quarter of the Sphere, Called in Arabic *rup-dagire*', consists of the description of the astrolabe quadrant (or 'Profatius quadrant' after the Jewish astronomer otherwise known as Jacob ben Madir ibn Tibbon, who first described it in Europe).

The second text, entitled 'Explanation of the Instrument Called *tjeip*', describes an analogue astrolabe drawn for all latitudes (the *rup-dagire* is conceived for a particular latitude). This second instrument is more versatile but less precise. The third text, titled 'Astrolabe Problems', presents the solution of classic problems such as determining the hour of sunset, the direction of the sunset, the time during the night, latitude, longitude, cardinal points, the hours of the rising and setting of the moon, the horoscope, the direction of Mecca and so on. To solve these problems some tables are needed, not indicated in the text. Chrysanthos adds a method for the multiplication of degrees, another for drawing up a horoscope and an Arabic–Greek glossary of terms relating to the astrolabe. This kind of scientific translation, from Arabic or Ottoman Turkish into Greek, is unique.

Although they were subjects of the Ottoman Empire, the Greeks had a separate educational system. The patriarch was responsible for the education of the Orthodox Christians, and schools were organized by the Greek communities themselves. Contacts with Ottoman science were therefore much less important than contacts with Italian science, as a consequence of the network of Greek communities and the belief that science had been transmitted to Europe by the ancient Greeks.

---

[21] Tsakoumis (1990).

Chrysanthos Notaras played an active role in a high school founded to provide translators for the Russian Empire. This school, called the 'Slavo-Hellenic-Latin Academy', was founded in Moscow in 1686 and financed by Prince Galitzin and the Greek Meletios Domestikos (below, p. 215). This Academy was the first Russian high-level educational institution. The first professors, the brothers Ioannikios and Sofronios Leichoudis, were sent from Padua by Dositheos Notaras, Patriarch of Jerusalem and the uncle of Chrysanthos. Chrysanthos was sent by his uncle to Moscow in 1692 in order to contact the tsar and also to supervise the teaching of the Leichoudis brothers at the Academy, as Dositheos considered this teaching too pro-Latin.

At this time, Chrysanthos copied – but did not translate – a very rare manuscript on astronomy and mechanics sent by the head of the Jesuit mission in China, Ferdinand Verbiest, to Tsar Alexei Mikhailovich.[22] This was the first important contact of Chrysanthos with the new European science, as Verbiest presented the achievements of science and technology to the tsar in order to introduce the Jesuit missions as useful in the modernization of the country. Following that contact, Chrysanthos would visit Paris, stay a few days at the Observatory with Jean Dominique Cassini, and write a book based on French sources, the *Introduction to Geography and Spheres*. This book was printed in Paris in 1716, after the author had succeeded his uncle as Patriarch of Jerusalem.[23]

To end the presentation of the translations of that period, we have also to mention two medical books. The first, written by Gerasimos Vlahos (one of the most important teachers in the Greek College in Venice), is strangely enough a translation of Hippocrates from Latin into Modern Greek. It should be noted that after the fall of the Byzantine Empire and the flight to Western Europe of Byzantine scholars with a large number of scientific manuscripts, the rediscovery of ancient Greek science by modern Greek scholars was often the result of their stay in Padua. Hence it was not unusual for a Greek text to be read in Latin by some of these scholars.[24] The second treatise, written at the end of the seventeenth century by the doctor Nicolaos Agrafiotis, is a book of medicaments translated from an unknown Italian source.[25]

---

[22] Nicolaïdis (1995).   [23] Nicolaïdis (2003).

[24] Not one manuscript of this translation is known. The information on Vlahos's translation is given in a manuscript medical dictionary written by Alexander Konstantinou Oikonomou in 1812: Karas (1992), vol. III, 41 and 78.

[25] Αντιδοταριον εξηγημενον από την ιταλικην γλωσσαν ... (Book of Antidotes Translated from Italian ...), Library of the Monastery of Sina, MS 1848. Karas (1992) has found five manuscripts of that text, four from the eighteenth century.

To conclude: so far as this second period, 1500–1700, is concerned, some translations from Italian scientific works appeared in Greek communities in the Ottoman and Venetian Empires, mainly in manuscript form. These translations were the product of Greeks who had studied at the University of Padua. The books were mainly textbooks; in the Greek communities of this time, the history of science is difficult to separate from the history of education. The number of these translations was limited, like the number of books on science and the number of scholars in this period. Scientific treatises as well as translations would become an important phenomenon in the Balkans after the middle of the eighteenth century, when the 'new science' would be introduced into the Greek Colleges, after the reform of the University of Padua in 1739 by Giovanni Poleni.[26]

During the first half of the fifteenth century, when Byzantium still existed as a weak but organized state with a group of noble scholars, translations into Greek aimed at introducing unknown knowledge to that milieu. Scholars debated whether Persian or Western European astronomy could describe the motion of the heavens with greater accuracy. Greek was the language in which Eastern and Western science met, Byzantium was still a cultural crossroads and science spread from Persia to Europe via Byzantine translations.

During the Ottoman period a scholarly milieu participating in the development of science did not exist any longer in the Greek communities. There were scholars who taught science in these communities and this teaching became a symbol of a long-desired revival of Hellenism. Looking back to the glorious past of Greece, these scholars sought ancient Greek science and discovered the new science in Italy. Translations of that period aimed at spreading the knowledge of ancient Greek science as it was taught in Italy and at the same time to make known new scientific developments. Greek scholars did not participate any longer in the making of science but only in the spread of European science towards the 'scientific periphery'. More than anything else, science teaching would integrate the Greek communities into European culture in the eighteenth century.

---

[26] A concise article on the reform: Talas (2004).

Ottoman encounters with European science: sixteenth- and seventeenth-century translations into Turkish

Feza Günergun

A scholarly community seems to have gradually emerged in Anatolia as Turkomans settled in the region from the eleventh century onwards. The *medrese*s, the schools (mainly teaching Islamic theology and Muslim juris-prudence) established between the twelfth and fourteenth centuries by the Seljuks, introduced Islamic religious and scientific culture to the Anatolian towns. These educational institutions created on the model of the *Nizamiye medrese*s, named after their founder the Seljuk vizier Nizamulmulk (reigned 1063–92), were widespread in the eastern part of the Islamic world.

The rulers of the Turkish principalities that surfaced after the Seljuk state weakened and collapsed carried on the tradition of founding *medrese*s where Islamic scientific culture flourished. The Ottoman state that emerged at the turn of the fourteenth century was one of these principal-ities and it welcomed and championed Islamic scientific culture until the nineteenth century, when science and technical knowledge transferred from Western Europe were finally taught in Ottoman educational institu-tions. Translations played a significant role not only in the introduction of the Islamic scientific knowledge that had developed between the ninth and fourteenth centuries, but also in transmitting science from Western Europe.

Ottoman scholarly life would thus evolve under the influence of two distinct cultures. While Islamic scientific culture dominated up to the end of the eighteenth century, Western European scientific and technical knowl-edge penetrated Ottoman space through translations and other means from the sixteenth century onwards. The new knowledge from the West gradually became established in the nineteenth century when Ottoman administrators undertook the modernization of the army and governmental institutions on the European model and founded modern educational institutions teaching European scientific and technical knowledge.

The principal Ottoman institutions where Islamic scientific culture flourished were the *medrese*s. Created by wealthy individuals as pious foundations, Ottoman *medrese*s taught Muslim jurisprudence together with Arabic, logic, the interpretation of the Quran, *hadith* (the sayings of the Prophet Muhammad), theology, Sufism and the mathematical sciences, including arithmetic, astronomy and occasionally physics. Although the curriculum of all *medrese*s did not include mathematical sciences, scholars from these institutions contributed to commenting on and propagating Islamic scientific texts within the Ottoman Empire.

Scholars who came from Baghdad, Cairo, Damascus, Herat, Samarkand and Tabriz to teach in Ottoman *medrese*s brought along not only their knowledge but also Islamic scientific texts. These scholars came to the Ottoman lands to seek patronage and earn their living or they were invited by Ottoman rulers. The mathematician and astronomer Ali Qushji (d. 1474) came from Samarkand to teach in Istanbul on the invitation of Sultan Mehmed II (reigned 1451–81).

During the socio-economic unrest following the death of Ulugh Beg in 1449, a large number of Iranian scholars as well as scholars from Khorasan and Transoxiana emigrated to Anatolia, seeking refuge in Ottoman lands. They obtained positions as advisers or physicians to the Ottoman sultans or as judges or teachers in *medrese*s. Young *medrese* graduates wishing to improve their knowledge often left Anatolia to join the entourage of famous scholars living in the above-mentioned centres.

SCIENTIFIC TEXTS IN ARABIC AND THEIR TURKISH TRANSLATIONS

The teaching language in the Anatolian *medrese*s was Arabic, the language of science in the Islamic world. For this reason, the works of many Islamic mathematicians and astronomers such as al-Cagmînî (d. 1221), Nasîr al-Dîn al-Tûsî (d. 1274), al-Samarkandî (fl. c. 1284), Ali Qushji (d. 1474) and Kadizâde-i Rumî (d. 1412) were mostly studied directly in Arabic. Their commentaries and the new works compiled after them were also written in Arabic. Turkish and Persian were also used in the compilation of scientific texts but to a lesser extent. Although Arabic was omnipresent in *medrese* teaching until the nineteenth century, Arabic and Persian scientific texts were rendered into Turkish, the spoken language of Anatolia and the administrative language of the Ottoman state, from the fourteenth century onwards.

In pharmacology, Ibn Beithar's (d. 1248) *Kitâbu'l-câmî' müfredâti'l-edviye* (*Materia medica*) was among the earliest works translated into Turkish. The translation, *Tercümetü'l-müfredât*, soon became popular. About thirty-five copies of various translations made in the following centuries are kept in several libraries in Turkey together with the thirty copies of Ibn Beithar's original work in Arabic.[1]

The fifteenth-century Turkish physician Celalüddin Hizir (known as Haci Pasha, d. 1413), who wrote most of his medical books in Arabic, compiled *Müntahab üs-sifa* (Selection of Medical Knowledge) in Turkish aiming to introduce his medical knowledge to a wider readership.[2] Muhammed b. Mahmûd-i Sirvânî, a physican from Shirvan, who practised in Anatolia in the first half of the fifteenth century, wrote in Arabic two books on health care and pharmaceutical products (ointments, oils, pills, powders, perfumes): the *Yakûbiyye* (Formulary of Yakub) and *Ravzatü'l-itr* (The Garden of Fragrances). Moreover, he made translations from Arabic into Turkish as well. He first translated his own medical book *Ilyâsiyye* from Arabic into Turkish, upon the order of Seljukid beg Ilyas to whom the original copy in Arabic had been dedicated.

According to his own account, Mahmûd-i Sirvânî learned about the properties of stones while practising medicine in Anatolia, and planned to write a book with the aim of protecting Muslims from counterfeiters. Thus in 1427 he translated the *Cevâhirnâme* (Book of Precious Stones) by the Islamic physician and mineralogist Ahmad ibn Yusuf al-Tifashi (d. 1253) upon the order of Umur Beg (d. 1461), a Turkish military chief. Mahmûd-i Sirvânî's other two books seem to have been originally written in Turkish: the *Sultâniyye* (The Sultan's Codex) on health care (presented to Ottoman Sultan Celebi Mehmed, reigned 1421–31) and the *Mürsid* (The Guide), a comprehensive work on eye diseases.[3] These few examples illustrate both the concurrent use of Arabic and Turkish among scholars and the patronage of scientific works by fifteenth-century Anatolian princes.

In surgical practice, a translation made by Sabuncuoglu Sherefeddin (b. 1385), from the *darüssifa* (hospital) in Amasya, a town in Asia Minor, is worthy of mention because it exemplifies the transmission of surgical techniques from the seventh to the fifteenth century through successive translations made in various languages. Given the title *Cerrâhiyet'ül-Hâniyye*

---

[1] A copy of this earliest anonymous translation is to be found in Istanbul University Library. Süleymaniye Library (Istanbul) contains a good number of copies of both the Arabic original work as well as copies of its translations: Sesen (1984).

[2] A copy is recorded in the Bibliothèque Nationale, Paris (Man. Turcs A. F. 170).

[3] Mahmûd-i Sirvânî (2004).

(Surgery for the Khans), it must be a Turkish translation of *al-Tasrîf* (The Collection), the renowned surgery book in Arabic by Abul Qasim al-Zahravi (936–1013). Parts of the latter were borrowed from the *Epitome* (Synopsis of Medicine in Seven Books) by the seventh-century Byzantine Greek physician Paulos Aeginata.

In astronomy, only a few translations were made into Turkish between the fourteenth and sixteenth centuries. This suggests that translating astronomy books from Arabic were not deemed necessary since these could be directly consulted by Ottoman scholars. A few books on time-keeping were translated from Arabic into Turkish for the use of *medrese* students less knowledgeable in Arabic than their masters.

The Persian treatise dealing with astrology and calendar-making by Nasîr al-Dîn al-Tûsî, the leading astronomer of the Maragha Observatory, was turned into Turkish twice, at the end of the fourteenth and the beginning of the fifteenth century. Known as *Sî fasl der marifet-i takvim* (The Thirty Chapters of Calendar Making), it must have been frequently used by Ottoman astronomers since more than twenty-five copies ranging from the fourteenth to the eighteenth century remain in libraries in Turkey. In the mid-sixteenth century, the Ottoman admiral Seydî Ali Reis (d. 1563) translated Ali Qushji's (d. 1474) astronomy book *er-Risaletü'l-fethiyye fi'l-hey'e* (Astronomical Treatise Glorifying the Triumph)[4] from Arabic into Turkish. The abridged translation containing additional information from other astronomy books was entitled *Hulâsatu'l-hey'e* (A Brief Account of Astronomy). Although the number of Turkish translations grew in number regularly in the following centuries, most of the books on astronomy and mathematics were still written in Arabic until the eighteenth century.

In the field of veterinary medicine, treatises on the ailments of horses (*baytarname*s) were translated from Arabic into Turkish from the sixteenth century, if not earlier. A standard sixteenth-century *baytarname* enumerated the properties of horses (characters, coat colours, how to detect the horse's age) and described their organs, breeding, training, diseases and therapy. Thus early Ottoman *baytarname*s usually combined information on hippology and hippiatry, while those of the seventeenth and eighteenth centuries merely dealt with equestrian diseases and their cure. Information on animals other than horses, such as camels, cattle and sheep, was occasionally given.

---

[4] Ali Qushji presented the treatise to Sultan Mehmed II (the Conqueror) following his victory against the Akkoyunlu state in 1473 in Otlukbeli, eastern Anatolia.

Books compiled by the *baitar*s (farriers or veterinarians) of the Abbasid and Mamluk courts were held in esteem by the Ottomans in the sixteenth century. The *Kitâb al-hail wal-baitara* (Book on Horses and Hippiatry) of Muhammed bin Ya'kûb b. Ahi Huzzâm al-Huttalî (d. 865), veterinarian at the Abbasid court, was translated into Turkish in the early sixteenth century. A copy of the anonymous and untitled Turkish translation is dated 1536. Nearly thirty years later, in 1562, the *Kâmil al-sinâ'atayn al baytara* (The Perfect Book on the Two Veterinary Arts) of Abu Bakr bin al-Badr bin al-Mundir Badr ad-Din al-Baitar, veterinarian at the court of the Mamluk Sultan al-Nasir Muhammad Ibn Qalawun (reigned 1293–1340), was turned into Turkish by Hüseyin bin Abdullah. Another Turkish translation made over a century later, in 1679, by Muhammed b. Cerkes indicates its ongoing influence.

The *Kitâb-i makbûl der hâl-i huyûl* (The Esteemed Book on the Various Conditions of Horses), compiled in Turkish by Sheikh Mehmed bin Mustafa (d. 1635), seems to be a popular seventeenth-century *baytarname*, since nearly twenty copies are currently extant. Known as Kadizâde, the author related that he was involved with the science of horsemanship since his childhood and had perused a number of *baytarname*s. Having heard that Sultan Osman II (reigned 1617–21) was a matchless horseman, he composed the *Kitâb-i makbûl* as an offering to the sultan. Kadizâde probably drew on Arabic, Turkish or Persian *baytarname*s since no European work on horses is known to have been translated until the second half of the nineteenth century, after the opening of veterinary classes in 1849 in the Military School in Istanbul. The fact that Tayyarzade Mehmed Ataullah (d. 1879), an accountant in the Ottoman army and the author of a five-volume work on the Ottoman Empire (*Tarih-i ata*, 1876), translated a *baytarname* from Arabic shows how devotion to classical Islamic literature on hippiatrics survived.

SIXTEENTH CENTURY: SEAMEN AND PHYSICIANS CONVEY EUROPEAN CARTOGRAPHICAL AND MEDICAL KNOWLEDGE

Ottoman works based on West European sources began to appear from the sixteenth century onwards, although the introduction of knowledge from Western Europe did not mean the abandonment of Islamic scientific culture, which continued to dominate, especially in the *medrese*s, until the nineteenth century. The expansionist policy of the sixteenth century led to the widespread use of western Mediterranean marine cartography by Ottoman seafarers, while the coming of Jewish physicians enabled the Ottomans to encounter the European medical practices of the Renaissance. However, the spread of knowledge took place not only through translations but also via direct contact between Ottoman and Western seamen and physicians. The campaigns launched in the Mediterranean by Pîrî Reis (1470–1554), the commander of the Ottoman fleet, and his contacts with Italian and Catalan sailors led him to compile a world map of which we only have a fragment depicting the shores of north-west Africa, the Iberian Peninsula and the eastern shores of Central and South America. This fragment is now called Pîrî Reis's Atlantic Ocean Chart (1513). A note in the south-west corner of the map explains that he used nearly twenty large maps, among them one Alexandrian, eight Arab, four Portuguese, one Indo-Chinese and one Chinese together with a map drawn by Columbus.

Pîrî Reis's second chart, the North Atlantic Chart (1528), which is also believed to be a fragment of a larger world map, depicts the southern tip of Greenland and the eastern shores of Newfoundland, the shores of Florida, some of the Caribbean Islands including the Antilles, Cuba and Haiti and the northern shores of South America.

Pîrî Reis's *Kitab-i bahriye* (Book on Navigation) together with his two fragmentary portolan charts partially depicting the Atlantic Ocean, are good examples of the circulation of cartographical and nautical information in the Mediterranean region in the early sixteenth century.[5] However, the exchange of information must have started earlier. *Kitab-i bahriye*, a portolan atlas, also bears the characteristics of the *isolario* genre in which the subject matter was divided into chapters including maps, and the historical aspects of places are emphasized. Both the draft (1521) and the revised version (1526) of *Kitab-i bahriye* are in Turkish. While giving full account of the Mediterranean shores, seaports and anchorages, it offers technical information that seamen would need when sailing in the Mediterranean. In short, it is a guide for mariners.

The 1526 version is written in both prose and verse, and includes ninety-two portolan charts. In the introductory part (972 couplets) Pîrî Reis describes the tides, the magnetic compass, the winds and the seven seas, discusses how portolan charts should be used and gives additional instructions and advice to seamen. In the following couplets he narrates the discovery of the Antilles by Christopher Columbus:

Nâm ile Antilye dinür bil ana	They call that country Antilye
Dinler isen dahîsinin diyem sana	If you will listen, I will tell you of it
Hem nice bulundu isit ol diyar	Hear also how that land was discovered
Serh edeyim tâ kim ola âsikâr	Let me explain so that it will be clear

---

[5] Forty-two copies of *Kitab-i bahriye* are extant in world libraries. Some copies are without charts, others include up to 200; Ozen, *Piri Reis and his Charts* (1998), 20–2.

Ceneviz'de bir müneccim var imis *Nâm ile Kolon ana dirler imis*	In Genoa there was an astrologer whose name was Columbus
Anun eline girer bir hos kitâb *Kalmis Iskender'den ol da irtiyâb*	A curious book came into his possession that without doubt was from the time of Alexander
Cümle deryâ ilmini bir bir tamâm *Cem' idüb yazmislar imis iy hümâm*	In that book they had collected and written down all that was known about navigation
Ol kitâb gelmis bu Efrenc iline *Bilmemisler lîkin anun hâline*	The book ultimately reached the land of the Franks but they knew not what was in it
Bulur okur bu Kolon ani iy yâr *Varur Ispanya begine ani sunar*	Columbus found this book and read it whereupon he took it to the King of Spain
Takrîr ider cümle ahvâli ana *Ol dahi gemi virür sonra buna*	And when he told the king all that was written therein the king gave him ships
Ol kitâb ile amel ider iy yâr *Varub Antilye'yi ider asikâr*	Good friend, employing that book Columbus sailed and reached the Antilles
Dahî sonra durmaz açar ol ili *Simdi meshûr eylemisdür ol yolu*	After that he ceased not but explored those lands Thus the route has become known to all
Hartisi tâkim anun geldi bize *Isbudur hal kim didim cümle size*	His map too reached us. That is the situation and I have told it all to you
Lîkin bunda bir mahal geldi bana *Bu da tezkîre ola girü ana*	We have now come to point at which I must summarize the rest

Pîrî Reis's works dominate this period, but three other atlases of portolan charts of the standard Mediterranean type have survived: the *Atlas* of Ali Macar Reis (Topkapi Palace Library); the anonymous *Atlas-i humayûn* (Imperial Atlas) preserved in the Archaeological Museum in Istanbul; and the *Deniz atlasi* (Sea Atlas) in the Walters Art Gallery in Baltimore. They all belong to the second half of the sixteenth century, and, together with the more refined copies of the *Kitab-i bahriye*, they reflect the vogue that this genre must have enjoyed among the more sophisticated Ottomans. The plainer, functional marine charts or atlases that no doubt existed have not survived except for such isolated examples as the Aegean sea-chart of Mehmed Reis ibn Menemenli.

Renaissance medical knowledge was mainly brought to the Ottoman Empire in the sixteenth century by Jewish physicians expelled from the Iberian Peninsula by the kings of Spain and Portugal. Some of these physicians had been educated in European universities. During the period, however, the access of Jews to European universities was restricted and even those who were fortunate enough to be admitted to a university were not awarded a degree at the end of their studies. An exception to this situation was the University of Padua, which allowed Jewish students to study and awarded them degrees. The Ottoman sultans allowed them to profess their religion and to treat non-Jewish patients.

One of the most renowned Jewish physicians of the Ottoman court in the early sixteenth century was Moses Hamon (d. 1554), the private physician of Suleiman the Magnificent, also known as 'The Lawgiver' (reigned 1520–66). His father, Joseph Hamon, had emigrated from Spain and entered the court of Sultan Beyazit II (reigned 1481–1512). The medical literature brought by these physicians probably allowed Shemseddin Itaqi to compile his treatise on anatomy, the *Risâle-i tesrih-i ebdân* (Treatise on the Anatomy of the Human Body) at the beginning of the seventeenth century.

Sixteenth-century European travellers to Asia Minor and the Middle East witnessed not only Jewish and Turkish but also Spanish and Italian physicians practising in Ottoman lands. Dispatched by Ferdinand I (1503–64) to Istanbul in 1554 as ambassador to Sultan Suleiman I, the Fleming Ogier Ghislain de Busbecq (1522–92) related in his *Turkish Letters* that before leaving Istanbul in 1562, he had sent a Spanish doctor named Albacare to the island of Lemnos. He had asked the physician to attend the annual ceremony organized for the opening of clay beds:

Before leaving Constantinople, I sent to Lemnos a Spanish physician called Albacare, so that he would be present at the customary ceremony on 6 August, when they open that marvellous earth. I told him to write an exact description of what happened, to inform himself precisely about the spot and if the earth needed care for its power to be preserved: I have no doubt that he will carry out this commission, unless there is some insuperable obstacle, the Turks do not always allow everyone to go there and I would have gone myself long ago if I had been allowed to do so.[6]

According to the French traveller Pierre Belon (1517–64), the small lumps of clay were stamped with the seal of the Ottoman administrator (*subasi*) of the island. They therefore bore the inscription *tin-i mahtum* in Arabic characters, literally meaning 'sealed earth' or *terra sigillata*. Also known as *Terra Lemnia* (from Lemnos), this drug was extremely popular for its various medicinal properties. Owing to its astringent and siccative effects, it was used to prevent haemorrhage, heal wounds and treat ulcers and gonorrhoea. It was also recommended as an antidote to food poisoning because of its emetic qualities.

---

[6] Ogier Ghislain de Busbecq (1581), *Epistolae quatuor* (Antwerp).

On his way back to Vienna in 1562, Busbecq was accompanied by Don Alvaro de Sandé, the Spanish commander who had fought against the Ottomans at the Battle of Djerba (1560). Captured by the Turks, Sandé was released thanks to Busbecq. Sandé had a Spanish physician whom he had 'bought'. The latter was possibly one of the captives brought from Djerba and later sold in Istanbul. Busbecq did not give his name but related the quarrel between this physician and a janissary while looking for accommodation at Tolna, a town south of Buda, in 1562.

In 1553, a year earlier than Busbecq, the sixty-year-old Hans Dernschwam (1494–1586), a Bohemian traveller, had left Vienna for Istanbul in the company of a delegation Ferdinand I sent to Suleiman I. Thanks to his services in the Fugger Company, Dernschwam had made a small fortune and could travel at his own expense together with his 'servant, coach, three horses and a purse full of gold coins'. He noted in his diary that he had seen many Jewish and Italian physicians but omitted to give their names:

> Turks use the prescriptions they inherited from their ancestors as well as those they get from Italian druggists. An Italian physician used to pay frequent visits to our ambassador [Busbecq?]. He knew Latin very well and had assisted several persons.[7]

SEVENTEENTH CENTURY: TRANSLATIONS FROM EUROPEAN CARTOGRAPHERS, ANATOMISTS AND IATROCHEMISTS

Their military campaigns in Central Europe in the seventeenth century gave the Ottomans the opportunity to become acquainted with famous Western scientific works. It is interesting to note, first, that most of the translations or compilations from European books were made into Turkish and not into Arabic, the language of the main scientific institution of the time, the *medrese*. Second, the translations were generally made by professional translators or government officials familiar with European languages.

The reason why *medrese* teachers were little involved in translating European books in the seventeenth century was that European scientific treatises could hardly be used in *medrese*s, given that their primary aim was to teach Islamic religion, Islamic law, the Arabic language and to a lesser extent the mathematical sciences (computing, timekeeping, the use of astrolabes etc.) These subjects were taught on the basis of the abundantly available Islamic mathematical works. Another reason for their lack of involvement was the unfamiliarity of *medrese* scholars with European languages. Their knowledge of Arabic, Persian and Turkish, as well as

---

[7] Hans Dernschwam (1923), *Tagebuch*, ed. Franz Babinger (Munich).

the availability of Islamic textbooks, might have led these scholars to place excessive trust in Islamic authors. Some members of *medrese*s made partial translations, however, or consulted or studied European works with the help of a translator. The latter was either a European with some knowledge of Turkish or a convert to Islam.

A number of seventeenth-century translators of European scientific texts into Turkish were officials (secretaries and translators in service) in the various military and civil offices of the state. They were either born Muslims or converts to Islam. A young clerk (*kâtib*) who obtained a job in a state office would be trained by senior officials, but he might also educate himself by reading books on grammar, rhetoric, history, geography, law and diplomacy as well as literary compositions. State offices acted at that time as a kind of educational institution. Bureaucrats trained in these offices, even though they were not as respected and influential as *medrese* members (the *ulema* class), produced valuable literary, historical and to a lesser extent scientific works.

Generally speaking, seventeenth- and eighteenth-century Turkish bureaucrats and scholars were knowledgeable in Turkish, Arabic and Persian. They did not feel the need to learn European languages because interpreters were employed in foreign affairs. In the translation of scientific books, scholars or bureaucrats had to cooperate with an interpreter. The Turkish translations of Mercator and Ortelius's atlases resulted from such a collaboration.

KÂTIB CELEBI'S CIHANNÜMÂ: TRANSLATIONS FROM GERHARD MERCATOR, ABRAHAM ORTELIUS AND OTHER EUROPEAN CARTOGRAPHERS

Best known in Europe as Hadji Khalifa, Kâtib Çelebi (1609–57) was the 'scholar-bureaucrat' par excellence who introduced sixteenth- and seventeenth-century European cartographical and geographical knowledge to the Ottoman Empire. *Cihannümâ* (Cosmorama), the comprehensive work he compiled in Turkish on the basis of both Islamic and European geography books and atlases, was substantial in shaping the Ottoman perception of geography.

An outstanding polygraph and bibliophile, Kâtib Çelebi was charmed by geography because it provided the opportunity, while seated comfortably at home, to journey around the world and to acquire more information than people who travel their life long. For him, geography was a part of astronomy and he believed that astronomy was necessary to understand the universe and God. Moreover, statesmen should be acquainted with the 'art of geography' since a knowledge of the subject was required for the success of military campaigns and in order to control the borders. Kâtib Çelebi stressed the importance of geography by giving an example from the Christian world: 'The "infidel" Europeans who considered the science of geography important were able to discover America and could sail up to India. Venice, a small Christian dukedom, could enter a sea (the Aegean) which is under Ottoman control and challenge an empire that rules in the West and the East.'[8]

Kâtib Çelebi, like other young Ottomans aspiring to become a bureaucrat, was enrolled as assistant at the age of fourteen in one of the accounting offices of the Council of State where he learned computation and *siyakat*, the writing style used in treasury accounts. Transferred to a military office, he participated for about ten years in the Ottoman military campaigns against the Safawids in Iraq and Iran. Returning to Istanbul, he spent most of his fortune buying books. While continuing to work in the office, he paid visits to *medrese* teachers to learn astronomy, mathematics, religious sciences and logic. He was a keen reader of biographies, bibliographies and history books.

The Ottoman campaigns in Crete against Venice (1645–59) drew Kâtib Çelebi's attention to naval history and geography. He first wrote *Tuhfetü'l-kibâr fi esfâri'l-bihâr* (Gift to the Nobility: A Chronicle of Naval Campaigns, 1645), in which he analysed former victories and defeats of the Ottoman navy, discussed the measures that might be taken for its improvement and described the neighbouring territories ruled by the Venetians, Albanians and Peloponnesians. Then, he decided to compile a comprehensive book on the geography of the world and set to work in 1645. He started to compose his book on the basis of Islamic geographical texts such as *al-Muhît* (The Ocean), *Tarih-i hind-i garbî* (The History of the Discovery of America), *Taqwim al-buldan* (Geography of Countries), *Menâzir ül-avâlim* (Panorama of the World) and *Kitab-i bahriye* (Book of Navigation).

As he worked, he realized that Islamic sources were not sufficient for his project. He stopped writing and tried to obtain European geography books and to learn their contents. He procured the *Atlas minor*, which was widely known in the European market. This was the popular version of the atlas of Gerhard Mercator (1512–94) printed by Josse Hondius (1546–1611).

---

[8] From Kâtib Çelebi's *Tuhfetü'l-kibar fi esfâri'l-bihâr* (Prominent Figures of Naval Campaigns, 1645) cited in Gökyay (1982), 12, 129.

Kâtib Çelebi also tried to procure the *Theatrum orbis terrarum* (1570) of Abraham Ortelius (1527–98) but he apparently only had access, at a later stage, to the catalogue of geographers attached to it. The translation of the *Atlas minor* from Latin into Turkish was made orally by Sheikh Mehmed Ihlasî, a French convert to Islam. Kâtib Çelebi wrote down the Turkish text, edited it and named the translation *Levâmi'al-nûr fî zulmat-i atlas minor* (Lights Glittering in the Darkness: Atlas Minor, 1654). He appended a bibliography of cartographers and geographers that he compiled from Ortelius's text.

Kâtib Çelebi now started to write *Cihannümâ* anew. In the second version (1654) he made use of the European geographical literature cited above and it is also likely that he procured new information from other sixteenth-century geography books and maps. *Cihannümâ* stimulated other Ottomans to write on geography; its printed version (1732), enriched by Ibrahim Müteferrika, aroused considerable interest in the eighteenth century.

Geography was not the only concern of Kâtib Çelebi. He wrote on Islamic, Ottoman and European history and compiled a bibliographical encyclopedia, the *Kesfü'z-zunûn an-esâmi'l-kütüb vel'l-fünun* (The Elimination of Doubts about Book Titles and Sciences) including about 14,500 book entries and 10,000 biographies.[9] The financial difficulties the Ottoman state faced in the mid-sixteenth century encouraged him to think about measures to be taken in order to secure the prosperity of the state and society. He compared society to the human body and had recourse to the Hippocratic doctrine of four humours to explain the 'illness' of society and the way to recover its 'health'. In *Düsturü'l-amel li islâhi'l-halel* (Principles of Action for Reform, 1653), one reads:

The human body is a combination of four humours, and functions through its senses and natural capabilities that are delivered to the competent hands of the human soul. Likewise, the structure of a society is made up of four elements, and its regulation and administration by means of statesmen (the senses and capabilities) is submitted to the competent hands of the glorious Sultan (the human soul). The four elements of society are scholars, soldiers, tradesmen and the populace. The scholars, forming an eminent class, may be compared to the blood, the most valuable humour of the body, as the heart is the source of the animal soul which is immaterial in essence, so thin and fine, and unable to flow, it is carried by blood vessels to the farthest ends of the body, to all organs and the arms and legs. Without doubt, as the body finds life in blood and benefits from it, scholars who

---

[9] Celebi (1835–8).

excel in knowledge of divine laws and belief in God receive the holy science (the soul) directly from Allah or from his mediator, and communicate it to the uneducated public (the arms and legs). Thus the body is nourished by the soul, and the people learn from the scholars. The soul provides for the strength and perseverance of the body; science determines the vigour and endurance of the society ... Soldiers represent phlegm, and tradesmen are like yellow bile. The people are similar to black bile; their nature is that of the earth, and vulgar ... The four humours increase and decrease to influence one another to uphold the health of the body. In the same manner, when the four classes of the society, civilized by creation, receive sustenance from each other, the order of society and the health of the state are set. The four humours should be in equilibrium in order to give a healthy disposition to the body. Should one of the humours increase or change in substance, it will be necessary to remedy it by decreasing or suppressing this humour.

The populace corresponds to black bile. It has been established by medicine and anatomy that during the digestion of a meal, when food is introduced into the stomach, the spleen secretes black bile, so that it is not left empty and no harm is done. If one compares the stomach to the imperial treasury, when the coffer is empty the poor people should be ready to pay and supply it. However, if the people are oppressed, and have no work and income, they cannot afford to do so. For this reason, the Sultans of the past paid great attention to protecting the people from the merciless, treating them with justice and taking care of them ... Phlegm (warriors) is necessary and of service, yet its excess and change of character is detrimental, showing that the order of society depends on the equilibrium of these classes ... The number of cavalry and the janissaries should be kept around twenty to thirty thousand, and the other orders allowed to increase. The increase in the total number of warriors will not constitute a burden, and can be relieved by reducing their salaries in accordance with ancient law, and by acceptable precautions ...

In conclusion: the solution to the problems of deficiency in the treasury, the size of the army and expenditure, and the weakness of the people (taking into account that nothing more can be levied from the them), is for the Sultan – may God protect him – as the refuge for the people to provide by any means available, a full years' revenue to repay the debt of the treasury, and entrust one of his dependable subjects to repay the loans ... Afterwards, the burden of a large army can be dealt with by reductions and other suitable measures ... Experienced pious persons who shun sin should be appointed to state offices, the foundation of the treasury. The cure for the weakness of the people is to reduce the taxes, to refrain from extracting from state services, and to place just persons with experience in positions to defy the merciless, so that the people can recover in a couple of years and the Ottoman state enjoy the prosperity it deserves.[10]

---

[10] Cited in Gökyay (1982), 233–48.

THE TRANSLATION OF BLAEU'S *ATLAS MAJOR*

When Justinus Colyer, the Dutch ambassador in Istanbul, presented the *Atlas major* to Sultan Mehmed IV (reigned 1648–87) in 1668, the Ottomans became acquainted with the most expensive and spectacular atlas of seventeenth-century Europe. This eleven-volume atlas was first published in Latin between the years 1662–72 by the Dutch cartographer and printer Joan Blaeu (1596–1673).

In 1675, about seven years after the atlas was presented to the Sultan, Ebubekir b. Behram üd-Dimashqi (d. 1691), a *medrese* scholar in the retinue of Köprülü Fazil Ahmed Pasha (Grand Vizier from 1661 to 1676), was charged with supervising the translation of this voluminous work of 3,000 pages and 600 maps.

Born in Damascus, Ebubekir came to Istanbul in 1661 and took part in the military campaign against the emperor (1663–4). Returning to Istanbul, he taught in a *medrese* for over twenty years. He was knowledgeable in geography, astronomy, mathematics and history. Besides his work on the *Atlas major*, he added a supplement to Kâtib Çelebi's *Cihannümâ*, compiled the *Risāle fi'l-cografya* (Treatise on Geography) in Arabic and an essay in Turkish dealing with the history and the administrative and military organization of the Ottoman state.

The translation of the *Atlas major* from Latin into Turkish took ten years. A translator or a team of translators and cartographers probably assisted Ebubekir Effendi. The teamwork resulted in a nine-volume abridged version popularly known as *Tercüme-i Atlas major* (The Translation of *Atlas major*). The meaning of the full title *Nusret el-Islâm ve'l-surûr fi tahrîri Atlas major* (The Joy of the Muslims for the Success of the Translation of *Atlas major*) captures not only the pleasure and the honour of the translators in finishing the translation but also the importance of the *Atlas major*'s being introduced to the Islamic world. Geographical information on Asia Minor and the Middle East based on Islamic geographical works was added to the text.

THE TRANSLATION OF EUROPEAN ASTRONOMICAL TABLES

The Ottomans showed great interest in European astronomical tables in the seventeenth century. In the early 1660s they procured the tables calculated by Nathalis Durret (1590–1650), a cosmographer at the French court. Dedicated to Cardinal Richelieu, these tables were first published in 1635 and a number of editions appeared later. Tezkireci Köse Ibrahim

Effendi, an Ottoman official working in the army and interested in astronomy, translated Durret's astronomical tables into Arabic. After comparing Durret's tables with those prepared by Ibn Yunus in 1004 for the longitude of Cairo, he found out that they were Durret's source. He finished the translation in 1663 in Belgrade, the seat of the Ottoman army during the campaign.

Later on, he compiled a Turkish version and named it *Secencel al-aflâk fi gâyet al-idrâk* (Mirror of the Heavens and the Summit of Perception). The very few copies in the libraries show that Ottoman astronomers did not favour Durret's tables. Although Cezmi Effendi (d. 1692), the judge of Belgrade, added supplementary material to the tables, Ottoman timekeepers and astrologers continued to use astronomical tables based on those of Ulugh Beg until the mid-eighteenth century, when Cassini's astronomical tables were translated into Turkish by Halifezâde Cinarî Ismail Effendi, also remembered for the sundials he constructed while acting as the time-keeper (*muwaqqit*) of the Laleli Mosque in Istanbul and for his translation of the astronomical tables of Alexis Clairaut (1713–65).

TRANSLATIONS FROM EUROPEAN MEDICAL TEXTS ON DISEASES AND THERAPIES

The image of the seventeenth-century Ottoman medical community is rather complex, considering the diversity of practitioners. The authority of the Islamic legacy is well exemplified by Seyyid Muhammed et-Tabib known as Emir Celebi (d. 1638), while Salih b. Nasrullah b. Sallum (d. 1669) was influential in the introduction of iatrochemical therapies, popular in seventeenth-century Europe. Both of them held the post of chief physician to the Sultan.

Born in Thrace, Emir Celebi studied medicine in Cairo and was the chief physician of the Qalawun hospital for several years. Brought to Istanbul by the admiral of the Ottoman fleet during the Mediterranean campaign of 1622, he became renowned for the remarkable cures he performed in his 'shop' in Unkapani, a district of Istanbul near the Golden Horn. The thirty copies of his *Enmûzecü't-tibb* (The Reference Book for Medicine, 1624) extant in libraries in Turkey witness that it was widely consulted until the nineteenth century.

A large part of the book consists of information on diseases and *materia medica*. It is considered to be the second most popular medical book among the Ottomans, after the *Müntahab üs-sifa* of Haci Pasha, the fifteenth-century physician previously mentioned. Emir Celebi advised physicians to add their own therapeutical experiences when writing their books and not to content themselves with repeating older accounts, to learn anatomy and to dissect the dead bodies of soldiers or monkeys or pigs. He compiled *Neticetü't-tibb* (The Synopsis of Medicine), a shorter version of *Enmûzecü't-tibb*, as a guide to his assistant, who in his absence would prescribe drugs to patients visiting his shop.

While the compilation and the copying of guides dealing with diseases and remedies based on traditional knowledge and personal experience were carried on, the growing popularity of iatrochemistry in seventeenth-century Europe led some Ottoman physicians to become interested in the Paracelsan way of treating diseases with mineral drugs. The fame of *Basilica chymica* – ten editions between 1609 and 1658 – by Oswald Croll (1580–1609), the greatest propagandist of the iatrochemical movement, and the reputation of Daniel Sennert (1572–1611), the private physician of the Prince of Saxony, reached Istanbul by the mid-seventeenth century.

Ottoman physicians, referring to European treatises or consulting their European colleagues practising in Istanbul, wrote books on iatrochemistry, calling it *tibb-i cedîd* (new medicine). Interest in iatrochemistry continued into the eighteenth century. Salih bin Nasrullah bin Sellum's work *Tibb al-cedîd al-kimyâî* (The New Chemical Medicine) was not a direct translation from Paracelsus, but a compilation from Paracelsan works enriched by Sellum's own experiences and his views on the treatment of diseases. The book explains the theories of *tria prima* and *signatures*, and gives a number of Paracelsan prescriptions.

Ottoman physicians, particularly those at court, translated medical texts dealing with diseases and their treatment into Arabic and Turkish. Salih b. Nasrullah bin Sellum (d. 1670), the private physician to Sultan Mehmed IV (reigned 1648–87) and the chief physician of the Fatih hospital (*darüssifa*), in his work *Gayet ül-beyan fi tedbir beden il-insan* (Highest Perfection in the Treatment of the Human Body, 1655) described diseases unfamiliar to the Ottomans until this time: the *chlorose*, the *skorbut* and the *plica polonica*. In the section on therapeutics, he mentioned Nicolas Myrepsos and may have used his *Dynameron* (1280).

In his book *Hamse-i Hayâti* (Five Books of Hayâti) dealing with diseases and their treatments, the chief physician Hayâtizâde Mustafa Feyzi (d. 1692), known as Moché ben Raphaël Abranavel before his conversion from Judaism to Islam, mentioned Daniel Sennert, Jean Fernel (1497–1558) and the French physician de la Rivière. He described syphilis according to the works of Girolamo Fracastoro (1483–1553) and other European physicians. He talked about the researches of Nicolas Monardes

(1493–1588) on medicinal plants he imported from the New World, described *plica polonica* and a fever frequently seen in Germany. His information was taken from the Spanish physician Luis Mercado (1520–1606) and Rodrigo Fonseca (1452–1530).

Ibn Sellum's and Hayâtizâde's books dealing with diseases and the new European therapeutics point to the interest by Ottoman physicians in practical knowledge, a tendency similar to the interest in European astronomical tables on the part of Ottoman astronomers. Seventeenth-century court physicans could have access to European medical knowledge by various means, but European physicians practising in Ottoman cities and Ottomans studying in European medical schools seem to have been the principal conveyors.

Although seventeenth-century Ottoman sources refer to *frenk* (European) physicians practising in various parts of the Empire, details about their names, origin, education, practice and designation as well as the cities in which they practised are often lacking. The information available generally concerns those who worked in the Imperial Palace or in the retinue of Ottoman high officials or foreign legations. One of these was Israel Conegliano (Conian) (b. 1650, Padua). Conegliano had settled in Istanbul in 1675 and became physician to a powerful man, Merzifonlu Karamustafa Pasha (1634–83), who commanded the Ottoman army in the Polish and Austrian campaigns and besieged Vienna in 1683. Conegliano also acted as the physician of the Venetian legation in Istanbul. Tobia Cohen (b. 1652, Metz) after studying medicine in Padua settled in Istanbul and became the private physician of Mehmed Rami Pasha (1654–1706), Grand Vizier and Minister of Foreign Affairs. An astute politician and a tough negotiator, Rami Pasha was the Ottoman representative at the Treaty of Karlowitz, concluding the 1683–97 war between the Ottomans and the Holy League (Austria, Poland, Venice, Russia). As for Daniel Fonséca (b. 1668, Oporto, Portugal – d. 1736, Izmir, Turkey), he arrived in Istanbul in 1680 after having studied medicine in Paris. He first became physician to the French embassy, served in Bucharest between 1710–14 and thereafter entered the retinue of Sultan Ahmed III (reigned 1703–30).

European physicians doubtlessly practised in cities other than Istanbul. Sir George Wheler (1650–1724) mentioned in his *Journey into Greece* (1682) that he met a certain Dr Pickering in 1675 during his visit to north-west Anatolia and that they conversed on *Tuttie* (*Tuitia*), a herb growing on Uludag (Mons Olympus). Unfortunately Wheler gave no other information about him except that he was practising medicine in Bursa.

A well-known seventeenth-century example of the transfer of medical knowledge via Ottomans studying abroad is Alexandre Mavrocordato (1641–1709) who prepared a thesis on the circulation of the blood (*Pneumaticon instrumentum circulandi sanguinis*) in Bologna in 1664. Unfortunately, this work had little effect on Ottoman medicine because it was not translated into Turkish, since Mavrocordato preferred to work subsequently as translator at the Council of State.

The next reference to William Harvey's account of the circulation of the blood would be made in 1771 in the Turkish translation of Hermann Boerhaave's *Aphorismi*. The translation, titled *Kitaat-i nekave fi terceme-i kelimât-i Boerhaave* (The Finest Pieces from the Translation of the Aphorisms of Boerhaave), was made at the command of Sultan Mustafa III by the court physican Suphizâde Abdülaziz Effendi (d. 1782) and a team knowledgeable in Latin, including the interpreter of the imperial embassy in Istanbul. To overcome the difficulties encountered in the translation, Gerard Van Swieten's *Commentaria in Hermanni Boerhaave aphorismos* (1742–72) were consulted. The Turkish translation of the *Aphorismi* was not published and only three copies exist in libraries in Istanbul.

Although medical knowledge from Europe was introduced and applied to some extent in the seventeenth century, commentaries on Ibn Sina's (Avicenna's) *Kânûn fi't-tibb* (Canon of Medicine) and other medieval Islamic medical works were still the reference texts for Ottoman physicians.

SHEMSEDDIN ITAQI'S *TESRIH-I EBDÂN*: THE INTRODUCTION OF SIXTEENTH-CENTURY EUROPEAN ANATOMICAL KNOWLEDGE INTO TURKISH MEDICAL LITERATURE

As far as the introduction of anatomical knowledge is concerned, a striking example combining traditional Islamic with sixteenth-century European knowledge is the seventeenth-century Turkish text entitled *Risâle-i tesrih-i ebdân* (Treatise on the Anatomy of the Human Body, 1632) by Shemseddin Itaqi (born in Shirvan, c. 1570). After studying various sciences in Iran for twenty years, Itaqi had to flee his country following the upheavals after Shah Tahmasp's death in 1576. He arrived in Istanbul during the reign of Murad IV (1623–32) and was presented to the Grand Vizier Topal Recep Pasha (d. 1632) who favoured him. The vizier's entourage asked him to compile a Turkish book of anatomy, emphasizing that such a book would be very useful. This statement shows that his book was the first Turkish treatise ever written on anatomy. For Ottoman physicians, the most esteemed texts on anatomy were the first section of Ibn Sina's medical encyclopedia *Kânûn fi't-tibb* and its commentary by Ibn Nefis. Both texts were in Arabic.

Itaqi's book included schematic figures taken from the fourteenth-century Persian physician Mansur ibn Muhammad ibn Ahmad's *Tesrih-i Mansûr* (Anatomy of Mansur) and plates inspired by the *Anatomia del corpo humano* of the Spanish anatomist Juan Valverde de Hamusco (1520–88). It is highly possible that he consulted the sixteenth-century medical books that were brought to Turkey by the above-mentioned Jewish physicians. Among them were physicians trained in Padua, distinguished for its teaching of 'modern' anatomy.

CONCLUSION

Access to and reliance on Arabic and Persian scientific texts from medieval Islam did not hinder Ottoman scholars from introducing information from European sources throughout the sixteenth and seventeenth centuries. Most translations from European scientific texts seem to have been made in the fields of medicine, geography and cartography and aimed to make known new therapies and drugs, newly discovered countries and the features of geographical areas previously unknown to the Ottomans. Kâtib Çelebi studied European works in order to have access to knowledge unavailable in medieval Islamic geographies.

These initiatives in acquiring and translating European scientific texts were not peculiar to Ottomans who were eager to introduce novelties from Europe. A substantial number of European scholars were interested in examining Islamic scientific texts from the mid-sixteenth century onwards. As Sonja Brentjes writes:

Efforts were made since the middle of the sixteenth century to publish, translate and exploit Arabic and Persian geographical manuscripts. At this time, a copy of *Taqwim al-buldan* by Abu'l-Fida was brought to Western Europe by Guillaume Postel. There it came first to be kept by the Palatine Library, Heidelberg. Other copies were brought during the sixteenth and seventeenth centuries to Italy, Austria, France and Britain. In the late sixteenth century, an incomplete copy of al-Idrisi's [1099–1166] *Geography* arrived in Italy where it became part of the Medicis's library. Both texts were repeatedly accessed by West European and Maronite scholars from the sixteenth until the late eighteenth centuries for the utilization of their information for cartography, geographical dictionaries, historiography and the revision of latitude and longitude values ...

The geographical coordinates given by Nasir al-Din al-Tusi, Ulugh Beg and Ali Qushji, as well as anonymous texts, were tapped by Jacob Golius, Adrien Reland, Gilbert Gaulmyn, Antoine Galland, John Greaves and Thomas Hyde. Several

Arabic, Persian and Syriac historical works were translated – at least in extracts – during the seventeenth and eighteenth centuries and scrutinized by cartographers for their geographical information . . .

Among the scholars who either printed the one or the other text in Arabic or in Latin translation, completely, or produced manuscript translations we find during the sixteenth and seventeenth centuries Bernardino Baldi, Wilhelm Schickard, John Greaves, Thomas Hyde, Laurent d'Arvieux in cooperation with M. De la Roque and Melchisédech Thévenot, the Maronites Johannes Hesronita, Gabriel Sionita and Abraham Ecchellensis . . . [Pierre] Gassendi can be taken as a token of the immense attraction the Ottoman Empire exercised on the French scholarly world during the seventeenth century. In 1629/30, he himself together with his friend François Luillier started to study Arabic hoping to access texts Gassendi's mentor and friend Nicolas Fabri de Peiresc had acquired from Cairo, Aleppo, Sayda and other Ottoman towns. Other friends, students or contemporaries of Gassendi . . . either learned (some) Arabic, Persian or Turkish to study texts of various genres, travelled to Muslim countries, or sought to acquire from there manuscripts and other material deemed necessary for their own research.[11]

Their mutual interest in the scientific knowledge produced in each other's cultural area should have led Europeans and Ottomans to exchange scientific and technical information as well as books on related issues. The fact that the number of translations into Turkish was not extensive was partly due to the adequacy of medieval Islamic works and their commentaries for the Ottoman scientific community. The knowledge these works embodied could apparently meet the needs of scholars and the government in the sixteenth and seventeenth centuries. The translation of works of European science gradually increased in the course of the eighteenth century and reached a peak in the nineteenth century, when versions from Latin and Italian were replaced by those from French.

[11] Brentjes (2001), 123–5.

CHAPTER 12

Translations of scientific literature in Russia from the fifteenth to the seventeenth century[1]

S. S. Demidov

At the beginning of the fifteenth century, Russia had no place on the map of Europe. At that period, the most important Russian states were: the Moscow Dukedom (*Moskovskoe Knyazhestvo*) and the Novgorod Republic (*Gospodin Velikii Novgorod*). Only in 1380, after the Battle of Kulikovo, did Russian soil begin to be liberated from the Tatar yoke. During the reign of Ivan III (1462–1505), the Russian state was established. The tsar's ambitions were revealed by the adoption of a new state emblem: the two-headed Byzantine eagle. In this way the Grand Duke declared Russia to be the heir to the Byzantine Empire, the centre of the Orthodox world. In the sixteenth century, the monk Filotei developed the theory of Moscow as being the third Rome ('and a fourth there shall not be').

From a cultural point of view, Russia in 1400 was an actively developing and very distant province of the Byzantine Empire, whose power was waning at that time. An Orthodox country, Russia was hostile to every idea coming from the West, especially if the idea was connected to Catholicism. This hostility increased after Rome's attempts to extend its influence to the East. It is in this context that we need to examine the problem of translations of Western scientific literature in the fifteenth and sixteenth centuries.

TRANSLATIONS IN RUSSIA IN THE FIFTEENTH AND SIXTEENTH CENTURIES

After the Grand Duke of Kiev St Vladimir (reigned 978–1015) became a Christian, Russia was introduced to the Christian world and drawn into European culture. During St Vladimir's era, a school was organized in

---

[1] The main secondary sources on this topic are (in chronological order) Rainov (1940), Yushkevich (1968), Kuzakov (1976), Kosheleva and Simonov (1981), Likhachev (1987–98), Kuzakov (1991), Fonkich (1999), Simonov (2000).

Kiev, following the model of Byzantine schools. In the time of Yaroslav the Wise (reigned 1019–54), many copies of manuscripts were made and libraries established at princely courts, in monasteries and in churches. At that time Russian literature was composed of translations or paraphrases of Byzantine works or the works of Orthodox Balkan Slavs, though original Russian works appeared very quickly, including the famous chronological treatise by Kirik of Novgorod. Among these texts we cannot find any dedicated to mathematics or to questions that we can consider as scientific, although religious texts referred to some topics that may be considered to belong to science.

The period of the fifteenth and sixteenth centuries is a continuation of the previous era. New copies and sometimes new translations of the most popular works of the previous period can be found. These works include the thirteenth-century text *The Book of Secrets of Enoch* (a translation of a lost Greek original which was a revision of some old texts in the Semitic language compiled in Palestine in the first or second century BC); the works of an ecclesiastical scholar of the fourth century, Epiphany of Cyprus, *The Questions of Vasilii and the Answers of Gregorii* and *The Lapidary*, which contained the description of the wondrous properties of twelve precious stones; *The Christian Topography* by Kosmas Indikoplov, a sixth-century monk from Alexandria; *Theology* by I. Damaskin; *The Six Days* (of creation) by Vasilii the Great; and the *Chronicle* by the ninth-century Greek monk Georgii Amartol.

In these works the ideas of the medieval Eastern Orthodox world about the construction of the cosmos, geography, animals and plants and meteorological phenomena were represented (sometimes in fantastic forms). At times it is possible to find information about the works of the ancient Greek philosophers. For example, from the works of Amartol the Russian reader could find the earliest information about the Democritean theory of atoms.

To these works can be added the fourth-century *Commentary on Genesis* by John Chrysostom (the translation into Serbian was made on Mt Athos in 1426); *The Six Days* by the fourth-century Syrian bishop Severian of Gavala; and *The Discussion of Panaghiostos with Azimyth* (a translation into Serbian from the Greek original). The Orthodox Panaghiostos and the heretic Azimyth discussed questions concerning the world's construction in particular. The authors divided the stars into good and evil ones, according to their astrological properties.

Astrological topics were popular in old Russia. It was possible to find some information in Ioan Exarch's *The Six Days*, which appeared in Russia in the tenth century, and in the romance by Pseudo-Kallisphenos,

Alexandria, which was translated into Russian in the eleventh century. At the end of the fifteenth century, this interest increased. Astrological information could be found in *The Mystery of Mysteries*, which was translated into Lithuanian Russian at the end of the fifteenth or the beginning of the sixteenth century (the translation was made from Hebrew, while the original eleventh-century text was in Arabic). Specialists connect the appearance of this work in Russia with the 'Jewish heresy' (*Zhidovstvuyushchikh*).

At the beginning of the sixteenth century, Western astrology began to penetrate into Russia. The doctor and astrologer of the Great Dukes Ivan III and Vasilii III, Nikolai Nemchin (born in Lübeck as Nikolaus Bülow), made the translation – or the paraphrase – of the *Almanach* edited in Germany in the first quarter of the sixteenth century by Schöffler. It was a calendar with astrological predictions, horoscopes and medical advice connected to heavenly phenomena.

The Orthodox Church was opposed to astrology and considered such books 'erroneous' or 'forbidden'. The fourteenth century was the beginning of the compiling of the Indexes of such forbidden works. These Indexes were continued until the seventeenth century.

However, from a cultural point of view, the sixteenth century was more than a 'continuation' of the previous century. During this period it is possible to trace the rise of intellectual activity. The number of manuscripts from the sixteenth century that exist today is almost the same as the number of manuscripts from all the preceding centuries. Theological discussions became more active and numerous.

The changes that can be observed in the economic, political and social life of Russia (the beginning of the formation of an all-Russian market, the organization of a monetary system, the development of the state apparatus, the evolution of the social structure and so on) demanded the modernization of society and the rise of its educational level. We also see the gradual rise of Russian interest in Western Europe, in its science and culture.

At the end of the sixteenth century there was a gradual rise in the number of translations (from Latin, German and, to a lesser extent, Polish) of Western books that contained information of a scientific nature. In the fifteenth and sixteenth centuries, the majority of the translators were monks. In the seventeenth century, by contrast, they were natives of Ukraine (mostly clergymen) or official translators from the Office of Foreign Affairs. Already in the sixteenth century a book on cosmography was translated by that Office. Following an order from the tsar himself, various medical collections were also translated.

The works which were translated were usually not the most important works in their fields. They normally represented the past intellectual activity of the West, but in one way and another these works corresponded to the essentially medieval consciousness of contemporary Russian readers.

ON THE EVE OF THE REFORMS OF PETER THE GREAT

The beginning of the seventeenth century was a turbulent era, terminated by the ascent of the House of Romanov. The century ended with the first reforms of Peter the Great, who transformed Russia into the Russian Empire (1721).

Such a result was possible only after a century of intensive development. During this century (especially its second half), an enormous increase in the educational efforts of the government may be seen. Schools were organized at different levels, including schools to prepare qualified personnel for the administration. As we can see from the recent research of Boris L. Fonkich, in the second half of the century the level of these schools and the number of their students increased immensely.

In 1667, two Greek scholars, Ioannikios and Sofronios Leichoudis, established the first Russian superior institution, the Slavo-Hellenic-Latin Academy. It should be emphasized that its name represents the two axes of its orientation. The Slavonic and Greek stress the Orthodox direction, while the Latin stresses the Western European direction. Among the students of this Academy should be named the most important figure in Russian intellectual history in the eighteenth century, Mikhail Lomonosov (1711–65), who entered it in 1736, walking from a distant fishing village on the coast of the White Sea. What would develop in the eighteenth century is clear, but for this development conditions which had been created in the previous century were indispensable.

The most important part of this enormous intellectual work was intensive activity in the translation of books. Prior to this century, scientific and technical information had been included in Orthodox literature only incidentally and at times in fantastic forms (with imaginary animals among real ones and so on), but now – gradually – this information came to express the spirit of the European Renaissance.

In 1625, the first theoretical manuscript on geometry appeared in Russian. Its author, Prince Albert Dolmatskii, was a Greek who had been born in Patras, lived in England and afterwards came to Moscow and began his career close to the tsar's court. In the preface to his treatise he wrote that he had utilized many sources for this work. The principal ones were John

Speidell's *Geometrical Extraction* (1616) and Peter Ramus's *Geometriae libri XXVII* (1569). Dolmatskii's treatise, we may assume, was included in the curriculum for the education of the Great Duke Aleksei Mikhailovich (later tsar and father of Peter the Great). The author expected, unfortunately in vain, that his manuscript would be published. 'The first edition on geometry', wrote A. P. Yushkevich in connection with this manuscript, 'appeared in Russia more than eighty years afterwards, but a manual of the same level was published later, after the foundation of the Academy of Sciences.'

To understand the spirit of the seventeenth century and the aspirations of the Russian government around the year 1600, it is extremely useful to become acquainted with the 'Rules of the Military, Artillery and Other Affairs', published in two volumes in 1777–81. These 'Rules' were compiled in Vasilii Shuiskii's reign in 1606 and that of Mikhail Feodorovich in 1620. The text of the 'Rules' begins with the observation that the tsar Vasilii Shuiskii 'ordered this book in German and Latin translated into Russian'. The principal source of the 'Rules' was a three-volume edition (Frankfurt, 1566–73) of the *Kriegsbuch* by Leonard Fronsperger. It was made by two translators in the Office of Foreign Affairs, M. Yuriev and I. Fomin. This work on the organization of military affairs, on arms and the art of artillery, on the method of preparing gunpowder and on fortification, reveals the scientific and technical level in Russia at the end of the sixteenth century. It demands a good mathematical background and includes important scientific knowledge on ballistics (the work of Niccolò Tartaglia), physics and chemistry.

The military and practical needs of the country demanded geographical information. That is why, in the middle of that century, the translators in the Office of Foreign Affairs, B. Lykov and I. Dorn, translated G. Mercator's *Atlas* (1590–6) in 230 chapters. In 1670 the translation of an unknown compilation from Mercator's works of German origin also appeared; the original contained seventy-six chapters and had been made around 1611. It is also known that a book called 'Cosmography' was translated in the seventeenth century from the *Theatrum orbis terrarum* (1571) of Ortelius.

Everything seems to indicate that Patriarch Nikon (appointed head of the Russian Church in 1652) wanted to extend his authority with the preparation of translations not only of clerical but also of scientific works. In the 1650s, translators from his circle, the monks Epiphanii Slavenetskii, Arsenii and Isaiya, began to translate from Latin the famous *Atlas* published in Amsterdam by Blaeu (1646–65). They translated the first four volumes. In the second half of the seventeenth century Hendrick

Doncker's *De groote nieuwe vermeerderde zee-atlas* (The Great New Enlarged Maritime Atlas, 1688) was also translated, together with Zuca Delind's *Descriptio orbis et omnium ejus rerum publicarum* (Description of the World and all its Commonwealths, 1668).

Also deserving to be mentioned is a book about animals by Ulisse Aldrovandi (*De quadrupedibus digitatis viviparis libri tres*, 1637), and the most important anatomical work from the Renaissance epoch, *De humani corporis fabrica* (1543) by Andreas Vesalius, a translation made by Epiphanii Slaventskii. Numerous medical books were also translated, including – and this is most interesting – the works of ancient authors, such as Aristotle. In this way did the spirit of the Renaissance appear in distant Moscow.

Only one aspect of the cultural life of that time has been discussed, but it is sufficient to evaluate the unprecedented concentration of intellectual resources in the seventeenth century, and the high level of intellectual life around the year 1700. At the beginning of the eighteenth century, Russia was mature enough for many changes in its intellectual and cultural life.

However, for a really radical transformation, for the adhesion of the country to the process of development in Western Europe, a revolution in the dominant mentality was necessary. Russia remained attached to its medieval culture. This attachment was actively supported by the Russian Orthodox Church, which considered Western European influence a risk for Orthodoxy, of which Moscow, the 'third Rome', was the vigilant guardian. To break down this tradition and to open the road to radical reforms, the outstanding abilities of Peter the Great were necessary. This story belongs to the eighteenth century. The first meetings of the Academy of Sciences of Petersburg took place in August 1725 – twenty-five years after the end of the period examined here.

Bibliography

This bibliography is confined to works of secondary literature cited in the text.

Ács, Pál (2000), 'Austrian and Hungarian Renegades as Sultan's Interpreters', in Bodo Guthmüller and Wilhelm Kühlmann (eds.), *Europa und die Türken in der Renaissance* (Tübingen), 307–16.

Allison, A. F. and D. M. Rogers (eds., 1989–94), *The Contemporary Printed Literature of the English Counter-Reformation between 1558–1640: An Annotated Catalogue* (Brookfield, VT).

Almagor, J. (1984), 'Pierre Des Maizeaux', in *The Role of Periodicals in the Eighteenth Century* (Leiden), 41–7.

Alventosa Sanchis, Joaquín (1963), 'Los escritores nordicos y los espirituales españoles', in *Corrientes espirituales en la España del siglo XVI* (Barcelona), 527–42.

Anchieta, José de (1984), *Lírica portuguesa e Tupí*, ed. Armando Cardoso (São Paulo).

Andrés Martín, Melquíades (1975), *Los recogidos: nueva visión de la mística española (1500–1700)* (Madrid).

Anglo, Sydney (2005), *Machiavelli: The First Century* (Oxford).

Asad, Talal (1986), 'The Concept of Cultural Translation in British Social Anthropology', in James Clifford and George E. Marcus (eds.), *Writing Culture: The Poetics and Politics of Ethnography* (Berkeley), 141–64.

Assmann, Jan (1996), 'Translating Gods', in Sanford Budick and Wolfgang Iser (eds.), *The Translatability of Cultures* (Stanford), 25–36.

Backus, Irena (1995), 'Erasmus and the Spirituality of the Early Church', in H. M. Pabel (ed.), *Erasmus's Vision of the Church* (Kirksville), 95–114.

Bahlcke, Joachim and Arno Strohmeyer (eds., 2002), *Die Konstruktion der Vergangenheit: Geschichtsdenken, Traditionsbildung und Selbstdarstellung im frühneuzeitlichen Ostmitteleuropa, Zeitschrift für historische Forschung*, supplement 29.

Baier, Walter (1977), *Untersuchungen zu den Passionsbetrachtungen in der Vita Christi des Ludolf von Sachsen* (Salzburg).

Baker, Mona (ed., 1998), *Routledge Encyclopaedia of Translation Studies* (London).

Bakhtin, Mikhail (1965), *Rabelais and his World* (English trans., Cambridge, MA, 1968).

Bakhuizen van den Brink, J. N. (1969), *Juan de Valdés, réformateur en Espagne et en Italie, 1529–1541* (Geneva).

Ballard, Michel (1992), *De Cicéron à Benjamin* (Paris).

Balsamo, Jean (1992), *Répertoire des traductions de l'italien 1570–1600* (Rome).

Balsamo, J. (1998), 'Traduire de l'italien: ambitions sociales et contraintes éditoriales à la fin du 16e siècle', in Dominique de Courcelles (ed.), *Traduire et adapter à la Renaissance* (Paris), 89–98.

Bareggi, Claudia Di Filippo (1988), *Il mestiere di scrivere* (Rome).

Barnard, John and Don F. McKenzie (eds., 2002), *The Cambridge History of the Book in Britain*, IV: *1557–1695* (Cambridge).

Baron, Hans (1955), *The Crisis of the Early Italian Renaissance: Civic Humanism and Republican Liberty in an Age of Classicism and Tyranny* (Princeton).

Bartl, Július (1996), 'Die Hussitenbewegung und ihre Auswirkungen in der Slowakei', in Karl Schwarz and Peter Švorc (eds.), *Die Reformation und ihre Wirkungsgeschichte in der Slowakei: kirche- und konfessionsgeschichtliche Beiträge* (Vienna), 9–21.

Basnett, Susan (1980), *Translation Studies* (3rd edn, London, 2002).

Bataillon, Marcel (1937), *Erasme en Espagne* (2nd edn, 3 vols., Geneva, 1991).

Bataillon, Marcel (1957), 'Gaspar von Barth interprète de la Célestine', *Revue de littérature comparée* 31, 321–40.

Bazzoli, Maurizio (1979), 'Giambattista Almici e la diffusione di Pufendorf nel settecento italiano', *Critica storica* 16.

Beebee, Thomas O. (1990), *Clarissa on the Continent: Translation and Seduction* (University Park, PA).

Beidelman, Thomas (ed., 1971), *The Translation of Cultures* (London).

Berman, Antoine (1984), *L'épreuve de l'étranger: culture et traduction dans l'Allemagne romantique* (Paris).

Bermann, Sandra and Michael Wood (eds., 2005) *Nation, Language and the Ethics of Translation* (Princeton).

Berry, Helen (2003), *Gender, Society and Print Culture in Late-Stuart England: The Cultural World of the Athenian Mercury* (London).

Bianchi-Giovini, Aurelio (1836), *Biografia di Paolo Sarpi* (Zürich).

Binns, J. W. (1990), *Intellectual Culture in Elizabethan and Jacobean England: The Latin Writings of the Age* (Leeds).

Binotti, Lucia (1996), 'Alfonso de Ulloa's Editorial Project: Translating, Writing and Marketing Spanish Best-Sellers in Venice', *Allegorica* 35–54.

Bitskey, István (1999), *Konfessionen und literarische Gattungen der frühen Neuzeit in Ungarn*, Debrecener Studien zur Literatur, vol. IV (Frankfurt).

Blassneck, Marcel (1934), *Frankreich als Vermittler Englisch-Deutscher Einflüsse im 17. und 18. Jht* (Leipzig).

Blois, Georges de (1875), *Louis de Blois* (English trans., London, 1878).

Bodenstedt, Sister Mary Immaculate (1955), *The Vita Christi of Ludolphus the Carthusian* (Washington DC).

Bodnárová, Milica (1998), 'Reformácia vo východoslovenských kráľovských mestách v 16. storočí' (The Reformation in East-Slovakian Royal Cities in the Sixteenth Century), in Ferdinand Uličný (ed.), *Reformácia na východnom Slovensku v 16.–18. storočí* (Reformation in Eastern Slovakia in the Sixteenth to Eighteenth Centuries) (Prešov), 19–38.

Bohannan, Laura (1971), 'Shakespeare in the Bush', repr. in James P. Spradley and David McCurdy (eds.), *Conformity and Conflict: Readings in Cultural Anthropology* (8th edn, New York, 1994).

Bolgar, Robert R. (1954), *The Classical Tradition and its Beneficiaries* (Cambridge).

Bonnant, Georges (1978), 'Typographies genevoises du XVIe au XVIIIe siècle', and 'La librairie genevoise en Allemagne jusqu'à la fin du XVIIIe siècle', in Beat Weber (ed.), *Cinq siècles d'imprimerie genevoise 1478–1978* (Geneva), 93–100, 131–66.

Borges, Jorge Luis (1936), 'Los traductores de las 1001 Noches', repr. in *Obras completas (1923–1972)* (Buenos Aires, 1974), 406–10.

Borowski, Andrzej (1999), 'General Theory of Translation in Old Polish Literary Culture', in G. Brogi Bercoff et al. (eds.), *Traduzione e rielaborazione nelle letterature di Polonia, Ucraina e Russia* (Alessandria), 23–38.

Botley, Paul (2004), *Latin Translation in the Renaissance* (Cambridge).

Bourdieu, Pierre (1972), *Outlines of a Theory of Practice* (English trans., Cambridge, 1977).

Bouza, Fernando (2001), *Corre manuscrito* (Madrid).

Brancaforte, Charlotte L. (1983), *Fridericius Berghius's Partial Latin Translation of Lazarillo* (Madison).

Bremond, Henri (1916–33), *Literary History of Religious Thought in France* (English trans., 3 vols., London and New York, 1929–37).

Brentjes, Sonja (2001), 'On the Relation Between the Ottoman Empire and the West European Republic of Letters (17th–18th Centuries)', in Ali Caksu (ed.), *Proceedings of the International Congress on Learning and Education in the Ottoman World* (Istanbul).

Brett, Annabel (1997), *Liberty, Right and Nature* (Cambridge).

Briesemeister, Dietrich (1978), 'La difusión europea de la literatura española en el siglo xvii a través de traducciones neolatinas', *Iberoromania* 7, 3–17.

Briesemeister, D. (1983), 'Die Lateinsprachige Rezeption der Werke von Teresa de Jesús in Deutschland', *Iberoromania* 18, 9–21.

Briesemeister, D. (1984), 'As traduções neolatinas de *Os Lusíadas*', in H. Bots and M. Kerkhof (eds.), *Forum litterarium* (Amsterdam and Marssen), 95–101.

Briesemeister, D. (1985), 'Französische Literatur in neulateinischen Übersetzungen', in Richard J. Schoeck (ed.), *Acta conventus neo-latini Bononiensis* (Binghamton), 205–15.

Briesemeister, D. (1990), 'Kaspar von Barth', in Alberto Martino (ed.), *Beiträge zur Aufnahme der Italienischen und Spanischen Literatur in Deutschland im 16. und 17. Jht* (Amsterdam and Atlanta), 257–88.

Brtáň, Rudo (1939), *Barokový slavizmus* (Baroque Slavism) (Liptovský Sv. Mikuláš).

Budick, Sanford and Wolfgang Iser (eds., 1996) *The Translatability of Cultures* (Stanford).

Burgess, Glenn (1992), *The Politics of the Ancient Constitution* (Basingstoke).

Burke, Peter (1967), 'Introduction', to Burke (ed.), *Sarpi* (New York).

Burke, Peter (1969), *The Renaissance Sense of the Past* (London).

Burke, Peter (1992), *The Fabrication of Louis XIV* (New Haven and London).

Burke, Peter (1995), *The Fortunes of the Courtier* (Cambridge).

Burke, Peter (2004), *Languages and Communities in Early Modern Europe* (Cambridge).

Burke, Peter (2006), 'The Jesuits and the Art of Translation in Early Modern Europe', in John O'Malley et al. (eds.), *The Jesuits*, II (Toronto), 24–32.

Burke, Peter (forthcoming), 'Translating the Turks', in Mel Richter and Martin Burke (eds.), *The History of Translation and Political Theory*.

Burrow, Colin (1997), 'Virgil in English Translation', in Charles Martindale (ed.), *Companion to Virgil* (Cambridge), 21–37.

Cañizares-Esguerra, Jorge (2001), *How to Write the History of the New World: Histories, Epistemologies and Identities in the 18th-Century Atlantic World* (Stanford).

Čaplovič, Ján (1972–84), *Bibliografia tlačí vydávaných na Slovensku do roku 1700 I–II* (Bibliography of Publications Printed in Slovakia until 1700) (Martin).

Celebi, Kâtip (Haji Khalfa) (1835–8), *Kesfü'z-zunûn an-esâmi'l-kütüb vel'l-fünun – Lexicon encyclopaedicum et bibliographicum* (7 vols., Leipzig and London).

Chaix, Gérald (1981), *Réforme et contre-réforme catholiques: recherches sur la Chartreuse de Cologne au XVIe siècle* (Salzburg).

Chan, Albert (2002), *Chinese Books and Documents in the Jesuit Archives in Rome: A Descriptive Catalogue, Japonica–Sinica I–IV* (Armonk, NY and London).

Charon, A. (1991), 'A. Paré et ses imprimeurs libraires', in B. Crenn (ed.), *Ambroise Paré et son temps* (Québec).

Chartier, Roger and Piero Corsi (eds., 1996), *Sciences et langues en Europe* (Paris).

Chen, Nancy N. (1999), 'Translating Psychiatry and Mental Health in Twentieth-Century China', in Liu, 305–27.

Cheyfitz, Eric (1991), *The Poetics of Imperialism: Translation and Colonization from The Tempest to Tarzan* (Oxford).

Chiappelli, Fredi (ed., 1985), *The Fairest Flower: The Emergence of National Consciousness in Renaissance Europe* (Florence).

Čičaj, Viliam (1996), 'Biblie v meštianskom prostredí stredného Slovenska' (Bibles within the Burgher's Environment of Central Slovakia), in Jana Skladaná (ed.), *Slovenská krest'anská a svetská kultúra* (Slovak Christian and Secular Culture) (Bratislava), 9–26.

Cioranescu, Alexandre (1938), *L'Arioste en France* (Paris).

Cochrane, Eric (1981), *Historians and Historiography in the Italian Renaissance* (Chicago).

Cognet, Louis (1949), *Les origines de la spiritualité française au XVIIe siècle* (Paris).

Cognet, Louis (1958), *Post-Reformation Spirituality* (English trans., New York, 1959).

Cognet, Louis (1968), *Introduction aux mystiques rhéno-flamands* (Paris).

Cohen, Paul (1997), *History in Three Keys* (New York).

Conway, Charles Abbott (1976), *The Vita Christi of Ludolph of Saxony and Late Medieval Devotion Centred on the Incarnation* (Salzburg).

Copeland, Rita (1991), *Rhetoric, Hermeneutics and Translation in the Middle Ages* (Cambridge).

Copenhaver, Brian (1988), 'Translation, Terminology and Style in Philosophical Discourse', in Charles Schmitt (ed.), *Cambridge History of Renaissance Philosophy* (Cambridge), 75–110.

Corbett, John (1999), *Written in the Language of the Scottish Nation: A History of Literary Translation into Scots* (Clevedon).

Couto, Dejanirah (2001), 'The Role of Interpreters, or *Linguas*, in the Portuguese Empire in the Sixteenth Century', online www.brown.edu/Departments/Portuguese_Brazilian_Studies/ejph/html/issue2/html

Crăciun, Maria, Ovidiu Ghitta and Graeme Murdock (eds., 2002), *Confessional Identity in East-Central Europe* (Aldershot).

Craigie, James (1950), 'Introduction', in *The Basilikon Doron of King James VI* (2 vols., Edinburgh).

Dagens, Jean (1952a), *Bérulle et les origines de la restauration catholique, 1575–1611* (Bruges).

Dagens, Jean (1952b), *Bibliographie chronologique de la littérature de spiritualité et de ses sources, 1501–1610* (Paris).

Daly, James (1979), *Sir Robert Filmer and English Political Thought* (Toronto).

Daniel, David P. (1979), 'The Acceptance of the Formula of Concord in Slovakia', *Archiv für Reformationsgeschichte* 70, 260–77.

Daniel, David P. (1980), 'The Influence of the Augsburg Confession in South-East Central Europe', *Sixteenth Century Journal* 11, 99–114.

Daniel, David P. (1995), 'Ikonoklazmus v 16. storočí na Slovensku' (Iconoclasm in Sixteenth-Century Slovakia), in Květoslava Kučerová and Eva Tkáčiková (eds.), *Náboženské a sociálne hnutia v Uhorsku a Čechách* (The Religious and Social Movements in Hungary and Czech Lands) (Bratislava), 120–7.

Daniel, David P. (1998), 'Publishing the Reformation in the Habsburg Monarchy', in R. Barnes (ed.), *Books Have their Own Destiny: Habent sua Fata Libelli* (Kirksville), 47–60.

Darnton, Robert (1982), *The Literary Underground and the Old Régime* (Cambridge, MA).

Dehergne, J. (1973), *Répertoire des Jésuites de Chine de 1552 à 1800* (Rome and Paris).

Delisle, Jean and Judith Woodsworth (eds., 1995), *Translators through History* (Amsterdam and Philadelphia).

De Mas, Enrico (1975), 'Le edizioni italiane delle opera di Bacone nella prima metà del '600', in De Mas, *Sovranità politica e unità cristiana nel Seicento anglo-veneto* (Ravenna), 151–214.

Desgraves, Louis (1984), *Répertoire des ouvrages de controverse entre Catholiques et Protestants en France 1598–1685* (2 vols., Geneva).

Desmed, R. (1964), 'Une traduction latine des *Fables* de La Fontaine', *Latomus* 23, 86–93.

Diller, A. (1972), 'Joannes Canabutzes and Michael Chrysococces', *Byzantion* 42, 257–8.

Dotoli, Giovanni (1983), 'Il *Mercure galant* di Donneau de Visé', *Quaderni del '600 francese* 5, 219–82.

Dunn-Lardeau, Brenda (ed., 1986), *Legenda aurea, sept siècles de diffusion* (Montréal and Paris).

Dupont-Ferrier, Gustave (1923), *Les jeunes de langues* (Paris).

Ďurovič, Ján P. (1940), *Evanjelická literatúra do tolerancie* (Lutheran Literature until the Toleration) (Martin).

Ďurovič, L'ubomír (1998), 'Slovenská vývinová línia spisovnej češtiny' (The Slovak Line of Development of Literary Czech), in *Pocta 650. výročí založení Univerzity Karlovy v Praze* (Homage to the 650th Anniversary of the Charles University in Prague) (Prague), 43–52.

Ďurovič, L'ubomír (2004), 'Rosa and Doležal', in Ján Bosák (ed.), L'ubomír Ďurovič: *O slovenčine a Slovensku: vybrané štúdie I* (L'ubomir Ďurovič: On the Slovak Language and Slovakia: Selected Writings I) (Bratislava), 225–32.

Ebel, Julia G. (1969), 'Translation and Cultural Nationalism in the Reign of Elizabeth', *Journal of the History of Ideas* 30, 593–602.

Eco, Umberto (2003), *Mouse or Rat? Translation as Negotiation* (London).

Elison, George (1988), *Deus Destroyed* (Cambridge, MA).

Etchegoyen, Gaston (1923), *L'amour divin: essai sur les sources de sainte Thérèse* (Bordeaux and Paris).

Evans, Ruth (1994), 'Translating Past Cultures?', in Roger Ellis and Ruth Evans (eds.), *The Medieval Translator*, vol. IV (Exeter), 20–45.

Even-Zohar, Itamar (1979), 'Polysystem Theory', *Poetics Today* 1, 237–310.

Fabian, Bernhard (1992), *The English Book in Eighteenth-Century Germany* (London).

Faisant, Claude (1979), 'Un des aspects de la réaction humaniste à la fin du XVIe siècle: la paraphrase latine des poètes français', in *Acta conventus neo-latini Amstelodamensis* (Munich), 358–70.

Feder, L. (1955), 'Latin Translations of *Paradise Lost*', *Neolatin News* 1, 16.

Feyel, Gilles (2000), *L'annonce et la nouvelle: la presse d'information en France sous l'ancien régime (1630–1788)* (Oxford).

Firpo, Luigi (1965), *Traduzioni dei Ragguagli di Traiano Boccalini* (Florence).

Fitzmaurice-Kelly, James (1897), '*El licenciado vidriero*', *Revue hispanique* 4, 54–70.

Fitzmaurice-Kelly, James (1906), *Cervantes in England* (London).

Folena, Gianfranco (1991), *Volgarizzare e tradurre* (Turin).

Fonda, E. A. (1979), 'As versões latinas de *Os Lusíadas*', *Convergência Lusiada* 1, 137–56.

Fonkich, Boris L. (1999), *Grecheskie rukopis europiskh sobranii* (Greek Manuscripts on European Topics) (Moscow).

Foucault, Michel (1966), *Les mots et les choses*, English trans. as *The Order of Things* (English trans., London, 1974).

Foulché-Delbosc, R. (1915), 'Bibliographie espagnole de Fray Antonio de Guevara', *Revue hispanique* 33 (New York and Paris).

Franková, Libuša (1993), 'Zástoj českých a moravských exulantov na kultúrnom rozvoji Slovenska v prvej polovici 17. storočia' (The Position of the Czech and Moravian Exiles within the Cultural Development of Slovakia in the First Half of the Seventeenth Century), in Michal Otčenáš and Peter Kónya (eds.), *Jakub Jakobeus: život, dielo a doba* (Jakub Jakobeus: His Life, Work and Period) (Prešov), 97–109.

Fuller, Ross (1995), *The Brotherhood of the Common Life and its Influence* (Albany).

Fulton, J. F. (1961), *A Bibliography of the Hon. Robert Boyle* (2nd edn, Oxford).

Garcia, Stéphane (2004), *Elie Diodati et Galilée: naissance d'un réseau scientifique dans l'Europe du XVIIe siècle* (Florence).

García Mateo, Rogelio (2002), *El misterio de la vida de Cristo en los Ejercicios ignacianos y en el Vita Christi Cartujano* (Madrid).

García Gutiérrez, José M. (1999), *La herejía de los alumbrados: historia y filosofía* (Madrid).

Gemert, Guillaume van (1979), *Aegidius Albertinus* (Amsterdam).

Gerber, Adolph (1911–13), *Nicolò Machiavelli: die Übersetzungen* (4 vols., Gotha).

Gernet, Jacques (1982), *Chine et christianisme: action et réaction* (Paris).

Gilot, M. (1975), *Les journaux de Marivaux, itinéraire moral et accomplissement esthétique* (Lille).

Gilot, M. and Jean Sgard (1981), 'Le journalisme masqué', in Pierre Rétat (ed.), *Le journalisme d'ancien régime* (Lyon), 285–313.

Girard, Pascale (1999), *Os religiosos ocidentais na China na época moderna* (Macau).

Glatzer, Nahum N. (ed., 1953), *Franz Rosenzweig* (2nd edn, New York, 1961).

Gökyay, Orhan Saik (1982), *Kâtip Celebi, Yasami, Kisiligi ve Yapitlarindan Secmeler* (Ankara).

Golinski, Jan (1998), *Making Natural Knowledge: Constructivism and the History of Science* (Cambridge).

Goodman, Grant K. (1967), *Japan and the Dutch, 1600–1853* (rev. edn, Richmond, VA, 2000).

Graeber, Wilhelm and Geneviève Roche (1988), *Englische Literatur des 17. und 18. Jht in französische Übersetzung und deutscher Weiterübersetzung* (Tübingen).

Grafton, Anthony (2001), *Alberti* (London).

Grafton, Anthony and Lisa Jardine (1990), '"Studied for Action": How Gabriel Harvey Read his Livy', *Past and Present* 129, 30–78.

Grant, W. Leonard (1954), 'European Vernacular Works in Latin Translation', *Studies in the Renaissance* 1, 120–56.

Grell, Ole P. (ed., 1998), *Paracelsus: The Man and his Reputation, his Ideas and their Transformation* (Leiden).

Grendler, Paul (1969), 'Francesco Sansovino and Italian Popular History', *Studies in the Renaissance* 16, 139–80.

Grey, Ernest (1973), *Guevara, a Forgotten Renaissance Author* (The Hague).

Groult, Pierre (1927), *Les mystiques des Pays-Bas et la littérature espagnole du seizième siècle* (Louvain).

Guillerm, Luce (1996), 'Les belles infidèles, ou l'auteur respecté', in M. Ballard and L. d'Hulst (eds.), *La traduction en France à l'âge classique* (Paris), 28–42.

Gustafson, W. W. (1933), 'The Influence of the *Tatler* and *Spectator* in Sweden', *Scandinavian Studies and Notes* 12, 65–72.

Guy, R. Kent (1987), *The Emperor's Four Treasuries: Scholars and the State in the Late Qianlong Period* (Cambridge, MA).

Haeghen, Ferdinand van der (1897–1907), *Bibliotheca Erasmiana* (Ghent).

Hallberg, Peter (2003), *Ages of Liberty* (Stockholm).

Hamilton, Alastair (1992), *Heresy and Mysticism in Sixteenth-Century Spain: The Alumbrados* (Cambridge).

Hammond, Gerald (1982), *The Making of the English Bible* (Manchester).

Hankins, James (1990), *Plato in the Italian Renaissance* (2 vols., Leiden).

Hankins, James (2003–4), *Humanism and Platonism in the Italian Renaissance* (2 vols., Rome).

Hansson, Stina (1982), '*Afsatt på Swensko': 1600-talets tryckta översättningslitteratur* (Göteborg).

Harrison, John (1978), *The Library of Isaac Newton* (Cambridge).

Hartner, W. (1971), 'Planetary Theories, Common Features in the Late Islamic and Renaissance Astronomy', Academia Nationale dei Lincei, Fondazione Alessandro Volta, *Atti dei convegni* 13, 609–29.

Hausmann, Frank-Rutger (1992), *Bibliographie der deutschen Übersetzungen aus dem italienischen bis 1730* (2 vols., Tübingen).

Hebenstreit-Wilfert, Hildegard (1975), 'Wunder und Legende: Studien zu Leben und Werk von Laurentius Surius, 1522–1578', thesis, University of Tübingen.

Heilbron, Johan (1999), 'Toward a Sociology of Translation: Book Translations as a Cultural World-System', *European Journal of Social Theory* 2, 429–44.

Henkel, W. (1972), 'The Polyglot Printing-Office of the Congregation', in J. Metzler (ed.), *Sacrae Congregationis de Propaganda Fide memoria rerum*, vol. I (Rome), 335–50.

Hermans, Theo (1985), 'Images of Translation: Metaphor and Images in the Renaissance Discourse on Translation', in Hermans (ed.), *The Manipulation of Literature* (New York), 103–35.

Hermans, Theo (1992), 'Renaissance Translation between Literalism and Imitation', in Harald Kittel (ed.), *Geschichte, System, literarische Übersetzung* (Berlin), 95–116.

Hieronymus, Frank (1995), 'Physicians and Publishers: The Translation of Medical Works in Sixteenth Century Basle', in J. L. Flood and W. A. Kelly (eds.), *The German Book 1450–1750* (London), 95–110.

Higashibaba, Ikuo (2001), *Christianity in Early Modern Japan* (Leiden).

Highet, Gilbert (1949), *The Classical Tradition* (Oxford).

Higman, Francis M. (1984), 'Les traductions françaises de Luther, 1524–50', in Jean-François Gilmont, *Palaestra typographica* (Paris), 15–27.

Higman, Francis M. (1994), 'Calvin's Works in Translation', in Andrew Pettegree, Alastair Duke and Gill Lewis (eds.), *Calvinism in Europe 1540–1620* (Cambridge), 82–99.

Hochstrasser, Tim J. (1993), 'Conscience and Reason: The Natural Law Theory of Jean Barbeyrac', *Historical Journal* 36, 289–308.

Holmes, James S. (1972), 'The Name and Nature of Translation Studies', repr. in his, *Translated! Papers on Translation and Translation Studies* (Amsterdam, 1988), 67–80.

Homza, Lu Ann (2000), *Religious Authority in the Spanish Renaissance* (Baltimore).

Hoornaert, Rodolphe (1922), *Sainte Thérèse écrivain: son milieu, ses facultés, son oeuvre* (Paris).

Howland, Douglas (2001), *Translating the West* (Honolulu).

Hsia, Adrian (2000), 'The Literary Reception of Martino Martini's *De Bello Tartarico* in Europe', in Roman Malek and Arnold Zingerle (eds.), *Martino Martini* (Nettetal), 115–25.

Hughes, Lindsey (1998), *Russia in the Age of Peter the Great* (New Haven).

Hunter, Michael and Edward B. Davis (eds., 1999), *The Works of Robert Boyle*, vol. I (London).

Hyma, Albert (1965), *The Christian Renaissance: A History of the 'Devotio moderna'* (Hamden, CT).

Iserloh, Erwin (1971), *Thomas von Kempen und die Kirchenreform im Spätmittelalter* (Kempen-Niederrhein).

Israel, Jonathan (2001), *Radical Enlightenment* (Oxford).

Jacquemond, Richard (1992), 'Translation and Cultural Hegemony: The Case of French-Arabic Translation', in Venuti, 139–58.

Jakobson, Roman (1959), 'On Linguistic Aspects of Translation', in R. A. Brower (ed.), *On Translation* (Cambridge, MA), 232–9.

Javitch, Daniel (1971), '*The Philosopher of the Court*: A French Satire Misunderstood', *Comparative Literature* 23, 97–124.

Johns, Adrian (1998), *The Nature of the Book* (Chicago).

Johns, Adrian (2002), 'Science and the Book', in John Barnard and Don F. McKenzie (eds.), *The Cambridge History of the Book in Britain*, IV: *1557–1695* (Cambridge), 274–303.

Jones, Joseph R. (1975), *Antonio de Guevara* (Boston).

Jones, Richard F. (1953), *The Triumph of the English Language* (Stanford).

Kahn, Didier (1998), 'Paracelsisme et alchimie en France à la fin de la Renaissance', thesis, University of Paris IV.

Karas, Y. (1992), Οι επιστήμες στην Τουρκοκρατία – χειρόγραφα και έντυπα (Science under Ottoman Rule – Manuscripts and Printed Books) (3 vols., Athens).

Karttunen, Frances (1994), *Between Worlds: Interpreters, Guides and Survivors* (New Brunswick).

Kastanis, N. (1998), Οψεις της νεοελληνικής μαθηματικής παιδείας (Aspects of Modern Greek Mathematical Culture) (Salonica).

Kastanis, N. (2004), Μια εισαγωγή στη νεοελληνική μαθηματική παιδεία (An Introduction to Modern Greek Mathematical Culture) http://users.auth. gr/~nioka/mia_eisagogi_sti_neoelliniki_math_paideia.html

Keipert, Helmut (1993), 'Anton Bernolák's Kodifikation des Slowaksichen im Lichte der theresianischen Schulschriften', in Karl Gutschmidt, Helmut

Keipert and Hans Rothe (eds.), *Slavistische Studien zum XI. Internationalen Slavistenkongreß in Preßburg/Bratislava* (Cologne-Weimar-Vienna), 233–46.

Kelly, Louis (1979), *The Faithful Interpreter: A History of Translation Theory and Practice in the West* (Oxford).

Keuning, Johannes (1973), *Willem Jansz. Blaeu: A Biography and History of his Work as a Cartographer and Publisher* (revised by Marijke Donkersloot-de Vrij, Amsterdam).

Kim, Sanngkeun (2004), *Strange Names of God: The Missionary Translation of the Divine Name and the Chinese Responses to Matteo Ricci's Shangti in Late Ming China, 1583–1644* (New York).

Kissel, W. (ed., 1999), *Kultur als Übersetzung* (Würzburg).

Kitagaki, Muneharu (1981), *Principles and Problems of Translation in Seventeenth-Century England* (Kyoto).

Kloepfer, Rolf (1967), *Die Theorie der literarischen Übersetzung* (Munich).

Körner, Martin (1988), 'Profughi italiani in Svizzera', in *Città italiane del '500 tra riforma e controriforma* (Lucca), 1–22.

Kósa, László (1999), *A Cultural History of Hungary: From the Beginnings to the Eighteenth Century* (Budapest).

Kosheleva, O. E. and R. A. Simonov (1981), 'Novoe o pervoi russkoi knige po teoreticheskoi geometrii XVII veka i eio avtore', in *Kniga: issledovaniya i materialy* 42, 63–73.

Köster, Uwe (1995), 'Rezeption und Gebrauchssituation katholischer Bibelübersetzungen', in Köster, *Studien zu den katholischen deutschen Bibelübersetzungen im 16., 17. und 18. Jahrhundert* (Münster), 232–69.

Kowalská, Eva (2001), *Evanjelické a.v. spoločenstvo v 18. storočí: hlavné problémy jeho vývoja a fungovania v spoločnosti* (The Lutheran Community in the Eighteenth Century: The Main Problems of its Development and Action in Society) (Bratislava).

Kuzakov, V. K. (1976), *Ocherki razvitya estestvennonauchnykh i tekhnicheskikn predstavlenii na Rusi v. X–XVII v.v.* (Essays on the Development of Science and Technology in Russia in the X–XVII Centuries) (Moscow).

Kuzakov, V. K. (1991), *Otechestvennaya istoriografiya istorii nauki v Rossii X–XVII v.v.* (Russian Historiography of the History of Science in the X–XVII Centuries) (Moscow).

Kvačala, Ján (1935), *Dějiny reformácie na Slovensku* (History of the Reformation in Slovakia) (Lipt. Sv. Mikuláš).

Kyas, Vladimír (1997), *Česká Bible v dějinách národního písemnictví* (The Czech Bible in the History of the National Literary Culture) (Prague).

Labrousse, Elisabeth (1963–4), *Pierre Bayle* (2 vols., The Hague).

Laeven, A. H. (1986), *Acta eruditorum* (Amsterdam).

Lai, Chang-Chung (1999), *Adam Smith across Nations* (Oxford).

Lambert, José (1993), 'History, Historiography and the Discipline', in Yves Gambier and Jorma Tommola (eds.), *Knowledge and Translation* (Turku), 3–25.

Lampsides, U. (1937), 'Georges Chrysococcis, le médecin et son oeuvre', *Byzantinische Zeitschrift*, 38.

Larner, John (1999), *Marco Polo and the Discovery of the World* (New Haven and London, 1999).

Larwill, Paul H. (1934), *La théorie de la traduction au début de la Renaissance* (Munich).

Lawrance, Jeremy (2001), 'Europe and the Turks in Spanish Literature of the Renaissance', in Nigel Griffin et al. (eds.), *Culture and Society in Habsburg Spain* (Woodbridge), 17–34.

Lawton, Harold W. (1926), 'Notes sur Jean Baudouin', *Revue de littérature comparée* 6, 673–81.

Lefevere, André (1992), *Translation, Rewriting and the Manipulation of Literary Fame* (London).

Legrand, Pierre (2005), 'Issues in the Translatability of Law', in Bermann and Wood, 30–50.

Lewis, Bernard (1999), 'From Babel to Dragomans', *Proceedings of the British Academy* 101, 37–54.

Lianeri, Alexandra (2006), 'Translation and the Language(s) of Historiography', in Theo Hermans (ed.), *Translating Others*, vol. I (Manchester).

Likhachev, D. S. (ed., 1987–98), *Slovar' knizhnikov i knizhnosti Drevnei Rusi* (Dictionary of Booklovers and the Book Culture in Ancient Russia) (3 vols., Petersburg).

Liu, Lydia H. (1995), *Translingual Practice: Literature, National Culture and Translated Modernity – China 1900–37* (Stanford).

Liu, Lydia H. (ed., 1999), *Tokens of Exchange* (Durham, NC).

Löfstedt, Bengt (1989), 'Notizen eines Latinisten zum *Leviathan* von Thomas Hobbes', *Arctos* 23, 133–43.

Long, Lynne (2001), *Translating the Bible: From the 7th to the 17th Century* (Aldershot).

Love, Harold (1993), *Scribal Publication in Seventeenth-Century England* (Oxford).

Luciani, V. (1936), *Francesco Guicciardini and his European Reputation* (New York).

Lücker, Maria Alberta (1950), *Meister Eckhart und die Devotio moderna* (Leiden).

McEwen, Gilbert D. (1972), *The Oracle of the Coffee-House: John Dunton's Athenian Mercury* (London).

McFarlane, I. D. (1978), 'Pierre de Ronsard and the Neo-Latin Poetry of his Time', *Res publica litterarum* 1.

McKenna, K. J. (1977), 'Catherine the Great's *Vsiakaia Vsiachina* and the *Spectator* Tradition of the Satirical Journal of Morals and Manners', Ph.D. thesis, University of Colorado.

Mackenzie, Cameron A. (2002), *The Battle for the Bible in England, 1557–1582* (New York).

McKitterick, David (2002), 'University Printing at Oxford and Cambridge', in John Barnard and Don McKenzie (eds.), *Cambridge History of the Book in Britain*, vol. IV (Cambridge), 189–205.

Mahmûd-i Sirvânî, Muhammed bin (2004) *Mürsid* (Ankara).

Malcolm, Noel (1984), *De Dominis, 1560–1624: Venetian, Anglican and Relapsed Heretic* (London).

Mannheim, Karl (1927), *Conservatism* (English trans., London, 1986).

Marichal, Juan (1971), 'Montaigne en España', in Marichal, *La Voluntad de estilo* (Madrid), 101–22.

Marker, Gary (1985), *Publishing, Printing and the Origins of Intellectual Life in Russia 1700–1800* (Princeton).

Marks, Richard Bruce (1974), *The Medieval Manuscript Library of the Charterhouse of St Barbara in Cologne* (Salzburg).

Marocchi, Massimo (1988), 'Spirituality in the Sixteenth and Seventeenth Centuries', in John O'Malley (ed.), *Catholicism in Early Modern History: A Guide to Research* (St Louis).

Marotti, Arthur M. (1995), *Manuscript, Print and the English Renaissance Lyric* (Ithaca).

Marsden, Richard (1996), 'Cain's Face, and Other Problems: The Legacy of the Earliest English Bible Translation', in *Reformation* 1, 29–51.

Martens, Wolfgang (1968), *Die Botschaft der Tugend: die Aufklärung im Spiegel der deutschen moralischen Wochenschriften* (Stuttgart).

Martin, Henri-Jean (1969), *Livre, pouvoir et société à Paris au XVIIe siècle* (Geneva).

Matthiessen, Francis O. (1931), *Translation: An Elizabethan Art* (Cambridge, MA).

Maxwell, Kenneth (2003), *Naked Tropics* (London).

Mayenowa, Maria R. (1984), 'Aspects of the Language Question in Poland', in Riccardo Picchio and Harvey Goldblatt (eds.), *Aspects of the Slavic Language Question*, vol. I (New Haven), 337–76.

Mercier, R. (1988), review of Pingree in *Byzantinische Zeitschrift* 81, 91–3.

Mignini, Filippo (ed., 2005), *Matteo Ricci: Dell'amicizia* (Macerata).

Milo, Daniel (1984), 'La bourse mondiale de la traduction: un baromètre culturel?', *Annales: économies, sociétés, civilisations* 39, 93–115.

Mišianik, Ján (1971), *Bibliografia slovenského písomníctva* (Bibliography of Slovak Literature) (Martin).

Moeller, Bernd (1987), 'Luther in Europe: His Works in Translation, 1517–46', in E. I. Kouri and Tom Scott (eds.), *Politics and Society in Reformation Europe* (London), 235–51.

Moore, Will G. (1930), *La réforme allemande et la littérature française* (Strasbourg).

Morgan, B. (1929), *Histoire du Journal des savants* (Paris).

Mornet, Daniel (1910), 'Les enseignements des bibliothèques privées (1750–1780)', *Revue d'histoire littéraire de la France* 17, 449–96.

Mounin, Georges (1955), *Les belles infidèles* (Paris).

Mrva, Ivan (1995), 'Heretické hnutia a uhorské zákony' (Heretical Movements and Hungarian Laws), in Květoslava Kučerová and Eva Tkáčiková (eds.), *Náboženské a sociálne hnutia v Uhorsku a Čechách* (The Religious and Social Movements in Hungary and the Czech Lands) (Bratislava), 42–56.

Mrva, Ivan (1999), 'Uhorsko, azylová krajina v období novoveku' (Hungary, the Land of Asylum in the Modern Period), *Česko-slovenská historická ročenka*, 17–25.

Mulligan, Lotte et al. (1979), 'Intentions and Conventions: Quentin Skinner's Method for the Study of the History of Ideas', *Political Studies* 27, 84–98.

Munday, Jeremy (2001), *Introducing Translation Studies* (London).

Nelson, C. and M. Seccombe (2002), 'The Creation of the Periodical Press', in John Barnard and Don F. McKenzie (eds.), *The Cambridge History of the Book in Britain*, IV: *1557–1695* (Cambridge), 533–50.

Neugebauer, Otto (1975), *A History of Ancient Mathematical Astronomy* (3 vols., Berlin-Heidelberg and New York).

Nicolaïdis, Ephthemios (1995), 'Les Grecs en Russie et les Russes en Chine: le contexte de la copie par Chrysanthos des livres astronomiques perdus de F. Verbiest', *Archives internationales d'histoire des sciences* 133, 271–308.

Nicolaïdis, Ephthemios (2003), 'Verbiest, Spathar and Chrysanthos: The Spread of Verbiest's Science to Eastern Europe', in W. F. Vande Walle and N. Golvers (eds.), *The History of the Relations between the Low Countries and China in the Qing Era (1644–1911)* (Leuven), 37–57.

Nida, Eugene A. (1939), *The Book of a Thousand Tongues* (rev. edn, New York, 1972).

Nieto, José C. (1970), *Juan de Valdés and the Origins of the Spanish and Italian Reformation* (Geneva).

Niranjana, Tejaswini (1992), *Siting Translation: History, Post-structuralism and the Colonial Context* (Berkeley).

Norton, Glyn P. (1984), *The Ideology and Language of Translation in Renaissance France* (Geneva).

Oldenburg, Henry (1965–77), *Correspondence*, ed. Rupert Hall (11 vols., Madison, WI), vol. IV.

Orcibal, Jean (1959), *La rencontre du Carmel Thérésien avec les mystiques du nord* (Paris).

Orcibal, Jean (1961), *Saint-Cyran et le jansénisme* (Paris).

Orcibal, Jean (1962), *La spiritualité de Saint-Cyran* (Paris).

Orcibal, Jean (1966), *Saint Jean de la Croix et les mystiques rhéno-flamands* (Bruges).

Ozen, Mine E. (1998), *Piri Reis and his Charts* (Istanbul).

Oz-Salzberger, Fania (1995), *Translating the Enlightenment: Scottish Civic Discourse in 18th-Century Germany* (Oxford).

Palau y Dulcet, Antonio (1948–77), *Manual de librero hispanoamericano* (28 vols., Oxford and Barcelona).

Pallares-Burke, Maria Lúcia (1993), 'Ousadia feminina e ordem burguesa', repr. in Pallares-Burke, *Nísia Floresta, O carapuceiro e outros ensaios de tradução cultural* (São Paulo, 1995).

Pallares-Burke, Maria Lúcia (1994a), 'A Spectator in the Tropics: A Case Study in the Production and Reproduction of Culture', *Comparative Studies in Society and History* 36, 576–701.

Pallares-Burke, Maria Lúcia (1994b), 'An Androgynous Observer in the Eighteenth-Century Press: *La Spectatrice, 1728–1729*', *Women's History Review* 3, 411–34.

Pallares-Burke, Maria Lúcia (1994–5), 'The Importance of Being Foreign: The *Journal Etranger* and the Eighteenth-Century Republic of Letters', *Journal of the Institute of Romance Studies* 3, 181–201.

Pallares-Burke, Maria Lúcia (1996), 'The *Spectator* Abroad: The Fascination of the Mask', *History of European Ideas* 22, 1–8.

Pallares-Burke, Maria Lúcia (2002), *The New History: Confessions and Conversations* (Cambridge).

Pallares-Burke, Maria Lúcia (2004), 'A Spectator of the Spectators: Jacques-Vincent Delacroix', in Hans-Jürgen Lüsebrink and Jeremy D. Popkin (eds.), *Enlightenment, Revolution and the Periodical Press* (Oxford).

Palmer, Martin E. (ed. and trans., 1996), *On Giving the Spiritual Exercises: The Early Jesuit Manuscript Directories and the Official Directory of 1599* (St Louis).

Pálsson, Gisli (ed., 1993), *Beyond Boundaries: Understanding Translation and Anthropological Discourse* (Oxford).

Pantin, Isabelle (1998), 'Langues', in R. Halleux and M. Blay (eds.), *Dictionnaire critique de la science classique* (Paris), 75–83.

Pantin, Isabelle (1999), 'New Philosophy and Old Prejudices: Aspects of the Reception of Copernicanism in a Divided Europe', *Studies in History and Philosophy of Science* 30, 237–62.

Pantin, Isabelle (2000), 'Galilée, l'église conquérante et la république des philosophes', in A. Mothu (ed.), *Révolution scientifique et libertinage* (Turnhout), 11–34.

Pantin, Isabelle (2003), 'La traduction latine des *Œuvres* d'Ambroise Paré', in Eveline Berriot-Salvatore (ed.), *Ambroise Paré (1510–1590): pratique et écriture de la science à la Renaissance* (Paris), 315–36.

Paschos, E. A. and P. Sotiroudis (eds., 1998), *The Schemata of the Stars* (Singapore).

Paz, Octavio (1971), *Traducción* (Barcelona).

Perini, Leandro (2002), *La vita e i tempi di Pietro Perna* (Rome).

Péter, Katalin (1991), 'The Struggle for Protestant Religious Liberty at the 1646–47 Diet in Hungary', in Robert J. W. Evans and T. V. Thomas Crown (eds.), *Church and Estates: Central European Politics in the Sixteenth and Seventeenth Centuries* (London), 261–8.

Peters, Robert (1967), 'Erasmus and the Fathers: Their Practical Value', *Church History* 36, 254–61.

Petsios, Constantinos (2004), 'Middle Age-Scholastic Aristotelism as Frame for the Teaching of Philosophy in Venice during the Seventeenth Century: The Case of Mathaios (Meletios) Typaldos', in G. N. Vlahakis and E. Nicolaidis (eds.), Βυζάντιο-Βενετία-Νεώτερος Ελληνισμός: μια περιπλάνηση στον κόσμο της επιστημονικής σκέψης (Byzantium-Venice-Modern Hellenism: A Journey Through the World of Modern Greek Scientific Thought) (Athens), 245–82.

Picwnik, M. H. (1979), *O anónimo: journal portugais du 18e siècle* (Paris).

Pingree, D. (1985–6), *The Astronomical Works of Gregory Chioniades* (2 vols., Amsterdam).

Plomer, H. R. (1922), *A Dictionary of the Printers and Booksellers who Were at Work in England, Scotland and Ireland from 1668 to 1725* (Oxford).

Pocock, John (1975), *The Machiavellian Moment: Florentine Political Thought and the Atlantic Republican Tradition* (Princeton).

Pocock, John (2003), *Barbarism and Religion*, vol. III (Cambridge).

Price, Mary B. and Lawrence M. Price (1934), *The Publication of English Literature in Germany in the 18th Century* (Berkeley).

Pym, Anthony (1993), 'Negotiation Theory as an Approach to Translation History: An Inductive Lesson from 15th-Century Castille', in Yves Gambier and Jorma Tommola (eds.), *Knowledge and Translation* (Turku), 27–39.

Pym, Anthony (1998), *Method in Translation History* (Manchester).

Pym, Anthony (2000), *Negotiating the Frontier: Translators and Intercultures in Spanish History* (Manchester).

Rafael, Vicente L. (1993), *Contracting Colonialism*, 2nd edn (Durham, NC, 1988).

Rainov, T. (1940), *Nauka v Rossii XI–XVII vekov* (Science in Russia in the XI–XVII Centuries) (Moscow and Leningrad).

Rau, F. (1980), *Zur Verbreitung und Nachahmung des Tatler und Spectator* (Heidelberg).

Raymond, Joad (1996), *The Invention of the Newspaper: English Newsbooks 1641–9* (Oxford).

Reames, Sherry L. (1985), *The Legenda Aurea: A Reexamination of its Paradoxical History* (Madison).

Reiss, Katharina and Hans J. Vermeer (1984), *Grundlegung einer allgemeinen Translationstheorie* (Tübingen).

Rennhofer, Friedrich (1961), *Bücherkunde des katholischen Lebens: bibliographisches Lexikon der religiösen Literatur der Gegenwart* (Vienna).

Rhein, Reglinde (1995), *Die Legenda aurea des Jacobus de Voragine: die Entfaltung von Heiligkeit in 'Historia' und 'Doctrina'* (Cologne).

Richter, Melvin (1990), 'Reconstructing the History of Political Languages: Pocock, Skinner and the *Geschichtliche Grundbegriffe*', *History and Theory* 29, 38–70.

Ries, Paul (1977), 'The Anatomy of a Seventeenth-Century Newspaper', *Daphnis* 6, 171–232.

Robbins, Caroline (1959), *The Eighteenth-Century Commonwealthman* (Cambridge, MA).

Robinson, Douglas (ed., 1997), *Western Translation Theory from Herodotos to Nietzsche* (Manchester).

Roche, Daniel (1989), *The Culture of Clothing: Dress and Fashion in the 'Ancien Regime'* (English trans., Cambridge, 1994).

Rösel, Hubert (1961), *Die tschechischen Drucke der Hallenser Pietisten* (Würzburg).

Rothe, Hans, Friedrich Scholz and Ján Dorul'a (eds., 2002), *Swaté Biblia Slowénské, aneb Pisma Swatého Cástka I–II* (The Holy Slovak Bible or the First and Second Part of the Bible) (Paderborn).

Rubel, Paula G. and Abraham Rosman (eds., 2003), *Translating Cultures: Perspectives on Translation and Anthropology* (Oxford).

Rudwick, Martin (1972), *The Meaning of Fossils* (London).

Rumbold, M. E. (1991), *Traducteur Huguenot: Pierre Coste* (Frankfurt).

Russell, Peter (1985), *Traducciones y traductores en la península ibérica (1400–1550)* (Barcelona).

Ryšánek, František (1954), *Slovník k Žilinské knize* (The Dictionary of the City Book of Žilina) (Bratislava).

Sainz Rodriguez, Pedro (1979), *La siembra mística del Cardenal Cisneros* (Madrid).

Sakai, Naoki (1997), *Translation and Subjectivity* (Minneapolis).

Sanchez Lora, José Luis (1988), *Mujeres, conventos y formas de la religiosidad barroca* (Madrid).

Scaglione, Aldo (ed., 1984), *The Emergence of National Languages* (Ravenna).

Schaffer, Frederic C. (1998), *Democracy in Translation* (Ithaca).

Schäffner, Christina (ed., 1999), *Translation and Norms* (Clevedon).

Schäfke, Werner (ed., 1991), *Die Kölner Kartause um 1500: Aufsatzband* (Cologne).

Schoneveld, Cornelis W. (1983), *Intertraffic of the Mind: Studies in 17th-Century Anglo-Dutch Translation* (Leiden).

Schoneveld, Cornelis W. (1984), 'The Dutch Translation of Addison and Steele's *Spectator*', in *The Role of Periodicals in the Eighteenth Century* (Leiden), 33–9.

Schott, H. and I. Zinguer (eds., 1998), *Paracelsus und seine internationale Rezeption in der Frühen Neuzeit* (Leiden).

Schröder, Thomas (1995), *Die ersten Zeitungen* (Tübingen).

Schweiger, Franz (1830–4), *Handbuch der classischer Bibliographie* (3 vols., Leipzig).

Scott, Mary Augusta (1916), *Elizabethan Translations from the Italian* (Boston and New York).

Seguin, Jean Pierre (1964), *L'information en France avant la périodique* (Paris).

Seidel Menchi, Silvana (1977), 'Le traduzioni italiane di Lutero nella prima metà del '500', *Rinascimento* 17, 31–108.

Sesen, Ramazan et al. (1984), *Fihris makhtutat el-tibb el-Islami fi maktabat turkiyya* (Catalogue of Islamic Medical Manuscripts in Libraries in Turkey) (Istanbul).

Sevcenco, I. (1962), *Etudes sur la polémique entre Théodore Métochite et Nicéphore Choumnos*, ed. Byzantion (Brussels).

Sgard, Jean (ed., 1976), *Dictionnaire des journalistes 1600–1789* (Grenoble).

Sgard, Jean (ed., 1991), *Dictionnaire des journaux 1600–1789* (Paris and Oxford).

Shackelford, Jole (2004), *A Philosophical Path for Paracelsian Medicine: The Ideas, Intellectual Context, and Influence of Petrus Severinus: 1540–1602* (Copenhagen).

Shore, Paul J. (1998), *The Vita Christi of Ludolph of Saxony and its Influence on the Spiritual Exercises of Ignatius of Loyola* (St Louis).

Simonov, R. A. (2000), 'Novye materially po istorii matematiki Drevnei Rusi' (New Materials on the History of Mathematics in Old Russia), *Istoriko-matematicheskie Issledovaniya* 5, 244–71.

Skinner, Quentin (1978), *The Foundations of Modern Political Thought* (Cambridge).

Skinner, Quentin and Martin van Gelderen (eds., 2002), *Republicanism, a Shared European Heritage* (Cambridge).

Skladaná, Jana (2002), 'Jazykový charakter mestských kníh zo 16.–18. storočia' (The Linguistic Character of the City Books from the Sixteenth to Eighteenth Centuries), in *Historické štúdie* 42, 159–64.

Smith, M. C. (1988), 'Latin Translations of Ronsard', in S. P. Revard et al. (eds.), *Acta conventus neo-latini Guelpherbytani* (Binghamton), 331–8.

Smolinsky, Heribert (1998), 'Sprachenstreit in der Theologie? Latein oder Deutsch für Bibel und Liturgie – ein Problem der katholischen Kontroverstheologen des 16. Jahrhunderts', in *Latein und Nationalsprachen in der Renaissance* (Wiesbaden), 181–200.

Soll, Jacob (2004), *Publishing the Prince: History, Reading and the Birth of Political Criticism* (Ann Arbor, MI).

Solon, P. (1968), 'The *Hexapterygon* of Michael Chrysokokkes', Ph.D. thesis, Brown University.

Solon, P. (1970), 'The *Six Wings* of Immanuel Bonfils and Michael Chrysokokkes', *Centaurus* 15, 1–20.

Sommervogel, Carlos (ed., 1890–1900), *Bibliothèque de la Compagnie de Jesus* (10 vols., Brussels).

Sopko, Július (1997), '*Devotio moderna* a jej podoby na Slovensku v 15. storočí' (*Devotio moderna* and its Manifestation in Slovakia), in Jozef Šimončič (ed.), *Trnavská univerzita 1635–1777* (University in Trnava 1635–1777) (Trnava), 281–94.

Spitz, Lewis (1963), *The Religious Renaissance of the German Humanists* (Cambridge, MA).

Stackelberg, Jürgen von (1971), 'Das Ende der "belles infidèles"', in Karl-Richard Bausch and Hans-Martin Gauger (eds.), *Interlinguistica* (Tübingen), 583–96.

Stackelberg, Jürgen von (1984), *Übersetzungen aus zweiten Hand* (Berlin).

Standaert, Nicolas (1985), 'Note on the Spread of Jesuit Writings in Late Ming and Early Qing China', *China Mission Studies (1550–1800) Bulletin* 7, 22–32.

Standaert, Nicolas (ed., 2002), *Handbook of Christianity in China*, vol. I: *635–1800* (Leiden).

Stankiewicz, Edward (1981), 'The "Genius" of Language in Sixteenth-Century Linguistics', in Jürgen Trabant (ed.), *Histoire de la linguistique* (Madrid and Berlin), 177–89.

Steiner, George (1975), *After Babel* (Oxford).

Steiner, T. R. (1975), *English Translation Theory 1650–1800* (Amsterdam).

Stephen, Leslie (1910), *English Literature and Society in the Eighteenth Century* (London).

Stilma, Astrid J. (2005), *A King Translated: James VI and I and the Dutch Interpretations of his Works, 1593–1603* (Amsterdam).

Stolt, Birgitte (1983), 'Luthers Übersetzungstheorie und Übersetzungspraxis', in H. Junghans (ed.), *Leben und Werk Martin Luthers* (Berlin).

Sturge, Kate (1997), 'Translation Studies in Ethnography', *Translator* 3, 21–38.

Suda, Max Josef (1996), 'Der Melanchthonschüler Leonhard Stöckel und die Reformation in der Slowakei', in Karl Schwarz and Peter Švorc (eds.), *Die Reformation und ihre Wirkungsgeschichte in der Slowakei: kirche- und konfessionsgeschichtliche Beiträge* (Vienna), 50–66.

Sudhoff, Karl (1894), *Bibliographia Paracelsica* (repr., Graz 1958).

Swerdlow, N. M. and Otto Neugebauer (1984), *Mathematical Astronomy in Copernicus' De Revolutionibus* (2 vols., New York).

Talas, Sofia (2004), 'Giovanni Poleni's *Teatro di filosofia sperimentale*', in G. N. Vlahakis and E. Nicolaidis (eds.), Βυζάντιο-Βενετία-Νεώτερος Ελληνισμός: μια περιπλάνηση στον κόσμο της επιστημονικής σκέψης (Byzantium-Venice-Modern Hellenism: A Journey Through the World of Modern Greek Scientific Thought) (Athens), 283–93.

Tarkiainen, Kari (1972), 'Rysstolkarna som yrkeskår, 1595–1661', *Historisk Tidskrift*, 490–521.

Tatakis, V. N. (1973), Νικόλαος Βλάχος ο Κρης (Nikolaos Vlahos the Cretan) (Venice).

Terracini, Benvenuto (1957), *Conflitti di lingua e di cultura* (2nd edn, Turin, 1996).

Tibenský, Ján (1992), 'Funkcia cyrilometodskej a veľkomoravskej tradície v ideológii slovenskej národnosti' (The Function of Cyril and Methodius and the Great Moravian Traditions in the Ideas of the Slovak Ethnic Group), *Historický časopis* 40, 579–94.

Tihanyi, Catherine (2004), 'An Anthropology of Translation', *American Anthropologist* 106, 739–42.

Tippelskirch, Xenia von (2003), 'Sotto controllo: letture femminili all'inizio dell'epoca moderna in Italia', Ph.D. thesis, European University Institute.

Tóth, István G. (1996), *Literacy and Written Culture in Early Modern Central Europe* (Budapest).

Tournay, G. (1981), 'Le versioni latine del Decamerone', in G. A. Tarugi (ed.), *Ecumenismo della cultura* (Florence), 125–6.

Toury, Gideon (1995), *Translation Studies and Beyond* (Amsterdam and Philadelphia).

Trabant, Jürgen (2000), 'Du génie aux genes des langues', in Henri Meschonnic (ed.), *Et le génie des langues?* (Saint-Denis), 79–102.

Tricaud, François (1969), 'Quelques questions soulevées par la comparaison du *Leviathan* latin avec le *Leviathan* anglais', in Reinhart Koselleck and Roman Schnur (eds.), *Hobbes-Forschungen* (Berlin), 237–44.

Tsakoumis, A. (1990), 'Chrysanthos Notaras, the Astronomer', in Ephemios Nicolaidis (ed.), Οι μαθηματικές επιστήμες στην Τουρκοκρατία (Mathematical Sciences under Ottoman Rule) (Athens), 129–222.

Tuck, Richard (1979), *Natural Rights Theories* (Cambridge).

Tuck, Richard (1993), *Philosophy and Government* (Cambridge).

Tully, James (ed., 1988), *Meaning and Context: Quentin Skinner and his Critics* (Cambridge).

Unger, Thorsten, Brigitte Schultze and Horst Turk (eds., 1995), *Differente Lachkulturen? Fremde Komik und ihre Übersetzung* (Tübingen).

Van Boheemen-Saaf, C. (1984), 'The Reception of English Literature in Dutch Magazines 1735–1785', in *The Role of Periodicals in the Eighteenth Century* (Leiden), 1–25.

Van Schoote, Jean-Pierre (1963), 'Les traducteurs des mystiques Rhéno-Flamands et leur contribution à l'élaboration de la langue dévote à l'aube du xviie siècle', *Revue d'ascétique et de mystique* 39, 319–37.

Vekene, Emil van der (1996), 'Johann Sleidan als Übersetzer', in *Johann Sleidan: Bibliographie* (Stuttgart), 305–38.

Venuti, Lawrence (ed., 1992), *Rethinking Translation* (London).

Venuti, Lawrence (1995), *The Translator's Invisibility* (London).

Vermij, R. (2002), *The Calvinist Copernicans: The Reception of the New Astronomy in the Dutch Republic, 1575–1750* (Amsterdam).

Veselý, Jindřich (2002), 'Český překlad od středověku do národního obrození' (Czech Translations from the Middle Ages until the National Awakening), in Milan Hrala (ed.), *Kapitoly z dějin českého překladu* (Chapters from the History of Czech Translations) (Prague), 11–29.

Viallon, Marie and Bernard Dompnier (2002), 'Introduction', to Paolo Sarpi, *Histoire du Concile de Trente* (Paris).

Vincent, Monique (1979), 'Le Mercure galant et son public féminin', *Romanistische Zeitschrift für Literaturgeschichte/Cahiers des littératures romanes* 3, 76–85.

Viti, Paolo (ed., 2004), *Leonardo Bruni, la perfetta traduzione* (text and Italian trans. of *De interpretatione recta*) (Naples).

Vivanti, Corrado (1974), 'Introduzione', to Paolo Sarpi, *Storia del Concilio Tridentino* (Turin).

Vogels, J. (1885), *Die ungedruckten lateinischen Versionen Mandevilles* (Krefeld).

Vos, Lambert (1992), *Louis de Blois, abbé de Liessies, 1506–1566: recherches bibliographiques sur son oeuvre* (Turnhout).

Wal, Marijke J. van der (2004), 'Simon Stevin, observateur et utilisateur de la langue', in *Simon Stevin (1548–1620): l'émergence de la nouvelle science* (Turnhout).

Wallner, G. (1982), 'De versionibus latinis poematis Klopstockiani', *Vox Latina* 18, 488–90.

Walter, Peter (1991), *Theologie aus dem Geist der Rhetorik: zur Schriftauslegung des Erasmus von Rotterdam* (Mainz).

Waquet, Françoise (1998), *Le latin ou l'empire d'un signe* (Paris).

Wassermann, Dirk (1996), *Dionysius der Kartäuser: Einführung in Werk und Gedankenwelt* (Salzburg).

Watts, Derek A. (1980), *Cardinal de Retz* (Oxford).

Webster, Charles (1975), *The Great Instauration* (2nd edn, Bern, 2002).

Webster, Charles (1979), 'Alchemical and Paracelsian Medicine', in Webster (ed.), *Health, Medicine and Mortality in the Sixteenth Century* (Cambridge), 301–34.

Westman, Robert S. (1984), 'The Reception of Galileo's *Dialogue*: A Partial World Census of Extant Copies', in Paolo Galluzzi (ed.), *Novità celesti e crisi del sapere* (Florence), 329–71.

White, James B. (1990), *Justice as Translation* (Chicago).

Willems, A. (1880), *Les Elzevier* (Brussels).

Wootton, David (1994), 'Introduction: The Republican Tradition: From Commonwealth to Common Sense', in David Wootton (ed.), *Republicanism, Liberty and Commercial Society 1649–1776* (Stanford), 1–41.

Worth, Valerie (1988), *Practising Translation in Renaissance France: The Example of Etienne Dolet* (Oxford).

Xu Zongze (1949), *Mingqingjian yesuhuishi yizhu tiyao* (Precis of Works and Translations by Jesuits in the Ming and Qing Periods) (repr. Beijing, 1989).

Yardeni, Myriam (1985), *Le refuge protestant* (Paris).

Yates, Frances (1944), 'Paolo Sarpi's History of the Council of Trent', *Journal of the Warburg and Courtauld Institutes* 7, 123–44.

Yushkevich, A. P. (1968), *Istoriya matematiki v. Rossii do 1917 goda* (History of Mathematics in Russia up to 1917) (Moscow).

Zach, Krista (2002), 'Protestant Vernacular Catechisms and Religious Reform in Sixteenth-Century East-Central Europe', in Crăciun et al., 49–63.

Zaunick, Rudolph (1977), *Der sächsische Paracelsist Georg Forberger* (Wiesbaden).

Zonta, Giuseppe (1916), 'Francesco Negri l'eretico', *Giornale storico della letteratura italiana* 67, 265–324.

Zuber, Roger (1968), *Les belles infidèles* (Paris).

Index

Abbot, George, Archbishop 138
Abdülaziz, Suphizâde, Effendi 209
Ablancourt, Nicolas Perrot d' 29–31, 126
  Tacitus 25
Abu Bakr bin al-Badr bin al-Mundir Badr
  ad-Din al-Baitar 196
Abu'l-Fida 210
Acosta, José de, *Natural and Moral History of the*
  Indies 130, 140
Acta eruditorum 145
Addison, Joseph 23, 69, 142, 147–8, 151, 156,
  157, 159
  Cato 148
Aegidius Albertinus 32, 69, 112
Aesop 39–40
Afentopoulo, Kaleb 183
Africa, accounts of 75
Agrafiotis, Nicolaos 190
Ahmad ibn Yusuf al-Tifashi 194
Ahmed II, Sultan 208
al-Cagmînî 193
al-Idrisi 210
al-Samarkandî 193
al-Tûsî, Nasîr al-Dîn 181, 182, 193, 195
al-Zahravi, Abul Qasim 194–5
Alba, Duke of 14
Alberti, Alberto di Giovanni 36
Alemán, Mateo, *Guzmán de Alfarache* 76
Aleni, Giulio 40, 41, 42–3, 45
Alexander the Great 18
Alexander VI, Pope 134–5
Alexei Mikhailovich, Tsar 190, 216
Alexis II Comnenus, (Byzantine) Emperor 181
Alfonso X 'the Wise' of Castile 15, 184–5
Ali Qushji 193, 195
Allestree, Richard 22
Almici, Giambattista 107
Almogáver, Gerónima Palova de 16
Alonso de Madrid 92
Alphonsine Tables 184–5
Amartol, Georgii 213

Ammirato, Scipione, *Discorsi sopra Cornelio*
  Tacito 76, 116
'amplification,' practice of 32, 134–5
Amyot, Jacques 2
Anchieta, José de 29
Andrewes, Lancelot 131–2
Andronicus II, (Byzantine) Emperor 181
Androvandi, Ulisse 217
Angela of Foligno 92
anthropology 8, 125
Antoine, Jean 173
aphorisms 134
Appian 30
Aquinas, Thomas, St 45, 95
  Summa theologica 39, 40–1, 47–9
Arabic, works in/translations from
  193–6
Aretino, Pietro 23, 67
  Letters 67
Argyropulos, Johannes 29
Ariosto, Ludovico 2, 19, 23, 24, 65
  Negromante 75
  Orlando furioso 10, 75
  I suppositi 75
Aristotle 29, 36, 115, 217
  translations into Chinese 42–3, 45, 50
Arnauld, Antoine 77
Aron, Pietro, *De institutione harmonica* 67
art, works on 77
astrology 213–14
astronomy 181–5, 188–90, 195, 205–6
Athenian Mercury 145, 147
atlases *see* cartography
Augustine, St 89
Auvergne, Gaspard d' 110, 113
Avicenna *see* Ibn Sina
Avila, Juan de 95
  Audi filia 92
Avila, Luis de 17
  Commentario 130, 140
Aylesbury, William 131

Bacon, Francis 23
  Advancement of Learning 168
  Considerations Touching a War with Spain 27
  Essays 27, 31, 77
  Henry VII 73, 129
Baker, Thomas 132
Bakhtin, Mikhail 36
Baldelli, Francesco 126, 132
Bandello, Matteo 30
Barbapiccola, Giuseppa-Eleonora 12
Barbeyrac, Jean 107, 121–4
  impact of works 123–4
  justification of translation method 122–3
Barclay, Alexander 131
Barezzi, Barezzo 16
Barksdale, Clement 107
Baron, Hans 110
Baronius, Cardinal 17
Barth, Caspar 69
Baxter, Richard 22
Bayle, Pierre 14, 145, 146
Bayly, Lewis, *Praxis of Piety* 27
Beaufort, Margaret 12
Bede, St, *History of the English Church* 127
Bedingfield, Thomas 131
Behn, Aphra 12
Bellarmino, Roberto, Cardinal 10, 17, 72, 104
Belleforest, François de 134
Belli, Costantino 129
Bellintani da Salò, Mattia 94, 95
Belon, Pierre 199
Belot, Octavie 12
Bembo, Pietro 79
Benavides, Florez de 135
Berman, Antoine 2
Bernegger, Matthias 74, 174
Bérulle, Pierre de, Cardinal 96
Bessarion, Basilius (Johannes), Cardinal 185
Béthune, Philippe de, *Le conseiller d'estat* 114
Beverland, Johannes 14
Beyazit II, Sultan 199
Bèze, Theodore 90
Bible translation(s) 2, 11, 17, 20, 24, 57–60,
    66, 88, 89–90, 100
  accessibility, debates on 52
  Chinese, lack of 41, 51
  choice of wording 34, 36
  Czech/Slovak 56, 57, 61–2, 64
  literality *vs* freedom, debate on 28
Biblical Institute (Halle) 61–2
Bibliothèque universelle et historique 145
Bidpai, fables of 27
Biehl, Dorothea 12
biography 125
Biringuccio, Vannoccio, *Pyrotechnica* 74

Birk, Sixt, *Susanna* 75
Bitiskius, Fridericus 173
Blaeu, Jan 165–6
Blaeu, Willem 165–6, 167
  Atlas major 205, 216
Blois, Louis de (Blosius) 91, 95
Blosius *see* Blois
Blundeville, William 114
Boccaccio, Giovanni, *Decameron*
    67, 75
Boccalini, Traiano 76, 116
Bodenstein, Adam von 166–7, 172
Bodin, Jean 69, 70
  The Republic 76, 108, 177
Bodmer, Johann Jakob 153, 154
Boeckler, Georg Andreas, *Theatrum
    machinarum* 74
Boerhaave, Hermann, *Aphorismi* 209
Bohannan, Laura 8
Boiastuau, Pierre 30
Boileau, Nicolas 18, 67, 69, 75
Boner, Hieronymus 132
Bonfils de Tarascon, Jacob 183–4
Bong'oron/Bonjorn *see* Yom-tob
The Book of Secrets of Enoch (anon.) 213
Borges, Jorge Luis 150, 159
Bornemisza, Péter 32–3
Bossuet, Jacques-Bénigne 136
  Variations 67
Botero, Giovanni 24
  Ragione di stato 76, 116
  Relazioni 21
Bouhours, Dominique 77
Boulliau, Ismale 181
Bourchier, John 111–12
Bourdieu, Pierre 24–5
bowdlerization 31–2
Boyer, Abel 146
Boyle, Robert 69, 74, 166, 171, 173, 177–8
  Spring of the Air 178–9
Bracciolini, Poggio 126
Brant, Sebastian, *Narrenschiff* 75
Breitinger, Johann Jakob 154
Bremond, Henri 95
Brent, Sir Nathaniel 138
Brentjes, Sonja 210–11
Briani, Girolamo 116
Briencour, Seigneur de 113
Briganti, Annibale 12
Brignon, Jean 15
Browne, Thomas 22
Brucker, Johann, *Historia critica philosophiae* 67
Bruni, Leonardo 12, 25, 26, 29, 35, 110, 125–6
Bryskett, Lodowick (Lodovico Bruschetto)
    14, 33

Bucer, Martin 17
Buchanan, George 119
   De iure regni apud Scotos 117
Budden, John 109
Buddhism 49
Budny, Szymon 28
Buglio, Ludovico, SJ 39, 40, 45, 47–8, 48–9
Bunyan, John, *The Pilgrim's Progress* 23
Burke, Peter 150
Burmann, Peter, the Elder 68, 77
Burnet, Gilbert 14, 22, 73, 129
Busbecq, Ogier Ghislain de 199–200
Busch, Wilhelm, *Max und Moritz* 68
Buys, Jan 15
Byrd, William 132
Byzantine Empire
   influence on Western science 185
   political decline 180, 191, 212

Caesar, C. Julius 127
Caffa, Carlo 133
Calvin, Jean 2, 10, 23, 28, 37, 72
Calvinists 17
Calvo, Ignacio 67
Cambini, Andrea 37
   History of the Turks 21
Camden, William 131–2, 138
Camões, Luis Vaz de 65
   Os Lusíadas 75
Campanella, Tommaso, *Città del sole* 76
Campion, Edmund 66
Campomanes, Count of 128–9
Canfield, Benedictus de (William Fitch) 95
Cappel, Guillaume 113
Caramuel y Lobkowicz, Juan 76
Carcavy, Pierre de 166, 174
Cardano, Girolamo 36
Carion, Johann 128, 132
Carleton, Sir Dudley 138
Carmichael, Gershom 107
Caroline, Queen, of England 131
Cartagena, Alonso de 29
Carter, Elizabeth 12–13
Carthusians of Cologne 90–1, 95, 99
cartography 201–5, 210–11, 216–17
   marine 196–8
Cary, Elizabeth 12
Cary, Henry *see* Monmouth
Cassini, Jean Dominique 190, 206
Castellion, Sébastien 28, 66
Castiglione, Baldassare, *Il cortegiano* 16, 19, 23, 24,
   32, 33, 67, 79, 113
Castiglione, Giuseppe 42
Castracani, Castruccio 73
Catherine II (the Great) of Russia 15–16, 18

Catherine of Genoa 95
Catherine of Siena 90, 92, 95
Catholicism
   Hungarian approach/traditions 63–4
   Latin translations of texts 72–3
   role of translation in development 83–5
   see also clergy
Caxton, William 16, 19, 29
Cecil, William 131
Celebi Mehmed, Sultan 194
Celestina (play) 23
censorship 124, 135–6
   see also bowdlerization; *Index of Forbidden
   Books*
Ceriol, Federico Furió 24, 76, 113–14
Cervantes, Miguel de 2, 65, 75
   Don Quixote 10, 21, 67
Cezmi Effendi 206
Chapelain, Jean 31
Chapman, George 36
Chappelain, Geneviève 12
Chappuys, Gabriel 13
Charles I of England 108, 110, 131
Charles IX of France 131
Charles V, (Holy Roman) Emperor 17
Charles V of France 15
Charrier, Jean 110
Châtelet, Emilie, Marquise du 12
China/Chinese language 39–51
   accounts of visits to 75
   cultural influence of translations 49–51
   decline of interest in European texts 51
   European interest in 21, 51
   methods of translation into 39–40, 46–7
   missions to 9–10
   translations from 46
   units of book production 47
Chionades, Gregory (George) 181–2
Chomedey, Jérôme de 135
Choumnos (Byzantine official) 180
Christian Fathers, translations of 88–9, 95
Chrysokokkes, George 181, 182
Chrysokokkes, Michael/Manuel 183–4
Chrysoloras, Demetrius 185
Chrysoloras, Emanuel, *Erotemata* 92
Churchill, Winston 137
Cicero, M. Tullius 26, 28, 42, 115
Cieklinski, Piotr, *Protrójny* 33
Cisneros, García de 92, 94
Clairaut, Alexis 206
Clarendon, Lord 129
Clarke, Samuel 74, 176
classical literature/era
   cultural traditions 104–5, 115
   translations 19, 29–30, 40, 42–4, 65, 126, 163

'classicizing' 80
Clavius, Christophorus 41–2, 50
Clement VIII, Pope 119–20
clergy
    central role in text production/translation 69, 84–5
    as focus of scholarship 85
Clerke, Bartholomew 79
Clifford, Lady Anne 132
Climacus, John 92
Cognet, Louis 95
Cohen, Tobia 208
coinages *see* neologisms
Coke, Sir Edward 132
Collodi, Carlo, *Pinocchio* 68
Cologne *see* Carthusians of Cologne
colonial rule, translation under 29
Columbus, Christopher 197–8
Colyer, Justinus 205
comedy, problems of translating 7
commercialism, as motive for translation/ publication 173, 176, 177–8
Commynes, Philippe de 12, 73, 129, 140
Concini, Bartolomeo 135
conduct books 76–7
Conegliano, Israel 208
confessional identity, importance of 53–4
Confucius 46, 77
constitution, theoretical studies 108–9
Contarini, Gasparo, *De magistratibus et republica Venetorum* 110–11
contraction (of translated texts) 31–2
Cook, Ann 12
Copernicus, Nicolaus 182
    influence of Eastern scientists 181, 182
    later writers' developments of theory 179, 188–9
Corneille, Pierre 75
Corydaleus, Theophylos 187
Coste, Pierre 14, 121, 146
Cotterell, Charles 131
Counter-Reformation 16–17
Couplet, Philippe 46
Courtin, Antoine de 107
Cowley, Abraham 31
'creative infidelity' 150, 159
Cremonini, Cesare 187
Croce, Benedetto 25
Croll, Oswald 207
Cromwell, Oliver 117
Cromwell, Thomas 18
Crusades
    literature from conquereed lands 184–5
    works on/interest in 127, 130
Cudworth, Ralph, *True Intellectual System of the Universe* 77

'cultural translation' 8–10, 133
    availability 103
    relationship with linguistic 10
    scientific 163
Cumberland, Richard 107, 122, 123
Curione, Celio Secundo 70, 78, 135
Curtius, Qunitus 18
Curtius Rufus, Q. 127
Cyril, St, Archbishop of Great Moravia 61
Czech Brethren 56–7, 61
Czech (language)
    (religious) use in Slovakia 54–5, 56–7, 58–60, 61–2, 64
    translations into 23–4, 56–7

Dacier, Anne 12
Dacres, Edward 110, 113
Dale, Thomas 33
Dalhem, Josquin 167, 175
Damaskin, I. 213
Daniel, Fr, *Cleandre et Eudoxus* 72
Dante Alighieri 65, 169
    The Divine Comedy 75
Dariot, Claude 167
Darnton, Robert 102
Davila, Enrico Caterina, *Civil Wars of France* 130, 140
de Bry, Theodor/Johann Theodor 16, 19, 75, 77
De Dominis, Marco Antonio, dedication to *History of the Council of Trent* 137–8
de Rogeau, Marcus 138–9
de Tournes, Samuel 77, 171, 173, 178
de Veer, Effert 117
de Witt, Johann 171
decontextualization *see* recontextualization
Dee, John 172
Defoe, Daniel, *Robinson Crusoe* 68
Dehergne, Joseph, SJ 44
Delacroix, Jacques-Vincent 142, 150–1, 155–9
    authorial/editorial persona 158–9
    comments on own work 152, 153, 157, 158–9
    governmental hostility to 158
Delind, Zuca 217
Della Casa, Giovanni, *Il galateo* 27
Della Porta, Giambattista 67
    Il astrologo 75
Denis the Carthusian (Denis Rijckel) 87
Dentrecolles, François-Xavier 41
Dering, Sir Edward 132
Dernschwam, Hans 200
des Essars, Herberay 111
Desaguliers, John 14
Descartes, René 77
    Géométrie 170–1, 178
Desmaizeaux, Pierre 14, 146

devotional texts
  centres of origin 86
  cultural context 99
  definition/range 85–6, 97–9
  means of transmission 97
  modern studies 97–100
  role in religious history 84
Diaz, Emmanuel 41, 45
dictionaries, bilingual 13–14
Dieu, Louis de 72
Diodati, Elio 70, 74, 174
Diodati, Jean 137–8, 139
Diodorus Siculus 127
Dionysius the Areopagite 89, 95
The Discussion of Panaghiostos with Azimyth 213
Dolce, Ludovico 113–14
Dolet, Etienne 16, 25
  La manière de bien traduire 25
Dolmatskii, Albert, Prince 215–16
Domenichi, Ludovico 110, 132
'domestication' 26–7, 29
  see also 'foreignization'
Domestikos, Meletios 190
Doncker, Hendrick 216–17
Donne, John 34
Dorn, Gerard 172, 175
Douglas, Gavin 19, 29
Drake, Francis 23
Draskovich, János 112
Dryden, John 30–1, 34, 35, 67
  Absalom and Achitophel 75
  Ovid 25
Du Bartas, Guillaume de Salluste, *La semaine* 67, 75, 76
Du Bellay, Joachim 25, 30–1, 169
Du Vergerre, Susanne 12
Duan Gun 43
Dulcken, Anton 69
Dunton, John 145
Dupuy, Pierre 138
D'Urfé, Honoré, *L'Astrée* 67
Durret, Nathalis 205–6
Dutch, translations from/into 23
Duvergier de Hauranne, Jean 96

Eastern European languages, translations from/into 23–4
Eborensis, Andreas 42
Ebreo, Leone 77
Ebubekir b. Behram üd-Dimashqi 205
Eckhart, Johannes, Meister 86, 87
Eco, Umberto 7
Eden, Richard 19
Edward IV of England 108–9
Effen, Justus van 149, 151, 152

elites, religious *see* clergy
Elizabeth I of England 12, 16, 18, 104, 116
Elsevier (publisher) 164, 174–5, 177
émigrés, role in translation 14–15
Emir Celebi (Seyyid Muhammed et-Tabib) 206–7
England, cultural/scientific importance 165
English, translations from/into 22–3
Enlightenment 37–8
Ens, Caspar 69
Epictetus 39–40, 42
Epiphany of Cyprus 213
Erasmus, Desiderius 10, 12, 20, 23, 87–9, 93
  impact on development of Protestantism 88
  Enchiridion militis christiani 32, 37, 93
  Institutio principis christiani 112
Euclid, *Elementa* 39, 47
Eugenikos, Marcos 184
Europe
  cultural transfers within 1, 10–11, 124
  political situation 103
European Community 1
European Science Foundation 1
Eusebius of Caesarea 127
Evans-Pritchard, Edward 8
Evats, W. 107
Even-Zohar, Itamar 2
Everart, Martin 115, 166
Exarch, Ioan, *The Six Days* 213

fashion, magazine coverage of 145
Fausto da Longiano, Sebastiano 112
Fazio, Bartolomeo 33
Fénelon, François 14, 18
  Télémaque 76
Fenton, Sir Geoffrey 26, 135–6
Feofan Prokopovich 72
Ferdinand I, (Holy Roman) Emperor 199
Ferguson, Adam, *Essay on the History of Civil Society* 38
Fernández, Alonso 32
Fernel, Jean 207
Ferus, Jiří 15
Ficino, Marsilio 89
fiction, translations of 75–6
Fielding, Henry 23
Fieschi, Count 33
Filmer, Sir Robert, *Patriarcha* 117–18
Filotei (monk) 212
Finé, Oronce 169
Fioravanti, Leonardo 165
Fischart, Johann 31, 32, 33, 36
FIT (Fédération Internationale des Traducteurs) 2–3
Fitch, William *see* Canfield, Benedictus de
Flacius, Matthias 28, 30

Florence (city-state) 110
Florio, John 2, 14, 116, 120
    translations of Montaigne 16, 25, 32,
      33–4, 36–7
Fonkich, Boris L. 215
Fonseca, Daniel 208
Fonseca, Rodrigo 208
Forberger, Georg 131, 134–5, 172, 173
foreign language(s), adoption of 54
    see also Czech
'foreignization' 26, 34
    vs 'domestication' 80
Fortescue, John, *De laudibus legum Angliae* 108–9
Foucault, Michel 35
Fracastoro, Girolamo 207
Frachetta, Girolamo 116
France
    as devotional centre 95–7, 98
    periodicals 144–5, 155
Francis I of France 90, 131
Francis Xavier, St 72
Francke, August Hermann 73
François de Sales, St 72, 95–6
Fraunce, Abraham 33
Frederick II of Prussia 113
French, translations from/into 22
Fréron, Élie-Catherine 155–6
Frobisher, Martin 23
Froidmont, Libert 174
Froissart, Jean, *Chroniques* 67, 73, 127
Fronsperger, Leonard 216
Fuchs, Leonard 168
Furtado, Francisco 42–3

Gage, Thomas 22
Gagliardi, Achille, *Brief Summary of Christian
    Perfection* 86, 94, 96
Galileo Galilei 10, 42, 74, 166, 170, 174–5,
    176–7, 179
Galitzin, Prince 190
Garneau, Michel 33
Garzoni, Tomaso, *La piazza universale* 31
Gassendi, Pierre 211
Gazette 144
    foreign imitations 144–5
Gazette de Leyde 143
Gentile, Scipio 70
Gentili, Alberico 106
Gentillet, Innocent 76
George I of England 108–9
German(y)
    civic/religious uses 55, 56
    theoretical movements 35
    translations from/into 23, 56
Gerson, Jean 85, 86

Gesenius, Justus 134
Geuder, Jacob 80
Geuffroy, Antoine 80
Giannotti, Donato 76
Gibbon, Edward 130
Giolito, Gabriel 16, 132
Giovio, Paolo 79–80
    History of His Own Time 130, 132, 140
Giraldi, Giambattista Cinthio 33
Girard, Albert 171
Girard, Pascale 44
Glazemaker, Jan Hendriksz 13
Glyzounis, Emanuel 186–7
God, renderings of name 9–10, 29, 48
Goethe, Cornelia 149
Goethe, Johann Wolfgang von 68, 149
Gohorry, Jacques 32, 110
Golding, Arthur 131
Goldoni, Carlo, *Pamela* 154
Gordon, Thomas 123
Górnicki, Łukasz 33
Góslicki, Wawrzyniec Grzymała, *De optimo
    senatore* 114
Gottsched, Louise 12, 149, 154
Goulart, Simon 115
Goupyl, Jacques 166
Gracián, Jeronomo, *Summary of the Virtues of
    St Joseph* 86
Graeber, Wilhelm 2
Graevius, Johann Georg 19, 68, 71, 73, 77
Grafton, Anthony 102
Granada, Luís de 10, 12, 40, 85, 92, 95
Grantrye, Pierre de 167
Gray, Thomas, *Elegy in a Country Churchyard* 21,
    67, 75
Greece
    political/social conditions under
      Ottomans 189
    scientific aspirations 191
Greek
    translations from *see* classical literature
    translations into 181–91
Greflingen, Georg 143
Gregory Nazianzus 88
Grimm, Friedrich Melchior, Baron 155
Grotius (de Groot), Hugo 104, 106, 122, 169
    De jure belli et pacis 107, 123
Guarini, Giovanni Battista, *Il pastor fido* 21, 67
Guerre, Martin 66
Guevara, Antonio de, *Reloj de príncipes* 76,
    111–12, 124
Guevara y Vasconcelos, Manuel de 128–9
Guiccardini, Francesco 20, 21, 23, 26, 38, 70, 76,
    78, 113, 131, 133, 134
    Dialogo del reggimento del Firenze 110

Guiccardini, Francesco (cont.)
  Storia d'Italia 125, 129, 131–2, 134–6, 137, 139, 140, 141
Guiccardini, Ludovico 21
Guillemeau, Jacques 167–8, 178
Gustav Adolf of Sweden 15–16, 18
Gyllengrip, Catharina 12
Gyllenstierna, Catharina/Maria 12

Haci Pasha (Celalüddin Hizir) 194, 206
Hagenaeus, Melchior 115
hagiographies *see* saints, lives of
Hakluyt, Richard 18, 19
Hall, Joseph 23
  Characters 27
Hamazaspean, Gabriel 112
Hamon, Joseph 199
Hamon, Moses 199
Han Lin 43
Hankins, James 110
Harphius (Hendrik Herp) 87, 90, 95
  The Mirror of Perfection 90
Harvey, Gabriel 102
Harvey, William 209
Hassard, Pierre 167
Hatton, Christopher 131, 132
Havercamp, Sigebert 69
Hayâtizâde Mustafa Feyzi 207–8
Haydocke, Richard 12
Hebrew, translations from 183–4
Helmont, Jan van 173
Henri III of France 177
Henry, Prince of Wales (son of James I) 118
Henry VIII of England 17–18
Herder, Johann Gottfried 35
Hermann, Philip 166
Hermans, Theo 2, 26, 28
Herp, Hendrik *see* Harphius
historical works (in translation) 73, 125–9
  areas of interest 128–9
  defined 125
  'export'/'import' languages 128, 130
  translators 132–3
history, 'translation' across 7–9
Hobbes, Thomas 22, 104, 106, 107–8, 122
  Leviathan 76
Hoby, Sir Thomas 19
Holberg, Ludvig 154–5
Holland, Philemon 132
Holmes, James 2
Holst, Pieter Volck 166
Homer, translations of 11, 35, 36
Hondius, Josse 202
Hooft, Pieter 126
Horace (Q. Horatius Flaccus) 18, 25

horses, care of *see* veterinary science
Horta, García de 12
Hortensius, Martinus 167, 174
Hostovinus, Balthasar 15
Hotman, François, *Francogallia* 109
Hotman, Jean 120
Huarte de San Juan, Juan 69
Huguenots 14, 121, 146
Humboldt, Wilhelm 34–5
Hume, David 77
Hungary
  civic/social elite (Magyars) 58, 63
  ethnic/linguistic divisions 55, 57–8, 60
  legislation 55–6, 62
  literary imports 56
  political conditions 59
  religious divisions 52
  see also Slovakia
Hus, Jan/Hussites 52, 54, 60
Huser, Johannes 172, 173
Hüseyin bin Abdullah 196
Huyghens, Christiaan 18
hymns 59–60

iatrochemistry 207
Ibn Beithar 194
Ibn Khaldun 127
Ibn Sina (Avicenna) 209–10
Ibn Yunus 206
Illuminism 92–4
'imitation,' theory/practice of 30–1
  debates on 153–9
Imperial Encyclopedia *(Siku quanshu)* 49–50
index entries 137, 139
Index of Forbidden Books 93, 113, 120, 128
  impact on translation/publication projects 177
  Russian Orthodox version 214
India, accounts of 75
Indikoplov, Kosmas 213
Innys, William/John 176
integrity, textual, religious importance 55–6, 57
intellectual property 33, 173
intention, importance of 16
interpreters 13, 14
  hereditary 13
inwerken, translation of term 93, 99–100
Isabella, Queen of Spain 91
Isengrin (publisher) 168
Islam *see* Muslim texts
Ismail, Halifezâde Cinarî, Effendi 206
Isselt, Michael 69
Italian, translations from/into 22–3, 73
Italy, visits to 104
Ivan III, Tsar 212

James I of England/VI of Scotland 12, 23, 104, 131
  Basilikon doron 118–21, 124
Japan, accounts of 75
Jardine, Lisa 102
Jerome, St 25, 28, 89
Jesuits 15, 17, 29, 39–51, 83–4, 99
  numbers/nationalities 44–5, 46
  role in Chinese missions/translations 44
  selection of texts 50
  timescale of translation production 45–6
Jews
  medical knowledge/texts 198–9
Jiménez (Ximenes) de Cisneros, Francisco,
  Cardinal 15, 91–2, 94
João IV of Portugal 76
John Chrysostom, St 213
John of the Cross, St 92, 94, 95
Johnson, Samuel, Dr 12, 154
Jones, William 115
Josephus, Flavius 126–7
Joubert, Laurent 168
Le journal encyclopédique 156
Le journal étranger 153–4
Journal des savants 144
  imitations 145
Jouvancy, Joseph de 72
Juan, Prince, of Spain 111
Justinus 127

Kadizâde-i Rumî (Sheikh Mehmed bin Mustafa)
  193, 196
Kangxi, (Chinese) Emperor 42, 43
Kant, Immanuel 77
Karaites (Jewish sect) 183
Karl IX of Sweden 18
Kâtib Çelebi 201–4, 205, 210
Kavoutzes, Ioannes 183
Keller, Christoph 134
Kempis, Thomas 12
  Imitatio Christi (attrib.) 20, 85, 86–7
Kennet, Basil 107, 122, 123
Kerbekius, Antonius 69
Kirik of Novgorod 213
Klesch, Daniel 56
Klopstock, Friedrich Gottlieb, *Messiah* 75
Koerbagh, Adriaan 9, 36
Kopievich, Ilya 18
Koran, translations of 27
Kralice Bible 58–9

La Beaumelle, Laurent de 150
La Chapelle, Seigneur de 76
La Fontaine, Jean de, *Fables* 75
La Grise, Berthault de 111
La Houssaye, Amelot de 113, 139

La Noue, François de 76
la Rivière, Étienne de 207
Lamoot, Jan 14
Languet, Hubert 117
Lansbergen, Jacob 174
Lansbergen, Philip 173–4, 179
Lansperger, Johannes Justus 91
Lapithe, George 185
Laredo, Bernardino de 92
Latin
  'competition' with vernacular 167–73, 175–6
  as cultural lingua franca 54–5, 104–5, 168,
    169–70
  as language of law 106
  as language of religion 55, 56, 84
Latin, translations from *see* classical literature
Latin, translations into 4, 19, 21, 65–80, 84,
    174–5, 179
  choice of material 66–7
  chronology 68
  quantity 65–6
  selection of material 71–7
  source languages 69
  translation methods 78–80
  translators 69–70
  see also 'classicizing'
Lauro, Pietro 132
Lauterbach, Conrad 126
Lauterbeke, George 109
law, works on 77, 106–9
Lazarillo de Tormes (anon.) 31
Le Ber, Charles 115
Le Courayer, Pierre-François 131, 139
Le Noble, Eustache 125
Leclerc, Jean 145
Lefèvre d'Étaples, Jacques 89–90
Leibnitz, Gottfried Wilhelm 51, 77
Leichoudis, Ioannikos/Sofronios 190, 215
Lenglet du Fresnoy, Nicolas 34
Leo Africanus 18
León, Luis de, *La perfecta casada (The Perfect
  Wife)* 98
Leunclavius, Johannes 80
Lewkenor, Lewes 111
Li Cibin 43
Li Zhizao 42, 43
libraries, contents of 131–2, 149
linguistic ability, role in European education 104
Lipsius, Justus 23
  Politicorum sive civilis doctrinae 115–16
literality, *vs* freedom 25, 26–30, 133
literary criticism 77
liturgy *see* prayers
Livy (T. Livius) 102
localization *see* transposition

Locke, John 10, 14, 18, 22, 23, 37–8, 145
   Concerning Human Understanding 27, 77, 121–2
   Two Treatises on Government 27, 76, 118
Lok, Ann 12
Lomazzo, Giovanni Paolo 12
Lomonosov, Mikhail 215
Longfellow, Henry Wadsworth, *Hiawatha* 68
Longobardo, Niccolò 48
Lopes de Castanheda, Fernão, *History of the*
   Discovery of the New World 130, 140
Lorraine, Cardinal of 15
Louis XIII of France 114
Louis XIV of France 8, 76, 108, 144
Loyola, Ignatius, St 15, 83–4, 87, 94
Lubomirski, Stanislas 72
Lucae e Camerino, Johannes 183
Lucena, Juan de 33
Ludolph of Saxony, *Life of Christ* 83, 87, 92, 94
Ludwig, Prince of Anhalt 12
Luillier, François 211
Lukaris, Cyril, Patriarch 187
Lull, Raymond 92
Lumley, Jane 12
Luther, Martin 2, 23, 60, 88, 172
   as Bible translator 17, 28
   translations from 10, 17, 20, 23, 37, 72
   Little Catechism 53, 57
   Sendbrief von Dolmetschen (Epistle on
      Translation) 25
Lutheran Church 53–4, 56
   conflicts with Calvinism 57
   presence in Hungary/Slovakia 59–62, 63–4
   (supposed) links with Hussism 54, 60

Macault, Antoine 131
Machiavelli, Niccolò 21, 23, 70, 76, 134
   Arte della guerra 33
   Discorsi 32, 110
   Istorie Fiorentine 67, 128, 130, 131, 140
   Il principe 31, 76, 78, 104, 105–6, 110, 113
Maffei, Giovanni Pietro 22
Magalhães, Gabriel de 47–8
magazines *see* periodicals
Magnus, Olaus 132
Maignan, Eloi 168
Maimbourg, Louis 67, 128
   History of the Crusades 130, 140
Maire, Jean 178
Malebranche, Nicolas 77
Malvezzi, Virgilio 76
Mansur ibn Muhammad ibn Ahmad 210
manuscripts 4, 15, 21–2, 34, 67, 126, 164
March, Ausias 75
Marcus Aurelius, (Roman) Emperor 111
Mardrus, Joseph Charles, *Arabian Nights* 150

Marguerite of Navarre 90
Mariana, Juan de 106
Marivaux, Pierre de 152
Marnix, Philip 131
Marshall, William 17–18
Marsilio of Padua 17
Martin, Henri-Jean 164
Martin, Jean 30
Martini, Martino 21
   De bello tartarico 129, 140
Mascardi, Agostino 33
Masník (Masnicius), Tobias 61
mathematics 186–7
Mavrocordato, Alexandre 209
Maximilian II, (Holy Roman) Emperor 177
Mazel, David 146
Medici, Lorenzo de' 116
medicine, works on 190, 194–5, 198–200, 206–10
   analogy with political theory 203–4
   see also veterinary science
*medrese*s (Ottoman schools) 192, 193, 196, 200–1
Mehmed Ataullah, Tayyarzade 196
Mehmed Ihlasî, Sheikh 203
Mehmed II, Sultan 193, 195
Mehmed IV, Sultan 205, 207
Mehmed Rami Pasha 208
Mehmed Reis ibn Menemenli 198
Melanchthon, Philip 128
Ménage, Gilles 30
Mendoza, Juan González de 21
Mercado, Luis 208
Mercator, Gerhard 201, 202, 216
   Le mercure galant 144, 145, 147
Mersenne, Marin 166
Merzifonlu Karamustafa Pasha 208
Methodius, St 61
Metochites (Byzantine official) 180
Meusevoet, Vincentius 13, 14
Mexia, Pedro, *Historia Caesarea* 67, 133
Micanzio, Fulgencio 137
Middle Ages 52, 86–7
   translation methods 26–7
   translation of texts from 127
Mikhail Feodorovich, Tsar 216
Milne, A. A., *Winnie the Pooh*, Latin version 19, 68
Milton, John 65, 67, 104
   Paradise Lost 21, 23, 75
Minadoi, Giovanni 80
Mirandola, Pico della 183
missionaries 9–10, 16–17, 29, 39–51, 99
misunderstanding, role of (mis)translation in 35–6
Mitros, Meletios, Bishop, 'Epitome of
   Astronomy' 188, 188–9
Molina, Luis de 106
Molinos, Miguel de 73

monarchy, theories of 109, 111–15, 124
Monardes, Nicolas 12, 207–8
Monmouth, Henry Cary, Earl of 111, 116, 133
Montaigne, Michel de 2, 121
  Essais 16, 21, 24, 25, 32, 33–4, 36–7
Montano, Benito Arias 66, 70
Montecuccoli, Raimondo de 76
Montesquieu, Charles-Louis de Secondat,
  baron de 10
  L'esprit des lois 37
Montgomerie, *The Cherry and the Plum* 75
Moravia, Great 60–1, 63–4
More, Thomas
  Utopia 21, 37
Morin, Jean-Baptiste 174
Mornay, Philippe du Plessis 117
Mornet, Daniel 149
Moulin, Louis de 74
Moyriac de Mailla, J. A. M. de 127
Muhammad, the Prophet 193
Muhammed b. Mahmûd-i Sirvânî 194
Muhammed bin Cerkes 196
Muhammed bin Ya'kûb b. Ahi Huzzâm
  al-Huttalî 196
Mulcaster, Robert 108
Murad IV, Sultan 209
Murner, Thomas 22
Murphy, Arthur, *The Orphan of China* 154
Muslim texts/science
  role in Ottoman thought/education 192–3,
    196, 200–1, 210
  Western translations 127
  see also Ottoman Empire
Mustafa III, Sultan 209
Müteferrika, Ibrahim 203
Mutius, Huldreich, *De Germanorum origine* 67
Myrepsos, Nicolas 207
The Mystery of Mysteries (anon.) 214

Nadal, Jerónimo 41
Nannini, Remigio 134
Napier, John 42
nationalism
  cultural 19, 169
  growth of 103
natural philosophy *see* science
Naudé, Gabriel 69, 77
  Considérations politiques sur les coups d'état 116
Nebrija, Antonio 70
Needham, Peter 68
negotiation, role in translation 9–10
Negri, Francesco 70
Nemchin, Nikolai 214
neologisms 36–7, 48–9, 78–80
Neri, Antonio, *De arte vitraria* 74

Netherlands
  cultural/scientific importance 164–6
  return of exiles 14–15
Newcastle, Duke of 73
newspapers *see* periodicals
Newton, Adam 78–9, 138
Newton, Isaac 10, 14, 33, 74
  Opticks 176
Nian Xiyao 42
Nicholas V, Pope 15
Nieremberg, Emmanuel 12
Nieremberg, Juan Eusebio 85, 99
Nieuhof, Jan 75
Nikon, Patriarch 216
nineteenth century, translation movements/
  theories 34–5
Nizamulmulk, Vizier 192
non-fiction, translation of 3, 11, 66–7
Norfolk, Duke of 131
North, Sir Thomas 2, 27, 112
Northampton, Elizabeth, Marchioness of 16
Norton, Thomas 28
Notaras, Chrysanthos 189–90
Notaras, Dositheos, Patriarch 190
Nouvelles de la république des lettres 145

Oldenburg, Henry 74
Origen, St 89
Ortega y Gasset, José 25
Ortelius, Abraham 201, 203, 216
Osman II, Sultan 196
Osuna, Francisco de 92
Ottoman Empire
  education system 185, 187, 189, 192–3 (*see also*
    *medrese*s)
  rise in power 180
  scientific attainments 189
  Western accounts of 75, 76, 79–80
  Western influence on science/culture 192,
    196–211
  Western physicians in 208

Padua (University) 199
  'school of' 187–8, 191
Palissy, Bernard 36
Pallavicino, Sforza, Cardinal 137
Palthen, Zacharias 11, 173
Panneel, Michael 14
Papánek, Juraj 63
Papavasilopoulos, Anastasios 186, 187
  manuscripts of texts 186
Paracelsus (Theophrastus von Hohenheim) 11, 73–4
  influence in East 207
  Latin translations 164, 166–7, 172–3, 175, 178
Paré, Ambroise 167–8, 170, 177, 178

Parry, Thomas 120
Parsons, Robert 119, 120
Paruta, Paolo, *Della perfettione della vita politica* 111
Pascal, Blaise 69
  Pensées 77
Patriotiske Tilskuer 153
Patrizzi, Francesco 77
patronage 15–16, 131
Paul, St, *Letter to the Romans* 89
Paul III, Pope 137
Paulos Aeginata 195
Paz, Octavio 8–9
The Pearl of the Gospel (anon.) 90, 95
Pedro IV of Aragon 184
Peiresc, Nicolas Claude 138, 211
Peletier du Mans, Jacques 25, 169
  Algèbre/De occulta parte numerorum 170
Pemberton, John 120
Pepys, Samuel 132
Perez, Miguel 85
periodicals
  book reviews 145–6
  borrowings from others 143–4
  criticisms of others 152
  development 143–6
  government sponsorship 144
  role in cultural exchange 144–6
  specialization 144–5
  women's 145, 150, 153
  see also The Spectator
Perkins, William 17, 23, 27, 72
Perna, Pietro 136, 167, 172–3, 175, 177
Perne, Andrew 131–2
Persian, translations from 181–2
Peter I (the Great), Tsar 15–16, 18, 20, 215, 217
Petereius, Theodore 69
Petrarch 23
Philip II of Spain 73, 91
Philip IV of Spain 12, 21
Philip V of Spain 12
Phillip, William 18
Philosophical Transactions of the Royal Society of London 145, 146, 171
philosophy, works on 77
Pibrac, Guy du Four, Seigneur de 67, 75
Piccolomini, Alessandro 166
Pieroni, Giovanni 174, 176, 177
Pindar 31
Pipino, Francesco 31, 32
Pirckheimer, Wilibald 88
Pîrî Reis 197–8
Pitiscus, Bartholomaeus 42
Plato 43–4
  Laws 109
  Republic 31

Plautus, T. Maccius, *Trinummus* 33
plays, translations of 32–3, 75
Plutarch 2, 115
Pocock, John 110, 133
poetry, translations of 75
Poirot, Louis de 41
Poland, political system 114
polemic 103
Poleni, Giovanni 191
'policy,' translatability of term 7–8
Polish, translations into 24
'political economy of translation' 22
political theory, works of
  context of creation 101–2
  distribution 102
  Eastern 203–4
  range of ideas 101
  translations into Latin 76
  transmission of ideas 102–3
  see also law; monarchy; 'reason of state'; republicanism; resistance
Poliziano, Angelo 126
Polo, Gil, *Diana* 75–6
Polo, Marco 21, 31, 32
Polybius 12, 126, 127
Pope, Alexander 11, 12–13, 154
  Essay on Man 21, 75
Porcacchi, Tommaso 132
Pory, John 18
Postel, Guillaume 210
Pozzo, Andrea 42, 50
prayers, translations of 40–1
printers 16
  absence (from certain areas) 56
Proclus 182
Procopius 12, 125–6
propaganda
  translatability of term 8
  works of 76
Protestants/Protestantism
  appropriation of Catholic texts 136, 138–9
  texts translated into Latin 72
  translations of Catholic texts by 72–3, 77
  see also Calvinists; Lutheran Church; Reformation
Pseudo-Kallisphenos, *Alexandria* 213–14
publication, centres of 70–1, 72, 164
Pufendorf, Samuel 18
  De jure naturae et gentium 107, 121–3
  De officio hominis et civis 107
  Introduction (Einleitung) 129, 140
Pym, Anthony 2

Quevedo, Francisco de 76

Rabelais, François 23, 31, 32, 33, 36
Raleigh, Walter 23
Ramus, Peter, *Geometriae libri XXVII* 216
Ramusio, Giovanni Battista 19
Rawlinson, Richard 34
'reason of state', theoretical works on 115–17
re-Catholicization, Hungarian programme of
    53–4, 55–6, 59, 62–3
recontextualization, processes of 10
Reformation 10, 37
    attitudes to Scriptures 52–3
    liturgical languages 55–6
refugees *see* émigrés
Regnault, Noël 33
religion
    controversies 96–7, 99, 124
    histories 130
    texts (and translations) 3, 16–17, 40–1, 61, 62–3,
        71–3
    Wars of 95, 109
    see also Bible; Catholicism; devotional texts;
        God; missionaries; prayers; Protestants;
        saints, lives of
Renaissance 10, 37, 163
Renaudot, Théophraste 144
republicanism, theories of 110–11, 115
resistance, political theory of 117–18
Retz, Jean François Paul de Gondi de,
    Cardinal 33
reviews *see* periodicals
Rhineland, religious traditions 86–91, 92–4
    links/clashes with Catholicism 90–1
Rho, Giacomo 42, 45
Ricci, Matteo 9, 15, 16, 39, 41–2, 45, 47, 48, 50
    Jiaoyou lun (De amicitia) 42
    *Jiren shipian (Ten Essays from a Remarkable
        Man)* 39–40
Richardson, Samuel 2, 23
    Pamela 34, 154
Richelieu, Armand Jean Duplessis, Cardinal
    114, 205
Ricius, Johannes 79
Rijckel, Denis *see* Denis the Carthusian
Rivadeneira, Pedro de 15
    *The Christian Prince (Tratado de la religión y
        virtudes que debe tener el príncipe cristiano)*
        76, 112–13
Robertson, William 130
    History of America 128–9
Roche, Geneviève 2
Rohan, Henri de 76
Rojas, Fernando de, *Celestina* 75
Ronsard, Pierre 75
    Franciade 67
Roper, Margaret 12

Rosemond, Jean-Baptiste de 14
Rosenzweig, Franz 8
Roseo da Fabriano, Mambrino 112
Ross, Alexander 174
Rowling, J. K., *Harry Potter and the Philosopher's
    Stone*, Latin version 68
Royal Society 74, 166, 169, 170, 175–6
    see also Philosophical Transactions . . .
royalty
    as patrons of translation 15–16
    as translators 12
Rudolph II, (Holy Roman) Emperor 177
Ruggieri, Michele 39
'Rules of the Military, Artillery and Other
    Affairs' 216
Russia
    educational projects 215
    literature 213–15
    political history 212, 215
    social/cultural development 214–17
    translation programmes 18–19, 190,
        214–17
Ruysbroeck, Jan van 87, 90
    Spiritual Espousals 90, 95

Saadi 75
Saavedra, Diego de 76
Sabellico, Marco Antonio 22
Sabuncuoglu Sherefeddin 194–5
Sa'duddin bin Hasan Can 127
Saint-Evremond, Charles de Marquetel de 14
Sainte-Marthe, Scévole de 67
St Petersburg
    Academy 13, 18–19, 217
    Gazette 145
saints, lives of 41, 71, 86, 98
Sales, François de, St *see* François de Sales
Salih b. Nasrullah b. Sallum 206, 207, 208
Sallust (C. Sallustius Crispus) 115, 127
Sambiasi, Francesco 42–3
Sandé, Don Alvaro de 200
Sarpi, Paolo 20, 38, 128
    History of Benefices 130, 133, 140
    History of the Council of Trent 16, 17, 78–9, 125,
        129, 131–2, 133, 136–9, 140
Savonarola, Girolamo 92
Saxo Grammaticus 127
Saxony, Elector of 131
    see also George I of England
Scalvo, Marco de 67
Scandinavia 24
    see also Sweden
Schall von Bell, Adam 42, 45
Schiller, Johann Christoph Friedrich von 68
Schirmbeck, Adam 69

Schlegel, August Wilhelm 8, 154–5
Schleiermacher, Friedrich 34–5
school textbooks 62–3, 186–7
Schooten, Franz van 170, 178
Schottius, Andreas 69
Schreck, Johann Terenz 42
Schroder, Eric 13, 18, 112, 120
Schwartz, Johann Ludwig 63
science
    transmission of information 163–4
scientific works 3, 163, 180–211
    most translated 165
    translation into Chinese 40, 41–2, 50
    translation into Latin 73–4
Scot, Reginald 36
Scott, Thomas 116
Scribanius, Carolus 67
scribes, responsibilities/freedoms of 34
Scupoli, Lorenzo, *Il combattimento spirituale* 72,
    94, 95
Second Scholastic 106
Seklucjan, Jan 25
Selden, John 108
Seljukid beg Ilyas 194
Seneca, L. Annaeus 42
Sennert, Daniel 207
Serlio, Sebastiano 37
Settle, Elkanah, *The Conquest of China* 129
Severian of Gavala, Bishop 213
Severinus, Petrus 173
Seydî Ali Reis 195
Seyssel, Claude de 132
    The French Commonwealth 76
    La grande monarchie de France 109
Shakespeare, William 7, 24
    Hamlet 8
    Macbeth 104
    The Taming of the Shrew 24
Shams al-Din al-Bukhari 181–2
Shemseddin Itaqi 199, 209–10
Sherlock, William 122
Shute, John 37
Sidney, Algernon, *Discourses Concerning
    Government* 118
Sidney, Mary 12, 33
Sidney, Philip 23, 104
    A Defence of Poetry 21
Sigismund III of Sweden/Poland 120
Siku quanshu see Imperial Encyclopedia
Silhon, Jean de, *Ministre d'état* 114
Silvanus, Johannes 53
Sipayllówna, Maria 12
Skinner, Quentin 110
Skylitzes, Ioannis, 'Introduction to the
    Cosmographical Sciences' 188

Sleidan, Johann 12, 73, 128
    Commentaries 129, 140
    Four World Empires 130, 140
Slovakia/Slovak people
    ethnic identity 53, 59–60, 62
    exiles from 61
    'first state of' 63
    language(s) 53, 54–6, 58, 59, 61–4 (*see also* Czech)
    religious identity/divisions 53–4, 59–60, 64
Smidt, Frans de 15
Smith, Adam, *The Wealth of Nations* 31–2, 38
Smith, Samuel 176
Smith, Sir Thomas, *De republica Anglorum* 109
Snellius, Willebrord 167
Solis, Antonio de, *History of the Conquest of
    Mexico* 130, 141
Sophocles, *Electra* 32–3
Sorbière, Samuel de 107
Soto, Domingo de 106
sound-approximation, as translation technique 48–9
Sousa, Perez de 116
Spain
    cultural hegemony within Europe 72, 106
    as devotional centre 91–4, 98
Spandugino, Theodoro 21
Spanish, translations from/into 23, 24
The Spectator 142
    appeal to readership 147–50
    authorial/editorial persona 152
    correspondence 153
    imitations 142, 148–53, 154–9
    influence of earlier trends 142, 146–7
    reliance on collaborators 152–3
    translations 148
speeches, collections of 133–4
Speidell, John, *Geometrical Extraction* 215–16
Spenser, Edmund 33
    The Shepherd's Calendar 21, 75
Speroni, Sperone 169
Sporck, Eleonora von 12
Sprat, Thomas 74
Staden, Heinrich von 75
Standaert, Nicolas 39, 49–50
Stapleton, Sir Robert 131
Steele, Richard 142, 147–8, 151, 156, 157, 159
Steiner, George 8
Stevens, John, Capt. 133
Stevin, Simon 165, 167, 169, 171
Stillingfleet, Edward 14
Stoppani, Giovanni Niccolò 70
Stoudites, Damaskinos, Bishop 183
Strada, Famiano 128
    De bello belgico 130, 141
Suarez, Francisco 106
Suleiman I 'the Magnificent', Sultan 199

Surius, Laurence 90–1
Suso, Heinrich 87
Sweden, translation campaign 18, 19
Swieten, Gerard van 209
synopsis, translation by 40
syntax, reproduction of original 35
Szafarzyński, Jacob 15

Tacitus, P. Cornelius 126
Tasso, Torquato 19, 24, 33, 65, 70
  Aminta 75
  Gerusalemme liberata 20–1, 75
Tauler, Johannes 87
technical language, translation of 9
technology 74
Teelinck, Willem 15
Teglio, Silvestro 31, 70, 78
Temple, William 22
Tende, Gaspard de 30
  Règles de la traduction 25
Teresa of Avila, St 72, 92, 94, 95
Terracini, Benvenuto 8
Tezkireci Köse Ibrahim Effendi 205–6
Thompson, Emmanuel 120
Thott, Birgitte 12
Thucydides 127
Topal Recep Pasha 209
Toury, Gideon 2
Toxites, Michael 172
Traheron, William 133
Tranovský, Juraj 59
'translatability' 7
Translation Studies 2–3
translation(s)
  bibliography 100
  choice of material 20–1
  collaborative 11, 46–7, 205
  cultural impact 35–8, 99–100, 173–5, 192
  defined 67
  historical role 1–3
  ideological grounds for 173–5, 176, 178–9 (*see also* translators: motives)
  inaccurate 56, 93 (*see also* misunderstanding)
  programmes 16–19, 120–1
  (proposed) areas of study 99–100
  role in cultural exchange 10, 97, 98, 102–3
  second-hand 27
  target readership 21–2, 70–1, 72, 84, 102, 106, 131–2, 164
  terminology 25–6
  theories/methods 11, 24–35, 105–6, 124, 150
translators
  amateur 12
  anonymous/pseudonymous 69
  categories 11–16

errors *see* misunderstanding; translation(s): inaccurate
  improvements on original 30
  motives 105, 118, 121, 124, 148 (*see also* commercialism; translation(s): ideological grounds for)
  nationalities 70
  omissions *see* bowdlerization; contraction
  oral *see* interpreters
  professional 12–13, 132–3, 200, 201
  reversal of authorial intent 33, 38
  teams *see* translation(s): collaborative
  see also clergy; royalty; women
transposition (of action/settings) 32–3
travel
  books on 21, 74–5
  role in European education 103–4
Trediakovsky, Vasilij 13
Trenchard, John 123
Trent, Council of 62, 124
Tuck, Richard 113
Tuning, Jan 167
Turkish
  original works in 197–8, 209–10
  translations into 193–6, 200–6, 207–8, 209, 211
Turks/Turkey *see* Ottoman Empire
Turler, Johannes 79
Tyler, Margaret 12

Ulloa, Alfonso de 16, 132
Ulugh Beg 193, 206
Umur Beg 194
Union of Brothers 58
universities
  admissions policy 198–9
  linguistic preferences 175–6
'untranslatability' 25
Urquhart, Sir Thomas 32
Utraquists 56–7, 61

Vagnoni, Alfonso 42–3, 45
Valdés, Juan/Alfonso de 93
Valla, Lorenzo 17, 89, 126
Valverde de Hamusco, Juan 210
van den Bos, Lambert 133
Varenius, Bernhardus 18
Varthema, Ludovico de 21
Vasilii Shuiskii, Tsar 216
Vasilii the Great 213
Vaughn, William 116
Vazquez del Marmol, Juan 91
Venice (city-state) 202
  Greek community 185
  political treatises from/on 110–11

Venuti, Lawrence 2, 26
Verbiest, Ferdinand 43, 45, 190
Vergil, Polydore 22
  History of Inventors 129, 132, 141
vernaculars
  defined 67
  increase in use/prestige 168–70
  (studies of) translations between 3–4, 22–4, 84,
    165–7
  see also Latin
Vesalius, Andreas 18
  De humani corporis fabrica 217
veterinary science 195–6
Vetter, Conrad 15
Vienne, Philibert de, *Le philosophe de court* 36
Vigenère, Blaise de 126
Vignola, Giacomo Barozzi da 18
Villehardouin, Geoffroy de 126, 130
Vindiciae contra tyrannos (anon.) 105–6, 117
Virgil (P. Vergilius Maro) 18, 35
  Aeneid 19, 29
Vladimir, St 212–13
Vlahos, Gerasimos
  'Harmonia definitive entium' 188
  translation of Hippocrates 190
Voltaire (François-Marie Arouet) 51, 155–6
  Henriade 75
  L'orphelin de la Chine 154
Vondel, Joost van, *Zungchin* 129
Voragine, Jacob, *Legenda aurea* 83, 86, 94

Waesberge, Jan van 165, 176
Wagenaer, Lucas Jansz, *Speculum nauticum* 74
Waldergrave, William 118
Walford, Benjamin 176
Walker, William 117
Wallenstein, Albrecht von 73

Wallis, John 169
  Algebra 171, 175
Wanckel, Johannes 112
war(s)
  news reports 143
  see also names of conflicts
Waucquier, Mateo Martinez 69
Webster, Charles 164, 172
Wei Douxu 43
Weisse, Christian 13
Welsaer, Mark 74
Weyer, Johan 36
Wheler, Sir George 208
White Mountain, Battle of 59
Willymat, William 119
Władislaw (Ladislaus), Prince 72
Wolff, Christian, *Cogitationes rationales* 77
women
  as patrons of translation 16
  role in devotional life 99
  as translators 12–13
  see also periodicals
Wood, Anthony, *History of Oxford* 67
word-for-word *see* literality
Wysocki, Simon 15

Xenophon 127
Ximenes, Cardinal *see* Jiménez de Cisneros
Xu Guangqi, Paul 39, 41, 43, 47
Xu Zongze 39

Yaroslav the Wise 213
Yom-tob, Jacob ben David 184
Yushkevich, A. P. 216

Zhu Sihan 43
Žilina, Synod of 57, 58–9